Executive Information Systems

Emergence • Development • Impact

edited by

Hugh J. Watson
University of Georgia

R. Kelly Rainer
Auburn University

George Houdeshel
Management of Information, Inc.

JOHN WILEY & SONS, INC.
New York • Chichester • Brisbane • Toronto • Singapore

Library of Congress Cataloging-in-Publication Data

Executive information systems : emergence development impact / edited
 by Hugh J. Watson, R. Kelly Rainer, George Houdeshel.
    p. cm.
   Includes bibliographical references and index.
   ISBN 0-471-55554-1
   1. Management information systems.   I. Watson, Hugh J.
 II. Rainer, R. Kelly (Rex Kelly)   III. Houdeshel, George.
 T58.6.E95   1992
 658.4'038—dc20   91-36471

Printed in the United States of America

10 9 8 7 6 5 4 3 2 1

Printed and bound by Courier Companies, Inc.

Preface

Prior to the 1980s, only a few companies such as Lockheed-Georgia and Northwest Industries had developed executive information systems (EIS). These firms were headed by CEOs who were dissatisfied with existing reporting systems and wanted better information to run their companies. These leaders were willing to assume a strong role in sponsoring and participating in the development of an EIS. These were not easy undertakings: The limits of existing technology were pushed, systems designers had little experience with applications of this kind, and other companies' experiences could not be drawn upon. Nonetheless, these companies developed systems that are now recognized as new members of the family of computer-based information systems.

Public awareness of the potential for executive information systems grew with Jack Rockart's and Michael Treacy's article, "The CEO Goes On-Line," which appeared in the January-February, 1982 issue of the *Harvard Business Review*. It described how a number of CEOs were regularly using computers in a hands-on manner. While their article was widely read, it drew mixed reactions. Some saw it as signaling the beginning of the assault on the last bastion of computer resistance—the executive suite. Others viewed it with considerable skepticism, believing that the executives described were isolated exceptions rather than an emerging trend.

It is not surprising that people were skeptical. Both management information systems (MIS) in the 1960s and decision support systems (DSS) in the 1970s had promised more than they delivered. MIS became an expanded set of scheduled, summary reports. DSS were used by staff and lower level managers to analyze specific decision-making tasks. Neither made senior executives hands-on computer users or became an integral part of how executives perform their jobs.

A major contributor to the growth of EIS was the appearance of vendor supplied EIS software in the mid 1980s. Pilot Executive Software's Command Center and Comshare's Commander EIS made it much easier for firms to develop an EIS. This software provided facilities for (relatively) easy screen design, data importation, user friendly front ends, and access to news services. Soon thereafter, other products became available as vendor supplied software lessened the technical problems of developing an EIS.

Jack Rockart along with David DeLong once again helped spread the EIS word with the publication of their 1988 book, *Executive Support Systems*. It summarized the experiences of 30 firms with an EIS and identified the benefits and issues associated with the development of such a system (for example, the role of the executive sponsor, managing the data, and handling political resistance). It was written for executives interested in having an EIS and information systems managers with major responsibilities for delivering one.

Two conferences have also contributed significantly to the growth of EIS. The first is The Institute of Management Science's (TIMS) annual DSS conference. When the conference began in 1981, its focus was limited to DSS, but over the years its scope has broadened to cover all applications that support decision making, including EIS. Starting with DSS-85, there have been EIS presentations. The second important conference is The EIS Institute which began in 1988. Currently, it is held twice a year in the United States and once in Canada and focuses exclusively on EIS. Both conferences have speakers with considerable EIS experience and presentations and exhibits by vendors of EIS software. They provide a "jump start" for firms that want to learn how to develop an EIS.

With the growing interest in EIS, more is being written about it. Scattered across a variety of writings are important concepts, understandings, insights, and experiences about how to successfully develop an EIS. A major problem, however, is that many of the best materials are difficult to identify, locate, and obtain. They are published in academic journals, trade publications, conference proceedings, and university working paper series. This problem motivated the publishing of this collection of readings.

This book is written for anyone who wants to learn about EIS. With the exception of several classic articles such as "The CEO Goes On-Line," all of the selections are recent and reflect current understanding and knowledge.

The book is divided into four parts:

- The Emergence of EIS
- The Nature of Executive Work
- Developing an EIS
- The Impact of EIS.

Interspersed throughout the book are detailed descriptions of EIS in a variety of organizations. These descriptions are intended to make EIS more real and less abstract. Chapters 2, 17, 19, 20, 24, 25 and 26 are especially rich in their descriptions.

This book is intended for both practitioners and students. A small but growing number of universities offer an EIS course at either the undergraduate or graduate level. This book can serve as the primary text in such a course. Most schools offer a DSS course and this book can be used as a supplementary text by instructors who want to include a comprehensive coverage of EIS.

We would like to express our appreciation to the authors of the selections in this book and to the publishers of the articles for allowing us to reprint them. Also, we would like to thank our graduate assistant, Tyona Lyons, for her help in preparing this book.

HUGH J. WATSON
R. KELLY RAINER
GEORGE HOUDESHEL

November, 1991

Contents

PART I.   THE EMERGENCE OF EIS   1

 1. The CEO Goes On-Line   3
    John F. Rockart and Michael E. Treacy

 2. The Management Information and Decision Support
    (MIDS) System at Lockheed-Georgia   13
    George Houdeshel and Hugh J. Watson

PART II.   THE NATURE OF EXECUTIVE WORK   33

 3. The Manager's Job: Folklore and Fact   35
    Henry Mintzberg

 4. Making Executive Information Systems More Effective   53
    Raymond McLeod, Jr. and Jack W. Jones

 5. User Expectations—The CEO's Perspective   71
    George L. Ball

PART III.   DEVELOPING AN EIS   77

 6. Executive Information Systems: A Framework for Development
    and a Survey of Current Practices   81
    Hugh J. Watson, R. Kelly Rainer, and Chang E. Koh

 7. Implementing an Executive Information System:
    Seven Steps for Success   107
    Craig Barrow

 8. Is Your ESS Meeting the Need?   117
    Gary K. Gulden and Douglas E. Ewers

 9. A Path Framework for Executive Information Systems   127
    Ido Millet, Charles H. Mawhinney, and Ernest A. Kallman

10. The Strategic Business Objectives Method for Guiding
    Executive Information Systems Development   145
    Linda Volonino and Hugh J. Watson

11. Determining Information Requirements for an
Executive Information System   161
   Hugh J. Watson and Mark Frolick

12. Selecting Information for an EIS: Experiences at
Lockheed-Georgia   177
   George Houdeshel

13. Selecting EIS Software: The Western Mining Corporation
Experience   191
   *Hugh J. Watson, Betty-Anne Hesse, Carolyn Copperwaite,
   and Vaughan deVos*

14. What Users Want Today   203
   Richard Laska and Alan Paller

15. Product Spotlight on EIS   211
   *Eileen Carlson, Michael L. Sullivan-Trainor, and
   Rudolph Pizzano*

16. Avoiding Hidden EIS Pitfalls. A Case Study:
What You See Isn't Always What You Get   237
   Hugh J. Watson

17. EIS Experiences at Marine Midland Bank, N.A.   245
   Linda Volonino and Stephen Robinson

18. Identifying the Attributes of Successful Executive
Support System Implementation   257
   David W. DeLong and John F. Rockart

19. How Rockwell Launched Its EIS   279
   David A. Armstrong

20. The People Factor in EIS Success   287
   David A. Armstrong

PART IV.   THE IMPACT OF EIS   **299**

21. Power Computing at the Top   301
   Lou Wallis

22. Moments of Executive Enlightenment   315
   John F. Rockart and David W. DeLong

23. EIS and the Collapse of the Information Pyramid   327
   David Friend

24. Executive Information Streamlines Greyhound
    Dial's Operations 337
    Execucom Systems Corporation

25. Putting Hertz Executives in the Driver's Seat 343
    Meghan O'Leary

26. Developing an ESS for the Michigan State Senate 349
    Caryl Holland

INDEX **355**

PART *I*

THE EMERGENCE OF EIS

Computer-based information systems (CBIS) that support the firm's top executives first appeared in the late 1970s. These systems are called executive information systems (EIS) or executive support systems (ESS).

The relatively recent advent of EIS results from several factors, including the nature of executives and improved hardware and software technology. Executives typically do not have keyboarding skills and do not have time to be trained in the use of a CBIS. Further, many executives have reached their present positions without using computers and are skeptical about the need to learn to use them at this late point in their careers. However, improvements in hardware and software (e.g., mice, touchscreens, color graphic monitors, menus) have made CBIS much easier for executives to use with minimal training.

Previous attempts to provide computer support for executives (e.g., management information systems (MIS) and decision support systems (DSS)) have not been highly successful. MIS produce detailed reports for lower level managers and staff personnel. DSS are mainly used by middle managers and staff for data analyses. The two articles in Part I demonstrate how executive information systems overcame many of the limitations associated with previous CBIS to provide support for the organization's top executives.

One of the earliest EIS articles is "The CEO Goes On-Line" by John Rockart and Michael Treacy. They note that the information flow to the apex of the corporate pyramid will be changed by EIS. The reason given is that corporate executives now are not just consumers of information; rather, through their EIS, they are participating in the process of defining the information they want and developing the systems to

1

deliver it. In "The Management Information and Decision Support (MIDS) System at Lockheed-Georgia," George Houdeshel and Hugh Watson describe one of the earliest, and longest lasting, EIS. The authors provide valuable insights into EIS evolution, components, benefits, and keys to success.

1

The CEO Goes On-Line

John F. Rockart
Michael E. Treacy

Computer terminals are no strangers to corporate offices. Clerks have had them for years. Middle managers are increasingly using them. So are key staff personnel. But the thought that the CEO and other top officers of a billion-dollar company might regularly spend time at their own terminals usually elicits an amused smile and a shake of the head. Somehow, the image of top executives hard at work at a keyboard just doesn't seem right.

After all, their day is supposed to be filled with meetings with key division officers, briefings, telephone conversations, conferences, speeches, negotiations. What is more, the classic research on what executives actually do shows them to be verbally oriented, with little use for "hard" information. According to Henry Mintzberg, "A great deal of the manager's inputs are soft and speculative—impressions and feelings about other people, hearsay, gossip, and so on. Furthermore, the very analytic inputs—reports, documents, and hard data in general—seem to be of relatively little importance."[1]

But consider:

- Ben W. Heineman, president and chief executive of Northwest Industries, spends a few hours almost every day at a computer terminal in his office. Heineman accesses reports on each of his nine operating companies and carries out original analyses using a vast store of data and an easy-to-use computer language. The terminal has become his most important tool for monitoring and planning activities.

- Roger E. Birk, president of Merrill Lynch, and Gregory Fitzgerald, chief financial officer, have access via computer terminals in their

Reprinted by permission of *Harvard Business Review, 60* (1) (January–February, 1982).

offices to a large number of continually updated reports on the company's worldwide operations. The system, to which a graphics capability has recently been added, was initiated by former president of Merrill Lynch and now Secretary of the Treasury Donald T. Regan as a vehicle for quickly generating information on the latest financial developments.

- John A. Schoneman, chairman of the board and CEO of Wausau Insurance Companies, and Gerald D. Viste, president and chief operating officer, use an on-line data base of information about their own business and those of competitors. At their terminals they develop numerical and graphic analyses that help determine the company's strategic direction.
- George N. Hatsopoulos, president of Thermo Electron, writes programs in the APL language to format data contained in several of his company's data bases. As a result, he can quickly study information about company, market, and economic conditions whenever he desires.

Although these examples do not yet represent common practice for senior corporate officers, they do suggest a trend toward greatly increased computer use in top-executive suites. In fact, during the past two years we have studied some 16 companies in which at least one of the three top officers, most often the CEO, directly accesses and uses computer-based information on a regular basis. In the pages that follow we present a status report on this rapidly growing phenomenon.

AN INFORMATION SYSTEM FOR EXECUTIVES

Top managers' use of computers is spreading for three primary reasons: user-oriented terminal facilities are now available at an acceptable price; executives are better informed of the availability and capabilities of these new technologies; and, predictably, today's volatile competitive conditions heighten the desire among top executives for ever more timely information and analysis.

Whatever its specific causes, this trend is indisputably a measured response to a widely perceived need or set of needs. Our study indicates that the actual patterns of executive computer use represent variations on only a few basic themes. Though these patterns evolved independently and may appear quite different, their similarities are striking—so striking in fact that they suggest the emergence in a number of companies of a new kind of executive information support (or "EIS") system.

From our observations, we can generalize a simple model of EIS structure and development into which fit all the individual systems we have seen. This model helps illuminate both the process of executive information support and the factors that determine its success.

All EIS systems share . . .

- . . . **a central purpose**

  Obviously, the top executives who personally use computers do so as part of the planning and control processes in their organizations. The provision of information to senior management for such purposes is certainly nothing new; the reason for EIS systems is to support a more effective use of this information. Those managers with terminals of their own have decided that they need a better understanding of the workings of their corporations. To achieve this, they have sought out the individually tailored access to the broader, more detailed sweep of data that only computers can provide.

- . . . **a common core of data**

  Although no two EIS systems are identical, each contains what we call a "data cube" (see Figure 1–1)—that is, data on important *business variables* (for example, the major general ledger accounting variables and, equally important, the nonfinancial substantive figures—such as unit sales by product line—that underlie and explain the accounting numbers) through *time* (budgeted, actual, and revised data on key variables is kept on a month-by-month basis for a number of past years, usually five, and is available in the form of projections for several years into the future) and by *business unit* (whatever the nature of those units—geographic, divisional, or functional).

  What sets this data cube apart from information traditionally gathered by staff members and included in reports to top management is the sheer breadth of its cross-functional sources and the depth of its detail. With such inclusive information at their fingertips, executives can of course work through traditional accounting comparisons of "actual," "last year," and "budget" for a single business unit. But they can also look at a few variables, such as working capital and its major components, across time for a single subsidiary or at a single variable—say, a product line's performance in physical units as well as dollars—across all subsidiaries.

  Further, a number of companies have extended these axes of data to include information, however incomplete, on major competitors, key customers, and important industry segments.[2] Much of this information can be purchased today in the form of any of the several thousand machine-processable data bases sold by information vendors. For competitive financial data, for example, one common source is Standard & Poor's Compustat tape, which provides ten years of data on 130 business variables for more than 3,500 companies.

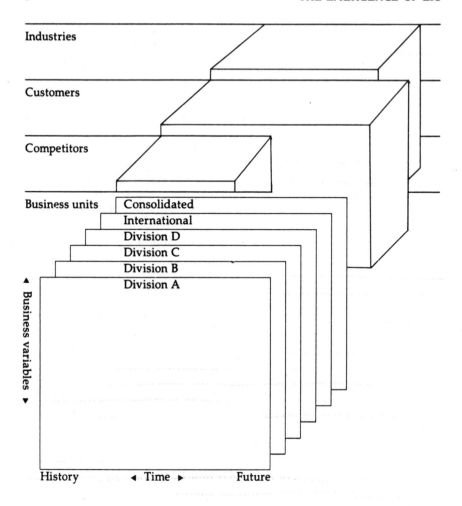

Figure 1-1.   *The Data Cube*

Operating data from a growing number of industries are readily available from industry associations or other published sources. Some of these sources—customer surveys, market sampling, and the like—are fairly "soft," but they are accurate enough for managerial planning and control purposes.

• . . . **two principal methods of use** —
The EIS systems in our study are used in two quite different ways by executives: (1) for access to the current status and projected trends of the business and (2) for personalized analyses of the available data. Let us look briefly at these two modes of use.

Status Access

When executives have "read only" access to the latest data or reports on the status of key variables, they can peruse the information requested but can do very little, if any, data manipulation. In industries where market conditions change rapidly, where there are many factors to watch, or where hour-to-hour operational tracking is important, the status access of this sort can be of great use. This is indeed the case at Merrill Lynch and at several other financial companies.

The status access approach also provides an easy, low-cost, and low-risk means to help an executive become comfortable with a computer terminal. At Owens-Illinois, for example, the first stage in the development of an EIS system will—for just these reasons—provide only status access for the CEO and other senior executives. Moreover, taking this approach can send a clear signal throughout an organization that top management intends to put more emphasis than it had in the past on quantitative analysis in the planning and control process. As one CEO put it, "The terminal on my desk is a message to the organization."

Personalized Analysis

Executives can, of course, use the computer not only for status access but also as an analytic tool. At Northwest Industries, Wausau, and Thermo Electron, senior managers have chosen the contents of the data bases available to them and have learned to do some programming themselves. Instead of merely having access to the data, they are able to do creative analyses of their own.

The type of analysis performed differs from manager to manager. Some merely compute new ratios or extrapolate current trends into the future. Some graph trends of particular interest to gain an added visual perspective. Some work with elaborate simulation models to determine where capital investments will be most productive. All, however, enjoy a heightened ability to look at, change, extend, and manipulate data in personally meaningful ways. But to make this approach effective, executives must be willing to invest much of their own time and energy in defining the needed data and in learning what the computer can do.

- . . . **a support organization**
  Finally, all the systems we observed depend on the provision of a high level of personal support to their executive users. This support is essential if those systems are to have a fair chance to demonstrate their full potential. Users require at least some initial training and ongoing assistance with computer languages. And they need help in establishing and updating data bases as well as in conceptualizing, designing, and improving their systems and their analyses.

In the organizations we observed, a group of EIS "coaches," often former consultants, gives EIS users continuing assistance. Their primary role is "to help" rather than "to do." Because such EIS coaches must be a different breed of expert from data processing analysts and because they need to be shielded from involvement in the normal run of EDP fire-fighting activities, the companies we studied have separated them organizationally from their regular data processing operations.

NORTHWEST INDUSTRIES: AN EXAMPLE

Perhaps the most impressive example of an EIS system, both in design and use, is that at Northwest Industries (1980 sales: $2.9 billion). The development of this system began in 1976 when Heineman decided that he needed a specially tailored data base to aid him in monitoring, projecting, and planning the progress of his nine operating companies. A great believer in the advantages of "not being the captive of any particular source of information," Heineman wanted to be able to analyze various aspects of the business himself but saw little opportunity to do so without a computer-based system to reduce data-handling chores.

In January 1977, the six top executives at Northwest were given access to an experimental system through which they could retrieve more than 70 reports and perform such limited analyses as compound growth calculations, variance analysis, and trend projections. By February, Heineman had reached the limits of the system's capabilities and was demanding more.

Additional capabilities came in the form of a new access and analysis language, EXPRESS, which facilitated not only simple file handling and data aggregation but also extensive modeling and statistical analyses of data series. To complement these improved capabilities, Northwest has since added to its executive data base:

- 350 financial and operational items of data on planned, budgeted, forecasted, and actual monthly results for each operating company for the past eight and the next four years.
- 45 economic and key ratio time series.
- Several externally subscribed data bases, including Standard & Poor's Compustat and DRI services.

Northwest's EIS system with its extensive and continually growing data base is now used by almost all managers and executives at corporate headquarters to perform their monitoring and analytic functions. But the

What Top Managers Are Saying about EIS Systems

"The system has been of infinite help in allowing me to improve my mental model of the company and the industry we're in. I feel much more confident that I am on top of the operations of our company and its future path."

"Your staff really can't help you think. The problem with giving a question to the staff is that they provide you with the answer. You learn the nature of the real question you should have asked when you muck around in the data."

"It saves a great deal of the time spent in communicating with functional staff personnel. Today, for an increasing number of problems, I can locate the data I want, and I can develop it in the form I want, faster than I could describe my needs to the appropriate staffer."

"Some of my best ideas come at fallow times between five in the evening and seven the next morning. Access to the relevant data to check out something right then is very important. My home terminal lets me perform the analysis while it's at the forefront of my mind."

"Comparing various aspects of our company with the competition is a very fast way of defining the areas in which I should place most of my attention. The system allows me to do exactly that."

"I think graphically. It's so nice to be able to easily graph out the data in which I'm interested. . . . And it's especially nice to be able to adjust the display to see the data in the exact perspective that best tells the story."

"I've always felt that the answers were in the detail. Now, at last, I can pore through some of that detail. That's my style. It used to mean long nights and plenty of staff and lots of frustration. Now it's somewhat easier. And frankly, it also saves me a great deal of staff time that was formerly spent on routine charting and graphing."

"I bring a lot of knowledge to the party. Just scanning the current status of our operations enables me to see some things that those with less time in the company would not see as important. Although the resulting telephone calls undoubtedly shake up some of my subordinates, I think in the long run this is helpful to them, too."

"The system provides me with a somewhat independent source for checking on the analyses and opinions presented both by my line subordinates and by my functional staffs. There is a great deal of comfort in being relatively independent of the analyses done by others."

"By working with the data I originally thought I needed, I've been able to zero in on the data I actually need. We've expanded our data base significantly, but each step has led to better understanding of our company and its environment."

"Frankly, a secondary, but very real, advantage of the use of the system by me is the signal it gives to the rest of the company that I desire more quantitatively oriented management of the organization. I want my subordinates to think more analytically, and they are. I feel we're on the way to becoming a significantly better-managed company."

driving force behind the system and its most significant user remains Heineman. Working with the system is an everyday thing for him, a natural part of his job. With his special knowledge of the business and with his newly acquired ability to write his own programs, Heineman sees great value in working at a terminal himself rather than handing all assignments to staff personnel.

"There is a huge advantage to the CEO to get his hands dirty in the data," he says, because "the answers to many significant questions are found in the detail. The system provides me with an improved ability to ask the right questions and to know the wrong answers." What is more, he finds a comparable advantage in having instant access to the data base to try out an idea he might have. In fact, he has a computer terminal at home and takes another with him on vacations.

Supporting Heineman and other Northwest executives are a few information systems people who function as EIS coaches. They train and assist users in determining whether needed data are already available and whether any additional data can be obtained. They also help get new information into the data base, train users in access methods, and teach them to recognize the analytic routines best fitted to different types of analyses. Only for major modeling applications do these coaches actually take part in the system design and programming process.

THE PROMISE OF EIS SYSTEMS

Most of America's top managers still have no terminal-based access whatsoever. They find the idea of working at a terminal a violation of their managerial styles and their view of their roles. They are perfectly comfortable asking staff to provide both manual and computer-generated analyses as needed. What is more, EIS systems provide no clear, easily defined cost savings. In fact, we know of no system that a traditional cost-benefit study would justify in straight labor-saving terms. Why, then, are managers implementing them in growing numbers?

Three principal reasons suggest themselves. Most significant is the assistance EIS systems offer analytically oriented top executives in their search for a deeper understanding of their companies and industries. We believe that many top managers are basically analytic and that they are now both aware of the new tools offered by EIS and finding them to their liking. (For some of their specific comments, see the ruled insert.)

Second, EIS systems can be structured to accommodate the information needs of the individual manager. Although the Merrill Lynch system, for example, is principally geared for status access, Gregory Fitzgerald, the chief financial officer, often writes his own programs to carry out personally tailored analyses.

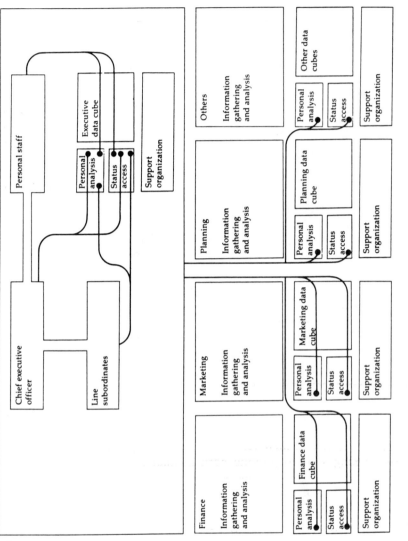

Figure 1-2. *A Conceptual Model of Executive Information Support*

11

Finally, the systems can start small (less than $100,000), providing support to a single data-oriented member of the corporate office. In fact, an EIS system can begin either at a line-executive level or as a system for the sole use of a particular functional staff, such as finance or marketing (see Figure 1–2). It can then evolve as others become interested, adding the data sets and access methods appropriate to each new user. This pattern of growth marks a logical progression since the executives, personal assistants, and key functional staffs in the corporate office form, in effect, an "executive information support organization" *jointly* responsible for preparing and analyzing the data needed at the corporate level. EIS support of an individual user enhances the information processing capability of the entire corporate office, for the data needed by different members of the office tend to overlap.

But EIS systems have the added advantage that they need grow and develop only as additional individuals "buy in." Unlike the huge, one-shot, multimillion-dollar projects necessary for such classic data processing systems as order entry or manufacturing control, EIS systems can evolve by increments in precise step with the distinct needs of each corporate office.

Not all senior managers, of course, will find an EIS system to their taste, but enough user-friendly technology now exists to accommodate the needs of those who wish to master a more data-intensive approach to their jobs.

REFERENCES

1. See Henry Mintzberg, "Planning on the Left Side and Managing on the Right," HBR July–August 1976, p. 49.
2. For one method of defining those variables that should be included, see John F. Rockart, "Chief Executives Define Their Own Data Needs," HBR March–April 1979, p. 81.

QUESTIONS

1. What are the primary reasons for the trend toward increased computer use by top executives?
2. What is a "data cube" and why is it a key ingredient of an EIS?
3. What are the common characteristics of an EIS?
4. What are EIS coaches and why are they important?
5. Why is the evolutionary development of an EIS an advantage?

2

The Management Information and Decision Support (MIDS) System at Lockheed-Georgia

George Houdeshel
Hugh J. Watson

Senior executives at Lockheed-Georgia are hands-on users of the management information and decision support system (MIDS). It clearly illustrates that a carefully designed system can be an important source of information for top management. Consider a few examples of how the system is used.

- The president is concerned about employee morale which for him is a critical success factor. He calls up a display which shows employee contributions to company-sponsored programs such as blood drives, United Way, and savings plans. These are surrogate measures of morale, and because they have declined, he becomes more sensitive to a potential morale problem.
- The vice president of manufacturing is interested in the production status of a C-5B aircraft being manufactured for the U.S. Air Force. He calls up a display which pictorially presents the location and assembly status of the plane and information about its progress

Previously published in *MIS Quarterly,* Volume 11, Number 1, March 1987. Copyright 1987 by the Society for Information Management and the Management Information Systems Research Center at the University of Minnesota. Used with permission.

relative to schedule. He concludes that the aircraft is on schedule for delivery.

- The vice president of finance wants to determine whether actual cash flow corresponds with the amount forecasted. He is initially concerned when a $10 million unfavorable variance is indicated, but an explanatory note indicates that the funds are enroute from Saudi Arabia. To verify the status of the payment, he calls the source of the information using the name and telephone number shown on the display and learns that the money should be in a Lockheed account by the end of the day.

- The vice president of human resources returns from an out-of-town trip and wants to review the major developments which took place while he was gone. While paging through the displays for the human resources area, he notices that labor grievances rose substantially. To learn more about the situation so that appropriate action can be taken, he calls the supervisor of the department where most of the grievances occurred.

These are not isolated incidents; other important uses of MIDS occur many times a day. They demonstrate that computerized systems can have a significant impact on the day-to-day functioning of senior executives.

The purpose of this article is to describe aspects of MIDS which are important to executives, information systems managers, and information systems professionals who are the potential participants in the approval, design, development, operation, and use of systems similar to MIDS. As a starting point, we want to discuss MIDS in the context of various types of information systems (i.e., MIS, DSS, and EIS), because its positioning is important to understanding its hands-on use by senior Lockheed-Georgia executives. We will describe how it was justified and developed, because these are the keys to its success. While online systems are best seen in person to be fully appreciated, we will try to describe what an executive experiences when using MIDS and the kinds of information that are available. Any computer system is made possible by the hardware, software, personnel, and data used and these will be described. Then we will discuss the benefits of MIDS. An organization considering the development of a system like MIDS needs to focus on key factors of success, and we will describe those factors that were most important to MIDS' success. As a closing point of interest, future plans for the evolution of MIDS will be discussed.

MIDS IN CONTEXT

Management information systems (MIS) were the first attempt by information systems professionals to provide managers and other organizational personnel with the information needed to perform their jobs effectively and efficiently. While originators of the MIS concept initially had high hopes and expectations for MIS, in practice MIS largely came to represent an expanded set of structured reports and has had only a minimal impact on upper management levels [11].

Decision support systems (DSS) were the next attempt to help management with its decision-making responsibilities. They have been successful to some extent, especially in regard to helping middle managers and functional area specialists such as financial planners and marketing researchers. However, their usefulness to top management has been primarily indirect. Middle managers and staff specialists may use a DSS to provide information for top management, but despite frequent claims of ease-of-use, top managers are seldom hands-on users of a DSS [4, 5].

With hindsight it is understandable why DSSs have not been used directly by senior executives. Many of the reasons are those typically given when discussing why managers do not use computers: poor keyboard skills, lack of training and experience in using computers, concerns about status, and a belief that hands-on computer use is not part of their job. Another set of reasons revolves around the tradeoff between simplicity and flexibility of use. Simpler systems tend to be less flexible while more flexible systems are usually more complex. Because DSSs are typically used to support poorly structured decision-making tasks, the flexibility required to analyze these decisions comes at the cost of greater complexity. Unless the senior executive is a "techie" at heart, or uses the system enough to master its capabilities, it is unlikely that the executive will feel comfortable using the system directly. Consequently, hands-on use of the DSS is typically delegated to a subordinate who performs the desired analysis.

Executive information systems (EIS), or executive support systems as they are sometimes called, are the least computerized attempt to help satisfy top management's information needs. These systems tend to have the following characteristics which differentiate them from MIS and DSS:

- They are used directly by top managers without the assistance of intermediaries.
- They provide easy online access to current information about the status of the organization.
- They are designed with management's critical success factors (CSF) in mind.
- They use state-of-the-art graphics, communications, and data storage and retrieval methods.

The limited reportings of EIS suggest that these types of systems can make top managers hands-on users of computer-based systems [2, 10,

12]. While a number of factors contribute to their success, one of the most important is ease-of-use. Because an EIS provides little analysis capabilities, it normally requires only a few, easy to enter keystrokes. Consequently, keyboard skills, previous training and experience in using computers, concerns about loss of status, and perceptions of how one should carry out job responsibilities are less likely to hinder system use.

MIDS is an example of an EIS. It is used directly by top Lockheed-Georgia managers to access online information about the current status of the firm. Great care, time, and effort goes into providing information that meets the special needs of its users. The system is graphics-oriented and draws heavily upon communications technology.

THE EVOLUTION OF MIDS

Lockheed-Georgia, a subsidiary of the Lockheed Corporation, is a major producer of cargo aircraft. Over 19,000 employees work at their Marietta, Georgia plant. Their current major activities are production of the C-5B transport aircraft for the U.S. Air Force, Hercules aircraft for worldwide markets, and numerous modification and research programs.

In 1975, Robert B. Ormsby, then President of Lockheed-Georgia, first expressed an interest in the creation of an online status reporting system to provide information which was concise, timely, complete, easy to access, relevant to management's needs, and could be shared by organizational personnel. Though Lockheed's existing systems provided voluminous quantities of data and information, Ormsby thought them to be unsatisfactory for several reasons. It was difficult to quickly locate specific information to apply to a given problem. Reports often were not sufficiently current, leading to organizational units basing decisions on information which should have been the same but actually was not. This is often the case when different reports or the same report with different release dates are used. Little action was taken for several years as Ormsby and information services personnel waited for hardware and software to emerge which would be suitable for the desired type of system. In the fall of 1978, development of the MIDS system began.

The justification for MIDS was informal. No attempt was made to cost-justify its initial development. Ormsby felt that he and other Lockheed-Georgia executives needed the system and mandated its development. Over time, as different versions of MIDS were judged successful, authorization was given to develop enhanced versions. This approach is consistent with current thinking and research on systems to support decision making. It corresponds closely with the recommendation to view the initial system as a research and development project and to evolve later versions if the system proves to be successful [7]. It also is in keeping with findings that accurate, timely and new kinds of information, an organizational champion, and managerial mandate are the factors which motivate systems development [6].

A number of key decisions were made early in the design of the system. First, an evolutionary design approach would be used. Only a limited number of displays would be created initially. Over time they would be modified or possibly deleted if they did not meet an information need. Additional screens would be added as needed and as MIDS was made available to a larger group of Lockheed-Georgia managers. Ease-of-use was considered to be of critical importance because of the nature of the user group. Most of the Lockheed-Georgia executives had all of the normal apprehensions about personally using terminals. In order to encourage hands-on use, it was decided to place a terminal in each user's office, to require a minimum number of keystrokes in order to call up any screen, and to make training largely unnecessary. Response time was to be fast and features were to be included to assist executives in locating needed information.

Bob Pittman was responsible for the system's development and he, in turn, reported to the vice president of finance. Pittman initially had a staff consisting of two people from finance and two from information services. The finance personnel were used because of their experience in preparing company reports and presentations to the corporate headquarters, customers, and government agencies. Their responsibility was to determine the system's content, screen designs, and operational requirements. The information services personnel were responsible for hardware selection and acquisition and software development.

Pittman and his group began by exploring the information requirements of Ormsby and his staff. This included determining what information was needed, in what form, at what level of detail, and when it had to be updated. Several approaches were used in making these determinations. Interviews were held with Ormsby and his staff. Their secretaries were asked about information requested of them by their superiors. The use of existing reports was studied. From these analyses emerged an initial understanding of the information requirements.

The next step was to locate the best data sources for the MIDS system. Two considerations guided this process. The first was to use data sources with greater detail than what would be included in the MIDS displays. Only by using data which had not already been filtered and processed could information be generated which the MIDS team felt would satisfy the information requirements. The second was to use data sources which had a perspective compatible with that of Ormsby and his staff. Multiple organizational units may have data seemingly appropriate for satisfying an information need, but choosing the best source or combination of sources requires care in order that the information provided is not distorted by the perspective of the organizational unit in which it originates.

The initial version of MIDS took six months to develop and allowed Ormsby to call up 31 displays. Over the past eight years, MIDS has evolved to where it now offers over 700 displays for 30 top executives and 40 operating managers. It has continued to be successful through many changes in the senior executive ranks, including the position of president. MIDS subsystems are currently being developed for middle managers in the various functional areas and MIDS-like systems are being implemented in several other Lockheed companies.

MIDS FROM THE USER'S PERSPECTIVE

An executive typically has little interest in the hardware or software used in a system. Rather, the dialog between the executive and the system is what matters. The dialog can be thought of as consisting of the command language by which the user directs the actions of the system, the presentation language through which the system provides the response, and the knowledge that the user must have in order to effectively use the system [1]. From a user's perspective, the dialog *is* the system, and consequently, careful attention was given to the design of the dialog components in MIDS.

An executive gains access to MIDS through the IBM PC/XT on his or her desk. Entering a password is the only sign-on requirement, and every user has a unique password which allows access to an authorized set of displays. After the password is accepted, the executive is informed of any scheduled downtime for system maintenance. The user is then given a number of options. He can enter a maximum of four keystrokes and call up any of the screens that he is authorized to view, obtain a listing of all screens that have been updated, press the "RETURN/ENTER" key to view the major menu, access the online keyword index, or obtain a listing of all persons having access to the system.

The main menu and keyword index are designed to help the executive find needed information quickly. Figure 2-1 shows the main menu. Each subject area listed in the main menu is further broken down into additional menus. Information is available in a variety of subject areas, including by functional area, organizational level, and project. The user can also enter the first three letters of any keywords which are descriptive of the information needed. The system checks these words against the keyword index and lists all of the displays which are related to the user's request.

Information for a particular subject area is organized in a top down fashion. This organization is used within a single display or in a series of displays. A summary graph is presented at the top of a screen or first in a series of displays, followed by supporting graphs, and then by tables and

MIDS MAJOR CATEGORY MENU

■ TO RECALL THIS DISPLAY AT ANY TIME HIT 'RETURN-ENTER' KEY.
■ FOR LATEST UPDATES SEE S1.

A MANAGEMENT CONTROL
MSI'S; OBJECTIVES;
ORGANIZATION CHARTS;
TRAVEL/AVAILABILITY/EVENTS SCHED.
CP CAPTURE PLANS INDEX

B C-5B ALL PROGRAM ACTIVITIES

C HERCULES ALL PROGRAM ACTIVITIES

E ENGINEERING
COST OF NEW BUSINESS; R & T

F FINANCIAL CONTROL
BASIC FINANCIAL DATA; COST
REDUCTION; FIXED ASSETS; OFFSET;
OVERHEAD; OVERTIME; PERSONNEL

H HUMAN RESOURCES
CO-OP PROGRAM EMPLOYEE
STATISTICS & PARTICIPATION

M MARKETING
ASSIGNMENTS; PROSPECTS;
SIGN-UPS; PRODUCT SUPPORT;
TRAVEL

O OPERATIONS
MANUFACTURING; MATERIEL;
PRODUCT ASSURANCE & SAFETY

P PROGRAM CONTROL
FINANCIAL & SCHEDULE
PERFORMANCE
MS MASTER SCHEDULING MENU

S SPECIAL ITEMS
DAILY DIARY; SPECIAL PROGRAMS

Figure 2-1. *The MIDS Main Menu*

19

text. This approach allows executives to quickly gain an overall perspective while providing back-up detail when needed. An interesting finding has been that executives prefer as much information as possible on a single display, even if it appears "busy," rather than having the same information spread over several displays.

Executives tend to use MIDS differently. At one extreme are those who browse through displays.

An important feature for them is the ability to stop the generation of a display with a single keystroke when it is not of further interest. At the other extreme are executives who regularly view a particular sequence of displays. To accommodate this type of system use, sequence files can be employed which allow executives to page through a series of displays whose sequence is defined in advance. Sequence files can either be created by the user, requested by the user and prepared by the MIDS staff, or offered by MIDS personnel after observing the user's viewing habits.

All displays contain a screen number, title, when it was last updated, the source(s) of the information presented, and a telephone number for the source(s). It also indicates the MIDS staff member who is responsible for maintaining the display. Every display has a backup person who is responsible for it when the primary person is on leave, sick, or unavailable for any reason. Knowing the information source and the identity of the responsible MIDS staff member is important when an executive has a question about a display.

Standards exist across the displays for the terms used, color codes, and graphic designs. These standards help eliminate possible misinterpretations of the information provided. Standard definitions have also improved communications in the company.

The importance of standard definitions can be illustrated by the use of the word "signup." In general, the term refers to a customer's agreement to buy an aircraft. However, prior to the establishment of a standard definition, it tended to be used differently by various organizational units. To marketing people, a signup was when a letter of intent to buy was received. Legal services considered it to be when a contract was received. Finance interpreted it as when a down payment was made. The standard definition of a signup now used is "a signed contract with a nonrefundable down payment." An online dictionary can be accessed if there is any question about how a term is defined.

Color is used in a standard way across all of the screens. The traffic light pattern is used for status: green is good; yellow is marginal; and red is unfavorable. Under budget or ahead of schedule is in green; on budget or on schedule is in yellow; over budget or behind schedule is in red. Bar graphs have a black background and yellow bars depict actual performance, cyan (light blue) is used for company goals and commitments to the corporate office, and magenta represents internal goals and objectives.

Organization charts use different colors for the various levels of management. Special color combinations are used to accommodate executives with color differentiation problems, and all displays are designed to be effective with black and white hard copy output.

Standards exist for all graphic designs. Line charts are used for trends, bar charts for comparisons, and pie or stacked bar charts for parts of a whole. On all charts, vertical wording is avoided and abbreviations and acronyms are limited to those on an authorized list. All bar charts are zero at the origin to avoid distortions, scales are set in prescribed increments and are identical within a subject series, and bars that exceed the scale have numeric values shown. In comparisons of actual with predicted performance, bars for actual performance are always wider.

Comments are added to the displays to explain abnormal conditions, explain graphic depictions, reference related displays, and inform of pending changes. For example, a display may show that signups for May are three less than forecasted. The staff member who is responsible for the display knows, however, that a downpayment from Peru for three aircraft is enroute and adds this information as a comment to the display. Without added comments, situations can arise which are referred to as "paper tigers," because they appear to require managerial attention though they actually do not. The MIDS staff believes that "transmitting data is not the same as conveying information" [8].

The displays have been created with the executives' critical success factors in mind. Some of the CSF measures, such as profits and aircraft sold, are obvious. Other measures, such as employee participation in company-sponsored programs, are less obvious and reflect the MIDS staff's efforts to fully understand and accommodate the executives' information needs.

To illustrate a typical MIDS display, Figure 2–2 shows Lockheed-Georgia sales as of November 1991. It was accessed by entering F3. The sources of the information and their Lockheed-Georgia telephone numbers are in the upper right-hand corner. The top graphs provide past history, current, and forecasted sales. The wider bars [in yellow] represent actual sales while budgeted sales are depicted by the narrower, [cyan] bars. Detailed, tabular information is provided under the graphs. An explanatory comment is given at the bottom of the display. The R and F in the bottom right-hand corner indicates that related displays can be found by paging in a reverse or forward direction.

Executives are taught to use MIDS in a 15 minute tutorial. For several reasons, no written instructions for the use of the system have ever been prepared. An objective for MIDS has been to make the system easy enough to use so that written instructions are unnecessary. Features such as menus and the keyword index make this possible. Another reason is that senior executives are seldom willing to take the time to read instructions. And most importantly, if an executive has a problem in

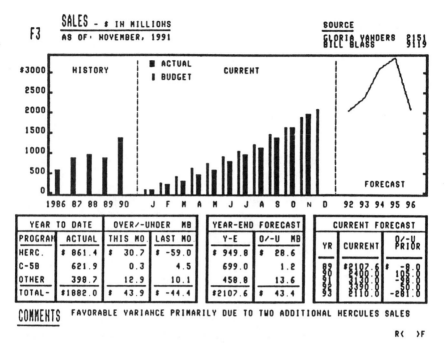

Figure 2-2. *Lockheed–Georgia Sales*

using the system, the MIDS staff prefers to learn about the problem and to handle it personally.

The IBM PC/XT on the executive's desk is useful for applications other than accessing MIDS displays. It can be used off-line with any appropriate PC software. It is also the mechanism for tying the user through MIDS to other computer systems. For example, some senior executives and even more middle managers want access to outside reference services or internal systems with specific databases. Electronic messaging is the most common use of the IBM PC/XT's for other than MIDS displays. The executive need only request PROFS from within MIDS and the system automatically translates the user's MIDS password to a PROFS password and transfers the user from the DEC 780 VAX host to the IBM mainframe with PROFS. After using PROFS' electronic mail capabilities, the transfer back to MIDS is a simple two keystroke process.

THE COMPONENTS OF MIDS

A number of component parts are essential to the functioning of MIDS: hardware, software, MIDS personnel, and data sources.

Hardware

A microcomputer from Intelligent Systems Corporation was used for the initial version of MIDS. Each day MIDS personnel updated the floppy disks which stored the displays. As more executives were given access to MIDS, it became impractical to update each executive's displays separately, and the decision was made to store them centrally on a DEC 11/34 where they could be accessed by all users. Executives currently interact with MIDS through IBM PC/XTs tied to a DEC 780 VAX. Next year MIDS will be migrated to an IBM 3081 as part of Lockheed's plan to standardize around IBM equipment. Because an objective of MIDS was to reduce the amount of paper, the generation of hard copy output has always been minimized. The only printers are in the MIDS office and include four Printronix 300 (black and white, dot matrix) and Xerox 6500 (color copier, laser unit, with paper and transparencies) printers.

Software

At the time that work on MIDS began, appropriate software was not commercially available. Consequently, the decision was made to develop the software in-house. Even though commercial EIS software such as Command Center and Metaphor are now available, none of it has justified a switch from what has been developed by the MIDS staff.

The software is used for three important tasks: creating and updating the displays; providing information about the system's use and status; and maintaining system security.

Creating and Updating the Displays

Each display has an edit program tailored to fit its needs. Special edit routines have been developed for graph drawing, color changes, scale changes, roll-offs, calculations, or drawing special characters such as airplanes. These edit functions are then combined to create a unique edit program for each display. This approach allows MIDS personnel to quickly update the displays and differs from off-the-shelf software which requires the user to answer questions for all routines, regardless of whether they are needed.

The edit software has other attractive features. There are computer-generated messages to the information analyst advising of other displays which could be affected by changes to the one currently being revised. Color changes are automatically made to a display when conditions become unfavorable. When the most recent period data is entered, the oldest period data is automatically rolled off of all graphs. The edit software has error checks for unlikely or impossible conditions.

Providing Information about the System's Use and Status

Daily reports are generated at night and are available the next morning for the MIDS staff to review. A daily log of system activity shows who requested what, when, and how. The log indicates everything but "why," and sometimes the staff even asks that question in order to better understand management's information needs. The log allows MIDS personnel to analyze system loads, user inquiry patterns, methods used to locate displays, utilization of special features, and any system and/or communication problems. Another report indicates the status of all displays, including the last time each display was updated, when the next update is scheduled, and who is responsible for the update. Yet another report lists all displays which have been added, deleted, or changed.

Weekly reports are generated on Sunday night and are available Monday morning for the MIDS staff. One report lists the previous week's users and the number of displays viewed by each executive. Another report lists the number of displays with the frequency of viewing by the president and his staff and others.

A number of reports are available on demand. They include an authorization matrix of users and terminals; a count of displays by major category and subsystem; a list of users by name, type of terminal, and system line number to the host computer; a list of displays in sequence; a list of display titles with their number organized by subject area; and a keyword exception report of available displays not referenced in the keyword file.

Maintaning System Security

Careful thought goes into deciding who has access to which displays. Information is made available unless there are compelling reasons why it should be denied. For example, middle managers might not be allowed to view strategic plans for the company.

System access is controlled through a double security system. Users can call up only displays which they are authorized to view and then only from certain terminals. This security system helps protect against unauthorized users gaining access to the system and the unintentional sharing of restricted information. As an example of the latter situation, a senior executive might be allowed to view sensitive information in his office, but be denied access to the information in a conference room or the office of lower management.

Personnel

The MIDS staff has grown from five to its current size of nine. Six of the staff members are classified as information analysts, two are computer analysts, and there is the manager of the MIDS group. The information analysts are responsible for determining the system's content, designing the screens, and keeping the system operational. Each information analyst is responsible for about 100 displays. Approximately 170 displays are updated daily by the MIDS staff. The computer analysts are responsible for hardware selection and acquisition and software development. While the two groups have different job responsibilities, they work together and make suggestions to each other for improving the system.

It is imperative that the information analysts understand the information that they enter into the system. Several actions are taken to ensure that this is the case. Most of the information analysts have work experience and/or training in the areas for which they supply information. They are encouraged to take courses which provide a better understanding of the users' areas. And they frequently attend functional area meetings, often serving as an important information resource.

Data

In order to provide the information needed, a variety of internal and external data sources must be used. The internal sources include transaction processing systems, financial applications, and human sources. Some of the data can be transferred directly to MIDS from other computerized systems, while others must be rekeyed or entered for the first time. Access to computerized data is provided by in-house software and commercial software such as DATATRIEVE. External sources are very important and include data from external databases, customers, other Lockheed companies, and Lockheed's Washington, D.C. office.

MIDS relies on both hard and soft data. Hard data comes from sources such as transaction processing systems and provides "the facts." Soft data often comes from human sources and results in information which could not be obtained in any other way; it provides meaning, context, and insight to hard data.

BENEFITS OF MIDS

A variety of benefits are provided by MIDS: better information; improved communications; an evolving understanding of information requirements; a test-bed for system evolution; and cost reductions.

The information provided by MIDS has characteristics which are important to management. It supports decision making by identifying areas which require attention, providing answers to questions, and giving knowledge about related areas. It provides relevant information. Problem areas are highlighted and pertinent comments are included. The information is timely because displays are updated as important events occur. It is accurate because of the efforts of the MIDS staff, since all information is verified before it is made available.

MIDS has also improved communications in several ways. It is sometimes used to share information with vendors, customers, legislators, and others. MIDS users are able to quickly view the same information in the same format with the most current update. In the past, there were often disagreements, especially over the telephone, because executives were operating with different information. PROFS provides electronic mail. The daily diary announces major events as they occur.

Initially identifying a complete set of information requirements is difficult or impossible for systems which support decision making. The evolutionary nature of MIDS' development has allowed users to better understand and evolve their information requirements. Having seen a given set of information in a given format, an executive is often prompted to identify additional information or variations of formats that provide still better decision support.

The current system provides a test-bed for identifying and testing possible system changes. New state-of-the-art hardware and software can be compared with the current system in order to provide information for the evolution of MIDS. For example, a mouse-based system currently is being tested.

MIDS is responsible for cost savings in several areas. Many reports and graphs which were formerly produced manually are now printed from MIDS and distributed to non-MIDS users. Some requirements for special reports and presentation materials are obtained at less cost by modifying standard MIDS displays. Reports that are produced by other systems are summarized in MIDS and are no longer printed and distributed to MIDS users.

THE SUCCESS OF MIDS

Computer-based systems can be evaluated on the basis of cost/benefit, frequency of use, and user satisfaction considerations. Systems which support decision making, such as MIDS, normally do not lend themselves to a quantified assessment of their benefits. They do provide intangible benefits, however, as can be seen in the following example.

Lockheed-Georgia markets its aircraft worldwide. In response to these efforts, it is common for a prospective buyer to call a company executive to discuss a proposed deal. Upon receipt of a phone call, the executive can call up a display which provides the following information: the aircraft's model and quantity; the dollar value of the offer; the aircraft's availability for delivery; previous purchases by the prospect;

the sales representative's name and exact location for the week; and a description of the status of the possible sale. Such a display is shown in Figure 2–3. All of this information is available without putting the prospective customer on hold, transferring the call to someone else, or awaiting the retrieval of information from a file.

When a user can choose whether or not to use a system, frequency of use can be employed as a measure of success. Table 2–1 presents data on how the number of users and displays and the mean number of displays viewed per day by each executive has changed over time. The overall picture is one of increased usage; currently an average of 5.5 screens are viewed each day by the 70 executives who have access to MIDS. Unlike some systems which are initially successful but quickly fade away, the success of MIDS has increased over time.

Frequency of use can be a very imperfect measure of success. The MIDS group recognizes that a single display which has a significant impact on decision making is much more valuable than many screens which are paged through with passing interest. Consequently, frequency of use is used as only one indicator of success.

MIDS personnel have felt no need to conduct formal studies of user satisfaction. The data on system usage and daily contact with MIDS users

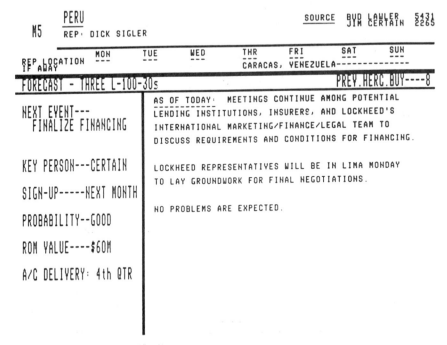

Figure 2-3. *The Status of a Sale*

Table 2-1. *MIDS Users, Displays and Displays Viewed*

Year	Number of Users	Number of Displays	Mean Number of Displays Viewed/ Per User/Per Day
1979	12	69	*
1980	24	231	*
1981	27	327	*
1982	31	397	3
1983	31	441	4
1984	49	620	4.2
1985	70	710	5.5

*Figures not available.

provide ample information on how satisfied users are with MIDS. User satisfaction can be illustrated by the experience of Paul Frech who was vice president of operations in 1979. When MIDS was offered to him, he had little interest in the system because he had well-established channels for the flow of information to support his job responsibilities. Shortly afterwards, Frech was promoted to the corporate headquarters staff in California. When he was again promoted to become the president of Lockheed-Georgia, MIDS had become a standard for executive information and he was reintroduced to the system. He has stated:

> I assumed the presidency of the Lockheed-Georgia Company in June 1984, and the MIDS system had been in operation for some time prior to that. The MIDS system enabled me to more quickly evaluate the current conditions of each of our operational areas and, although I had not been an advocate of executive computer systems, the ease and effectiveness of MIDS made it an essential part of my informational sources.

Because Frech and other senior executives have come to rely on MIDS, middle managers at Lockheed-Georgia and executives at other Lockheed companies want their own versions of MIDS. Within Lockheed-Georgia there is a feeling that "If the boss likes it, I need it." Currently, MIDS personnel are helping middle functional area managers develop subsystems of MIDS and are assisting other Lockheed companies with the development of similar systems.

KEYS TO THE SUCCESS OF MIDS

Descriptions of successful systems are useful to people responsible for conceptualizing, approving, and developing similar systems. Perhaps even more important are insights about what makes a system a success. We will identify the keys to MIDS' success here, but it should be remembered that differences exist among executive information systems, organizations, and possibly the factors that lead to success.

1. *A Committed Senior Executive Sponsor.* Ormsby served as the organizational champion for MIDS. He wanted a system like MIDS, committed the necessary resources, participated in its creation, and encouraged its use by others.

2. *Carefully Defined System Requirements.* Several considerations governed the design of the system. It had to be custom-tailored to meet the information needs of its users. Ease-of-use, an absolutely essential item to executives who were wary of computers, was critical. Response time had to be fast. The displays had to be updated quickly and easily as conditions changed.

3. *Carefully Defined Information Requirements.* There has been a continuing effort to understand management's information requirements. Displays have been added, modified, and deleted over time. Providing information relevant to managements' CFSs has been of paramount importance.

4. *A Team Approach to Systems Development.* The staff that developed, operates, and evolves MIDS combines information systems skills and functional area knowledge. The computer analysts are responsible for the technical aspects of the system while the information analysts are responsible for providing the information needed by management. This latter responsibility demands that the information analysts know the business and maintain close contact with information sources and users.

5. *An Evolutionary Development Approach.* The initial version of MIDS successfully addressed the most critical information needs of the company president and strengthened his support for the system. There is little doubt that developing a fully integrated system for a full complement of users would have resulted in substantial delays and less enthusiasm for the system. Over the years, MIDS has expanded and evolved as more users have been provided access to MIDS, management's information requirements have changed, better ways to analyze and present information have been discovered, and improved computer technology has become integrated into the system.

6. *Careful Computer Hardware and Software Selection.* The decision to proceed with the development of MIDS was made when good color terminals at reasonable prices became available. At that time graphics software was very limited and it was necessary to

develop the software for MIDS in-house. The development of MIDS could have been postponed until hardware and software with improved performance at reduced cost appeared, but this decision would have delayed providing management with the information needed. Also affecting the hardware selection was the existing hardware within the organization and the need to integrate MIDS into the overall computing architecture. While it is believed that excellent hardware and software decisions have been made for MIDS, different circumstances at other firms may lead to different hardware and software configurations.

FUTURE PLANS FOR MIDS

MIDS continues to evolve along the lines mentioned previously: expansion through subsystems to lower organizational levels; expansion to other Lockheed companies; and hardware changes to make MIDS more IBM compatible. Improvements in display graphics are also planned through the use of a video camera with screen digitizing capabilities. A pilot program for voice input is currently being sponsored by the vice president of engineering.

A number of other enhancements are also projected. A future version of MIDS may automatically present variance reports when actual conditions deviate by more than user defined levels. Audio output may supplement what is presented by the displays. The system may contain artificial intelligence components. There may be large screen projection of MIDS displays with better resolution than is currently available. The overriding objective is to provide Lockheed-Georgia management with the information they need to effectively and efficiently carry out their job responsibilities.

REFERENCES

1. Bennett, J. "User-Oriented Graphics, Systems for Decision Support in Unstructured Tasks," in *User-Oriented Design of Interactive Graphics Systems*, S. Treu, (ed.), Association for Computing Machinery, New York, New York, 1977, pp. 3–11.

2. DeLong, D. W. and Rockart, J. F. "Identifying the Attributes of Successful Executive Support System Implementation," *Transactions from the Sixth Annual Conference on Decision Support Systems*, J. Fedorowicz, (ed.), Washington, D.C., April 21–24, 1986, pp. 41–54.

3. El Sawy, O. A. "Personal Information Systems for Strategic Scanning in Turbulent Environments: Can the CEO Go On-Line?" *MIS Quarterly*, Volume 9, Number 1, March 1985, pp. 53–60.

4. Friend, D. "Executive Information Systems: Success, Failure, Insights and Misconceptions." *Transactions from the Sixth Annual Conference on Decision Support Systems,* J. Fedorowicz, (ed.), Washington, D.C., April 21–24, 1986, pp. 35–40.

5. Hogue, J. T. and Watson, H. J. "An Examination of Decision Makers' Utilization of Decision Support System Output," *Information and Management,* Volume 8, Number 4, April 1985, pp. 205–212.

6. Hogue, J. T. and Watson, H. J. "Management's Role in the Approval and Administration of Decision Support Systems," *MIS Quarterly,* Volume 7, Number 2, June 1983, pp. 15–23.

7. Keen, P. G. W. "Value Analysis: Justifying Decision Support Systems," *MIS Quarterly,* Volume 5, Number 1, March 1981, pp. 1–16.

8. McDonald, E. "Telecommunications," *Government Computer News,* February 28, 1986, p. 44.

9. Rockart, J. F. "Chief Executives Define Their Own Data Needs," *Harvard Business Review,* Volume 57, Number 2, January–February 1979, pp. 81–93.

10. Rockart, J. F. and Treacy, M. E. "The CEO Goes On-Line," *Harvard Business Review,* Volume 60, Number 1, January–February 1982, pp. 32–88.

11. Sprague, R. H., Jr. "A Framework for the Development of Decision Support Systems," *MIS Quarterly,* Volume 4, Number 4, December 1980, pp. 10–26.

12. Sundue, D. G. "GenRad's On-line Executives," *Transactions from the Sixth Annual Conference on Decision Support Systems,* J. Fedorowicz, (ed.), Washington, DC, April 21–24, 1986, pp. 14–20.

QUESTIONS

1. What features were incorporated into MIDS to encourage hands-on use?

2. If you were placed in charge of developing an EIS, how would you determine the information requirements? Be specific.

3. Discuss the reasons for standardization across the EIS for terms used, color codes, and graphic designs.

4. List and discuss five ways in which the development of MIDS benefited Lockheed-Georgia.

5. How would you measure the success of an EIS? Justify your choice of methods.

PART *II*

THE NATURE OF EXECUTIVE WORK

As was stated previously, corporate executives have only recently begun to use EIS. One of the reasons is the nature of the work they perform.

The three articles in Part II lay the foundation for understanding what the job of the executive actually involves. These selections were written prior to recent EIS successes in terms of supporting executives in their jobs.

Henry Mintzberg, in "The Manager's Job: Folklore and Fact," describes the jobs of all managers as a complex blend of ten roles. He notes that managers work at a rapid pace, performing activities that are brief, varied, and discontinuous. Further, he recognizes that managers rely very little on formal management information systems. Mintzberg illustrates the difficulty of providing computer support to top executives.

In their article, "Making Executive Information Systems More Effective," Raymond McLeod and Jack Jones discuss the variety of information sources that executives can access. These sources include five written and six oral media. They state that executives favor verbal over written media and note that executives consider computer reports to be only moderately valuable. The article suggests that an EIS will be a valued tool if it can accomplish three things: (1) it must provide and integrate external and internal information; (2) it must offer information with richness (e.g., soft, human, contextual information to enhance hard information); and (3) it must overcome problems typical of traditional MIS hard copy reports by providing accurate, timely, concise, and relevant information.

George Ball, in "User Expectations: The CEO's Perspective," describes what a typical CEO (using himself as an example) wants from computer-based information systems. He points out that a successful EIS should help the firm obtain a strategic advantage and that it should filter the information reaching the executive. Ball also notes the functions that information systems personnel should perform in building and maintaining an EIS.

3

The Manager's Job: Folklore and Fact

Henry Mintzberg

If you ask managers what they do, they will most likely tell you that they plan, organize, coordinate, and control. Then watch what they do. Don't be surprised if you can't relate what you see to these words.

When a manager is told that a factory has just burned down and then advises the caller to see whether temporary arrangements can be made to supply customers through a foreign subsidiary, is that manager planning, organizing, coordinating, or controlling? How about when he or she presents a gold watch to a retiring employee? Or attends a conference to meet people in the trade and returns with an interesting new product idea for employees to consider?

These four words, which have dominated management vocabulary since the French industrialist Henri Fayol first introduced them in 1916, tell us little about what managers actually do. At best, they indicate some vague objectives managers have when they work.

The field of management, so devoted to progress and change, has for more than half a century not seriously addressed *the* basic question: What do managers do? Without a proper answer, how can we teach management? How can we design planning or information systems for managers? How can we improve the practice of management at all?

Our ignorance of the nature of managerial work shows up in various ways in the modern organization—in boasts by successful managers who never spent a single day in a management training program; in the turnover of corporate planners who never quite understood what it was the manager wanted; in the computer consoles gathering dust in the

---

Reprinted by permission of *Harvard Busilness Review,* 53 (4) (July–August, 1975).

back room because the managers never used the fancy on-line MIS some analyst thought they needed. Perhaps most important, our ignorance shows up in the inability of our large public organizations to come to grips with some of their most serious policy problems.

Somehow, in the rush to automate production, to use management science in the functional areas of marketing and finance, and to apply the skills of the behavioral scientist to the problem of worker motivation, the manager—the person in charge of the organization or one of its subunits—has been forgotten.

I intend to break the reader away from Fayol's words and introduce a more supportable and useful description of managerial work. This description derives from my review and synthesis of research on how various managers have spent their time.

In some studies, managers were observed intensively; in a number of others, they kept detailed diaries; in a few studies, their records were analyzed. All kinds of managers were studied—foremen, factory supervisors, staff managers, field sales managers, hospital administrators, presidents of companies and nations, and even street gang leaders. These "managers" worked in the United States, Canada, Sweden, and Great Britain.

A synthesis of these findings paints an interesting picture, one as different from Fayol's classical view as a cubist abstract is from a Renaissance painting. In a sense, this picture will be obvious to anyone who has ever spent a day in a manager's office, either in front of the desk or behind it. Yet, at the same time, this picture throws into doubt much of the folklore that we have accepted about the manager's work.

FOLKLORE AND FACTS ABOUT MANAGERIAL WORK

There are four myths about the manager's job that do not bear up under careful scrutiny of the facts.

Folklore: The manager is a reflective, systematic planner. The evidence on this issue is overwhelming, but not a shred of it supports this statement.

Fact: Study after study has shown that managers work at an unrelenting pace, that their activities are characterized by brevity, variety, and discontinuity, and that they are strongly oriented to action and dislike reflective activities. Consider this evidence:

Half the activities engaged in by the five chief executives of my study lasted less than nine minutes, and only 10% exceeded one hour.[1] A study of 56 U.S. foremen found that they averaged 583 activities per eight-hour shift, an average of 1 every 48 seconds.[2] The work pace for both chief executives and foremen was unrelenting. The chief executives met a steady stream of callers and mail from the moment they arrived in the morning until they left in the evening. Coffee breaks and lunches were inevitably work related, and ever-present subordinates seemed to usurp any free moment.

A diary study of 160 British middle and top managers found that they worked without interruption for a half hour or more only about once every two days.[3]

Of the verbal contacts the chief executives in my study engaged in, 93% were arranged on an ad hoc basis. Only 1% of the executives' time was spent in open-ended observational tours. Only 1 out of 368 verbal contacts was unrelated to a specific issue and could therefore be called general planning. Another researcher found that "in *not one single case* did a manager report obtaining important external information from a general conversation or other undirected personal communication."[4]

Is this the planner that the classical view describes? Hardly. The manager is simply responding to the pressures of the job. I found that my chief executives terminated many of their own activities, often leaving meetings before the end, and interrupted their desk work to call in subordinates. One president not only placed his desk so that he could look down a long hallway but also left his door open when he was alone—an invitation for subordinates to come in and interrupt him.

Clearly, these managers wanted to encourage the flow of current information. But more significantly, they seemed to be conditioned by their own work loads. They appreciated the opportunity cost of their own time, and they were continually aware of their ever-present obligations—mail to be answered, callers to attend to, and so on. It seems that a manager is always plagued by the possibilities of what might be done and what must be done.

When managers must plan, they seem to do so implicitly in the context of daily actions, not in some abstract process reserved for two weeks in the organization's mountain retreat. The plans of the chief executives I studied seemed to exist only in their heads—as flexible, but often specific, intentions. The traditional literature notwithstanding, the job of managing does not breed reflective planners; managers respond to stimuli, they are conditioned by their jobs to prefer live to delayed action.

Folklore: The effective manager has no regular duties to perform. Managers are constantly being told to spend more time planning and delegating and less time seeing customers and engaging in negotiations. These are not, after all, the true tasks of the manager. To use the popular analogy, the good manager, like the good conductor, carefully orchestrates everything in advance, then sits back, responding occasionally to an unforeseeable exception. But here again the pleasant abstraction just does not seem to hold up.

Fact: Managerial work involves performing a number of regular duties, including ritual and ceremony, negotiations, and processing of soft information that links the organization with its environment. Consider some evidence from the research:

A study of the work of the presidents of small companies found that they engaged in routine activities because their companies could not afford staff specialists and were so thin on operating personnel that a single absence often required the president to substitute.[5]

One study of field sales managers and another of chief executives suggest that it is a natural part of both jobs to see important customers, assuming the managers wish to keep those customers.[6]

Someone, only half in jest, once described the manager as the person who sees visitors so that other people can get their work done. In my study, I found that certain ceremonial duties—meeting visiting dignitaries, giving out gold watches, presiding at Christmas dinners—were an intrinsic part of the chief executive's job.

Studies of managers' information flow suggest that managers play a key role in securing "soft" external information (much of it available only to them because of their status) and in passing it along to their subordinates.

Folklore: The senior manager needs aggregated information, which a formal management information system best provides. Not too long ago, the words *total information system* were everywhere in the management literature. In keeping with the classical view of the manager as that individual perched on the apex of a regulated, hierarchical system, the literature's manager was to receive all important information from a giant, comprehensive MIS.

But lately, these giant MIS systems are not working—managers are simply not using them. The enthusiasm has waned. A look at how managers actually process information makes it clear why.

Fact: Managers strongly favor verbal media, telephone calls and meetings, over documents. Consider the following:

In two British studies, managers spent an average of 66 percent and 80 percent of their time in verbal (oral) communication.[7] In my study of five American chief executives, the figure was 78 percent.

These five chief executives treated mail processing as a burden to be dispensed with. One came in Saturday morning to process 142 pieces of mail in just over three hours, to "get rid of all the stuff." This same manager looked at the first piece of "hard" mail he had received all week, a standard cost report, and put it aside with the comment, "I never look at this."

These same five chief executives responded immediately to 2 of the 40 routine reports they received during the five weeks of my study and to 4 items in the 104 periodicals. They skimmed most of these periodicals in seconds, almost ritualistically. In all, these chief executives of good-sized organizations initiated on their own—that is, not in response to something else—a grand total of 25 pieces of mail during the 25 days I observed them.

An analysis of the mail the executives received reveals an interesting picture—only 13% was of specific and immediate use. So now we have another piece in the puzzle: not much of the mail provides live, current information—the action of a competitor, the mood of a government legislator, or the rating of last night's television show. Yet this is the information that drove the managers, interrupting their meetings and rescheduling their workdays.

Consider another interesting finding. Managers seem to cherish "soft" information, especially gossip, hearsay, and speculation. Why? The reason is its timeliness; today's gossip may be tomorrow's fact. The manager who misses the telephone call revealing that the company's biggest customer was seen golfing with a main competitor may read about a dramatic drop in sales in the next quarterly report. But then it's too late.

To assess the value of historical, aggregated, "hard" MIS information, consider two of the manager's prime uses for information—to identify problems and opportunities[8] and to build mental models (e.g., how the organization's budget system works, how customers buy products, how changes in the economy affect the organization). The evidence suggests that the manager identifies decision situations and builds models not with the aggregated abstractions an MIS provides but with specific tidbits of data.

Consider the words of Richard Neustadt, who studied the information-collecting habits of President Roosevelt, Truman, and Eisenhower: "It is not information of a general sort that helps a President see personal stakes; not summaries, not surveys, not the *bland amalgams*. Rather . . . it is the odds and ends of *tangible detail* that pieced together in his mind illuminate the underside of issues put before him. To help himself he must reach out as widely as he can for every scrap of fact, opinion, gossip, bearing on his interests and relationships as President. He must become his own director of his own central intelligence."[9]

The manager's emphasis on this verbal media raises two important points. First, verbal information is stored in the brains of people. Only when people write this information down can it be stored in the files of the organization—whether in metal cabinets or on magnetic tape—and managers apparently do not write down much of what they hear. Thus the strategic data bank of the organization is not in the memory of its computers but in the minds of its managers.

Second, managers' extensive use of verbal media helps to explain why they are reluctant to delegate tasks. It is not as if they can hand a dossier over to subordinates; they must take the time to "dump memory"—to tell subordinates all about the subject. But this could take so long that managers may find it easier to do the task themselves. Thus they are damned by their own information system to a "dilemma of delegation"—to do too much or to delegate to subordinates with inadequate briefing.

Folklore: Management is, or at least is quickly becoming, a science and a profession. By almost any definition of *science* and *profession*, this statement is false. Brief observation of any manager will quickly lay to rest the notion that managers practice a science. A science involves the enaction of systematic, analytically determined procedures or programs. If we do not even know what procedures managers use, how can we prescribe them by scientific analysis? And how can we call management a profession if we cannot specify what managers are to learn? For after all, a profession involves "knowledge of some department of learning or science" (*Random House Dictionary*).[10]

Fact: The managers' programs—to schedule time, process information, make decisions, and so on—remain locked deep inside their brains. Thus, to describe these programs, we rely on words like *judgment* and *intuition,* seldom stopping to realize that they are merely labels for our ignorance.

I was struck during my study by the fact that the executives I was observing—all very competent—are fundamentally indistinguishable from their counterparts of a hundred years ago (or a thousand years ago). The information they need differs, but they seek it in the same way—by word of mouth. Their decisions concern modern technology, but the procedures they use to make those decisions are the same as the procedures used by nineteenth century managers. Even the computer, so important for the specialized work of the organization, has apparently had no influence on the work procedures of general managers. In fact, the manager is in a kind of loop, with increasingly heavy work pressures but no aid forthcoming from management science.

Considering the facts about managerial work, we can see that the manager's job is enormously complicated and difficult. Managers are overburdened with obligations yet cannot easily delegate their tasks. As a result, they are driven to overwork and forced to do many tasks superficially. Brevity, fragmentation, and verbal communication characterize their work. Yet these are the very characteristics of managerial work that have impeded scientific attempts to improve it. As a result, management scientists have concentrated on the specialized functions of the organization, where it is easier to analyze the procedures and quantify the relevant information.[11]

But the pressures of a manager's job are becoming worse. Where before managers needed to respond only to owners and directors, now they find that subordinates with democratic norms continually reduce

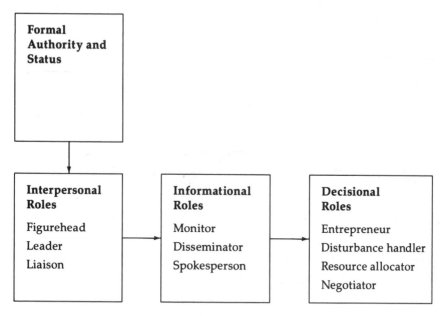

Figure 3-1. *The Manager's Roles*

their freedom to issue unexplained orders, and a growing number of outside influences (consumer groups, government agencies, and so on) demand attention. Managers have had nowhere to turn for help. The first step in providing such help is to find out what the manager's job really is.

BACK TO A BASIC DESCRIPTION OF MANAGERIAL WORK

Earlier, I defined the manager as that person in charge of an organization or subunit. Besides CEOs, this definition would include vice presidents, bishops, foremen, hockey coaches, and prime ministers. All these "managers" are vested with formal authority over an organizational unit. From formal authority comes status, which leads to various interpersonal relations, and from these comes access to information. Information, in turn, enables the manager to make decisions and strategies for the unit.

The manager's job can be described in terms of various "roles," or organized sets of behaviors identified with a position. My description, shown in "The Manager's Roles," comprises ten roles. As we shall see, formal authority gives rise to the three interpersonal roles, which in turn give rise to the three informational roles; these two sets of roles enable the manager to play the four decisional roles.

INTERPERSONAL ROLES

Three of the manager's roles arise directly from formal authority and involve basic interpersonal relationships. First is the *figurehead role*. As the head of an organizational unit, every manager must perform some ceremonial duties. The president greets the touring dignitaries. The foreman attends the wedding of a lathe operator. The sales manager takes an important customer to lunch.

The chief executives of my study spent 12 percent of their contact time on ceremonial duties; 17 percent of their incoming mail dealt with acknowledgments and requests related to their status. For example, a letter to a company president requested free merchandise for a crippled school-child; diplomas that needed to be signed were put on the desk of the school superintendent.

Duties that involve interpersonal roles may sometimes be routine, involving little serious communication and no important decision making. Nevertheless, they are important to the smooth functioning of an organization and cannot be ignored.

Managers are responsible for the work of the people of their unit. Their actions in this regard constitute the *leader* role. Some of these actions involve leadership directly—for example, in most organizations the managers are normally responsible for hiring and training their own staff.

In addition, there is the indirect exercise of the leader role. For example, every manager must motivate and encourage employees, somehow reconciling their individual needs with the goals of the organization. In virtually every contact with the manager, subordinates seeking leadership clues ask: "Does she approve?" "How would she like the report to turn out?" "Is she more interested in market share than high profits?"

The influence of managers is most clearly seen in the leader role. Formal authority vests them with great potential power; leadership determines in large part how much of it they will realize.

The literature of management has always recognized the leader role, particularly those aspects of it related to motivation. In comparison, until recently it has hardly mentioned the *liaison* role, in which the manager makes contacts outside the vertical chain of command. This is remarkable in light of the finding of virtually every study of managerial work that managers spend as much time with peers and other people outside their units as they do with their own subordinates—and, surprisingly, very little time with their own superiors.

In Rosemary Stewart's diary study, the 160 British middle and top managers spent 47 percent of their time with peers, 41 percent of their time with people inside their unit, and only 12 percent of their time with their superiors. For Robert H. Guest's study of U.S. foremen, the figures were 44 percent, 46 percent, and 10 percent. The chief executives of my study averaged 44 percent of their contact time with people outside their organizations, 48 percent with subordinates, and 7 percent with directors and trustees.

The contacts the five CEOs made were with an incredibly wide range of people: subordinates; clients, business associates, and suppliers; and peers—managers of similar organizations, government and trade organization officials, fellow directors on outside boards, and independents with no relevant organizational affiliations. The chief executives' time with and mail from these groups is shown in "The Chief Executive's Contacts." Guest's study of foremen shows, likewise, that their contacts were numerous and wide-ranging, seldom involving fewer than 25 individuals, and often more than 50.

INFORMATIONAL ROLES

By virtue of interpersonal contacts, both with subordinates and with a network of contacts, the manager emerges as the nerve center of the organizational unit. The manager may not know everything but typically knows more than subordinates do.

Studies have shown this relationship to hold for all managers, from street gang leaders to U.S. presidents. In *The Human Group*, George C. Homans explains how, because they were at the center of the information flow in their own gangs and were also in close touch with other gang leaders, street gang leaders were better informed than any of their followers.[12] As for presidents, Richard Neustadt observes: "The essence of [Franklin] Roosevelt's technique for information-gathering was competition. 'He would call you in,' one of his aides once told me, 'and he'd ask you to get the story on some complicated business, and you'd come back after a couple of days of hard labor and present the juicy morsel you'd uncovered under a stone somewhere, and *then* you'd find out he knew all about it, along with something else you *didn't* know. Where he got this information from he wouldn't mention, usually, but after he had done this to you once or twice you got damn careful about *your* information.'"[13]

We can see where Roosevelt "got this information" when we consider the relationship between the interpersonal and informational roles. As leader, the manager has formal and easy access to every staff member. In addition, liaison contacts expose the manager to external information to which subordinates often lack access. Many of these contacts are with other managers of equal status, who are themselves nerve centers in their own organization. In this way, the manager develops a powerful database of information.

Processing information is a key part of the manager's job. In my study, the CEOs spent 40 percent of their contact time on activities devoted

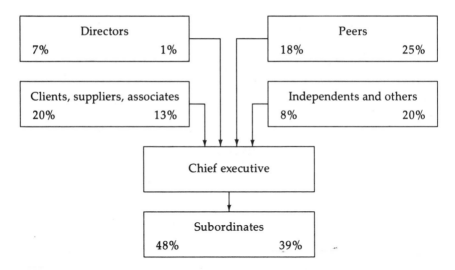

Note: The first figure indicates the proportion of total contact time spent with each group and the second figure, the proportion of mail from each group.

Figure 3–2.   *The Chief Executive's Contacts*

exclusively to the transmission of information; 70 percent of their incoming mail was purely informational (as opposed to requests for action). Managers don't leave meetings or hang up the telephone to get back to work. In large part, communication *is* their work. Three roles describe these informational aspects of managerial work.

As *monitor,* the manager is perpetually scanning the environment for information, interrogating liaison contacts and subordinates, and receiving unsolicited information, much of it as a result of the network of personal contacts. Remember that a good part of the information the manager collects in the monitor role arrives in verbal form, often as gossip, hearsay, and speculation.

In the *disseminator* role, the manager passes some privileged information directly to subordinates, who would otherwise have no access to it. When subordinates lack easy contact with one another, the manager may pass information from one to another.

In the *spokesperson* role, the manager sends some information to people outside the unit—a president makes a speech to lobby for an organization cause, or a foreman suggests a product modification to a supplier. In addition, as a spokesperson, every manager must inform and satisfy the influential people who control the organizational unit. For the foreman, this may simply involve keeping the plant manager informed about the flow of work through the shop.

The president of a large corporation, however, may spend a great amount of time dealing with a host of influences. Directors and shareholders must be advised about finances; consumer groups must be assured that the organization is fulfilling its social responsibilities; and government officials must be satisfied that the organization is abiding by the law.

DECISIONAL ROLES

Information is not, of course, an end in itself; it is the basic input to decision making. One thing is clear in the study of managerial work: the manager plays the major role in the unit's decision-making system. As its formal authority, only the manager can commit the unit to important new courses of action; and as its nerve center, only the manager has full and current information to make the set of decisions that determines the unit's strategy. Four roles describe the manager as decision maker.

As *entrepreneur*, the manager seeks to improve the unit, to adapt it to changing conditions in the environment. In the monitor role, a president is constantly on the lookout for new ideas. When a good one appears, he initiates a development project that he may supervise himself or delegate to an employee (perhaps with the stipulation that he must approve the final proposal).

There are two interesting features about these development projects at the CEO level. First, these projects do not involve single decisions or even unified clusters of decisions. Rather, they emerge as a series of small decisions and actions sequenced over time. Apparently, chief executives prolong each project both to fit it into a busy, disjointed schedule, and so that they can comprehend complex issues gradually.

Second, the chief executives I studied supervised as many as 50 of these projects at the same time. Some projects entailed new products or processes; others involved public relations campaigns, improvement of the cash position, reorganization of a weak department, resolution of a morale problem in a foreign division, integration of computer operations, various acquisitions at different stages of development, and so on.

Chief executives appear to maintain a kind of inventory of the development projects in various stages of development. Like jugglers, they keep a number of projects in the air; periodically, one comes down, is given a new burst of energy, and sent back into orbit. At various intervals, they put new projects on-stream and discard old ones.

While the entrepreneur role describes the manager as the voluntary initiator of change, the *disturbance handler* role depicts the manager involuntarily responding to pressures. Here change is beyond the manager's control. The pressures of a situation are too severe to be ignored—a strike looms, a major customer has gone bankrupt, or a supplier reneges on a contract—so the manager must act.

Leonard R. Sayles, who has carried out appropriate research on the manager's job, likens the manager to a symphony orchestra conductor who must "maintain a melodious performance,"[14] while handling musicians' problems and other external disturbances. Indeed, every manager must spend a considerable amount of time responding to high-pressure disturbances. No organization can be so well run, so standardized, that it has considered every contingency in the uncertain environment in advance. Disturbances arise not only because poor managers ignore situations until they reach crisis proportions but also because good managers cannot possibly anticipate all the consequences of the actions they take.

The third decisional role is that of *resource allocator.* The manager is responsible for deciding who will get what. Perhaps the most important resource the manager allocates is his or her own time. Access to the manager constitutes exposure to the unit's nerve center and decision maker. The manager is also charged with designing the unit's structure, that pattern of formal relationships that determines how work is to be divided and coordinated.

Also, as resource allocator, the manager authorizes the important decisions of the unit before they are implemented. By retaining this power, the manager can ensure that decisions are interrelated. To fragment this power encourages discontinuous decision making and a disjointed strategy.

There are a number of interesting features about the manager's authorization of others' decisions. First, despite the widespread use of capital budgeting procedures—a means of authorizing various capital expenditures at one time—executives in my study made a great many authorization decisions on an ad hoc basis. Apparently, many projects cannot wait or simply do not have the quantifiable costs and benefits that capital budgeting requires.

Second, I found that the chief executives faced incredibly complex choices. They had to consider the impact of each decision on other decisions and on the organization's strategy. They had to ensure that the decision would be acceptable to those who influence the organization, as well as ensure that resources would not be overextended. They had to understand the various costs and benefits as well as the feasibility of the proposal. They also had to consider questions of timing. All this was necessary for the simple approval of someone else's proposal. At the same time, however, the delay could lose time, while quick approval could be ill-considered and quick rejection might discourage the subordinate who had spent months developing a pet project.

One common solution to approving projects is to pick the person instead of the proposal. That is, the manager authorizes those projects presented by people whose judgment he or she trusts. But the manager cannot always use this simple dodge.

The final decisional role is that of *negotiator*. Managers spend considerable time in negotiations: the president of the football team works out a contract with the holdout superstar; the corporation president leads the company's contingent to negotiate a new strike issue; the foreman argues a grievance problem to its conclusion with the shop steward.

These negotiations are an integral part of the manager's job, for only he or she has the authority to commit organizational resources in "real time" and the nerve-center information that important negotiations require.

THE INTEGRATED JOB

It should be clear by now that these ten roles are not easily separable. In the terminology of the psychologist, they form a gestalt, an integrated whole. No role can be pulled out of the framework and the job be left intact. For example, a manager without liaison contacts lacks external information. As a result, that manager can neither disseminate the information that employees need nor make decisions that adequately reflect external conditions. (This is a problem for the new person in a managerial position, since he or she has to build up a network of contacts before making effective decisions.)

Here lies a clue to the problems of team management.[15] Two or three people cannot share a single managerial position unless they can act as one entity. This means that they cannot divide up the ten roles unless they can very carefully reintegrate them. The real difficulty lies with the informational roles. Unless there can be full sharing of managerial information—and, as I pointed out earlier, it is primarily verbal—team management breaks down. A single managerial job cannot be arbitrarily split, for example, into internal and external roles, for information from both sources must be brought to bear on the same decisions.

To say that the ten roles form a gestalt is not to say that all managers give equal attention to each role. In fact, I found in my review of the various research studies that sales managers seem to spend relatively more of their time in the interpersonal roles, presumably a reflection of the extrovert nature of the marketing activity. Production managers, on the other hand, give relatively more attention to the decisional roles, presumably a reflection of their concern with efficient work flow. And staff managers spend the most time in the informational roles, since they are experts who manage departments that advise other parts of the organization. Nevertheless, in all cases, the interpersonal, informational, and decisional roles remain inseparable.

TOWARD MORE EFFECTIVE MANAGEMENT

This description of managerial work should prove more important to managers than any prescription they might derive from it. That is to say, *the managers' effectiveness is significantly influenced by their insight into their own work.* Performance depends on how well a manager understands and responds to the pressures and dilemmas of the job. Thus managers who can be introspective about their work are likely to be effective at their jobs. The questions in "Self-Study Questions for Managers" may sound rhetorical; none is meant to be. Even though the questions cannot be answered simply, the manager should address them.

Let us take a look at three specific areas of concern. For the most part, the managerial logjams—the dilemma of delegation, the database centralized in one brain, the problems of working with the management scientist—revolve around the verbal nature of the manager's information. There are great dangers in centralizing the organization's data bank in the minds of its managers. When they leave, they take their memory with them. And when subordinates are out of convenient verbal reach of the manager, they are at an informational disadvantage.

The manager is challenged to find systematic ways to share privileged information. A regular debriefing session with key subordinates, a weekly memory dump on the dictating machine, maintaining a diary for limited circulation, or other similar methods may ease the logjam of work considerably. The time spent disseminating this information will be more than regained when decisions must be made. Of course, some will undoubtedly raise the question of confidentiality. But managers would be well advised to weigh the risks of exposing privileged information against having subordinates who can make effective decisions.

If there is a single theme that runs through this article, it is that the pressures of the job drive the manager to take on too much work, encourage interruption, respond quickly to every stimulus, seek the tangible and avoid the abstract, make decisions in small increments, and do everything abruptly.

Here again, the manager is challenged to deal consciously with the pressures of superficiality by giving serious attention to the issues that require it, by stepping back in order to see a broad picture, and by making use of analytical inputs. Although effective managers have to be adept at responding quickly to numerous and varying problems, the danger in managerial work is that they will respond to every issue equally (and that means abruptly) and that they will never work the tangible bits and pieces of information into a comprehensive picture of their world.

To create this comprehensive picture, managers can supplement their own models with those of specialists. Economists describe the functioning of markets, operations researchers simulate financial flow processes, and behavioral scientists explain the needs and goals of people. The best of these models can be searched out and learned.

In dealing with complex issues, the senior manager has much to gain from a close relationship with the organization's own management scientists. They have something important that the manager lacks—time to probe complex issues. An effective working relationship hinges on the resolution of what a colleague and I have called "the planning dilemma."[16] Managers have the information and the authority; analysts have the time and the technology. A successful working relationship between the two will be effected when the manager learns to share information and the analyst learns to adapt to the manager's needs. For the analyst, adaptation means worrying less about the elegance of the method and more about its speed and flexibility.

Analysts can help the top manager schedule time, feed in analytical information, monitor projects, develop models to aid in making choices, design contingency plans for disturbances that can be anticipated, and conduct "quick and dirty" analyses for those that cannot. But there can be no cooperation if the analysts are out of the mainstream of the manager's information flow.

The manager is challenged to gain control of his or her own time by turning obligations into advantages and by turning those things he or she wishes to do into obligations. The chief executives of my study initiated only 32% of their own contacts (and another 5% by mutual agreement). And yet to a considerable extent they seemed to control their time. There were two key factors that enabled them to do so.

First, managers have to spend so much time discharging obligations that if they were to view them as just that, they would leave no mark on the organization. Unsuccessful managers blame failure on the obligations. Effective managers turn obligations to advantages. A speech is a chance to lobby for a cause; a meeting is a chance to reorganize a weak department; a visit to an important customer is a chance to extract trade information.

Second, the manager frees some time to do the things that he or she—perhaps no one else—thinks important by turning them into obligations. Free time is made, not found. Hoping to leave some time open for contemplation or general planning is tantamount to hoping that the pressures of the job will go away. Managers who want to innovate initiate projects and obligate others to report back to them. Managers who need certain environmental information establish channels that will automatically keep them informed. Managers who have to tour facilities commit themselves publicly.

THE EDUCATOR'S JOB

Finally, a word about the training of managers. Our management schools have done an admirable job of training the organization's specialists—management scientists, marketing researchers, accountants, and organizational development specialists. But for the most part, they have not trained managers.[17]

Management schools will begin the serious training of managers when skill training takes a serious place next to cognitive learning. Cognitive learning is detached and informational, like reading a book or listening to a lecture. No doubt much important cognitive material must be assimilated by the manager-to-be. But cognitive learning no more makes a manager than it does a swimmer. The latter will drown the first time she jumps into the water if her coach never takes her out of the lecture hall, gets her wet, and gives her feedback on her performance.

In other words, we are taught a skill through practice plus feedback, whether in a real or a simulated situation. Our management schools need to identify the skills managers use, select students who show potential in these skills, put the students into situations where these skills can be practiced and developed, and then give them systematic feedback on their performance.

My description of managerial work suggests a number of important managerial skills—developing peer relationships, carrying out negotiations, motivating subordinates, resolving conflicts, establishing information networks and subsequently disseminating information, making decisions in conditions of extreme ambiguity, and allocating resources. Above all, the manager needs to be introspective in order to continue to learn on the job.

No job is more vital to our society than that of the manager. The manager determines whether our social institutions will serve us well or whether they will squander our talents and resources. It is time to strip away the folklore about managerial work and study it realistically so that we can begin the difficult task of making significant improvements in its performance.

REFERENCES

1. All the data from my study can be found in Henry Mintzberg, *The Nature of Managerial Work* (New York: Harper & Row, 1973).
2. Robert H. Guest, "Of Time and the Foreman," *Personnel*, May 1956, p. 478.

3. Rosemary Stewart, *Managers and Their Jobs* (London: Macmillan, 1967); see also Sune Carlson, *Executive Behavior* (Stockholm: Strombergs, 1951).

4. Francis J. Aguilar, *Scanning the Business Environment* (New York: Macmillan, 1967), p. 102.

5. Unpublished study by Irving Choran, reported in Mintzberg, *The Nature of Managerial Work*.

6. Robert T. Davis, *Performance and Development of Field Sales Managers* (Boston: Division of Research, Harvard Business School, 1957); George H. Copeman, *The Role of the Managing Director* (London: Business Publications, 1963).

7. Stewart, *Managers and Their Jobs;* Tom Burns, "The Directions of Activity and Communication in a Departmental Executive Group," *Human Relations 7*, no. 1 (1954): 73.

8. H. Edward Wrapp, "Good Managers Don't Make Policy Decisions," HBR September-October 1967, p. 91. Wrapp refers to this as spotting opportunities and relationships in the stream of operating problems and decisions; in his article, Wrapp raises a number of excellent points related to this analysis.

9. Richard E. Neustadt, *Presidential Power* (New York: John Wiley, 1960), pp. 153–154; italics added.

10. For a more thorough, though rather different, discussion of this issue, see Kenneth R. Andrews, "Toward Professionalism in Business Management," HBR March-April 1969, p. 49.

11. C. Jackson Grayson, Jr., in "Management Science and Business Practice," HBR July-August 1973, p. 41, explains in similar terms why, as chairman of the Price Commission, he did not use those very techniques that he himself promoted in his earlier career as a management scientist.

12. George C. Homans, *The Human Group* (New York: Harcourt, Brace & World, 1950), based on the study by William F. Whyte entitled *Street Corner Society*, rev. ed. (Chicago: University of Chicago Press, 1955).

13. Neustadt, *Presidential Power*, p. 157.

14. Leonard R. Sayles, *Managerial Behavior* (New York: McGraw-Hill, 1964), p. 162.

15. See Richard C. Hodgson, Daniel J. Levinson, and Abraham Zaleznik, *The Executive Role Constellation* (Boston: Division of Research, Harvard Business School, 1965), for a discussion of the sharing of roles.

16. James S. Hekimian and Henry Mintzberg, "The Planning Dilemma," *The Management Review*, May 1968, p. 4.

17. See J. Sterling Livingston, "Myth of the Well-Educated Manager," HBR January-February 1971, p. 79.

QUESTIONS

1. Discuss the 10 managerial roles and include the three groups of roles. How can an EIS affect each role, if at all?

2. Mintzberg notes that managers have three problems that may prevent them from being effective. These problems are:

   (1) Finding systematic ways to share information

   (2) Giving attention to issues that require it and attempting to see the broad picture by making use of analytical inputs

   (3) Gaining control of his time.

   How can an EIS help managers with each of these problems?

3. Mintzberg stated in 1975 that managers favor verbal media and avoid formal management information systems. What characteristics of executive information systems might change this statement?

4

Making Executive Information Systems More Effective

Raymond McLeod, Jr.
Jack W. Jones

Computer-based management information systems (MIS) and decision support systems (DSS) have been promoted as necessary ingredients to good decision making. Many people believe, however, that managers do not really use such systems. If that is true, then where do managers get their information, and what do they do with it once they get it?

These are important questions, yet little effort has been made to answer them. It is time to investigate the structure that relates executive decision making to the total spectrum of information flows. This article reviews the information systems of five senior executives and suggests ways that all managers can improve their systems.

THE MANAGER'S INFORMATIONAL AND DECISIONAL ROLES

In his book *The Nature of Managerial Work,* Henry Mintzberg identified ten roles that are inherent in the manager's job.[1] Three of these roles (*figurehead, leader, liaison*) are interpersonal; they involve the manager in ceremonial duties and in interactions with subordinates and persons outside the unit. Three roles (*monitor, disseminator, spokesperson*) are informational;

the manager gathers and distributes information both externally and internally (within his or her own unit). Four roles are decisional; the manager uses the gathered information to improve the unit (*entrepreneur*), handle disturbances (*disturbance handler*), allocate the unit's resources (*resource allocator*), and negotiate agreements (*negotiator*).

This concept is appealing to information and decision scientists because it stresses the informational and decisional aspects of management. However, Mintzberg, writing in 1973, did not emphasize computer-based systems. Rather, he identified five general media—documents, scheduled and unscheduled meetings, telephone calls, and observational tours—that managers employ to do their job.

We believe that Mintzberg was on the right track. Managers *do* use more than computer information, and they *do* use their information in making decisions. But in his efforts to describe overall management activity, Mintzberg did not address the various information sources available

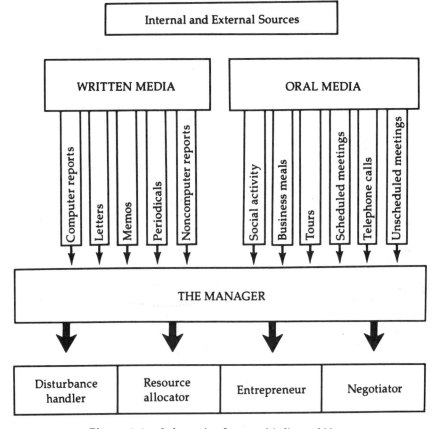

Figure 4-1. *Information Sources, Media, and Uses*

to the manager, and his five media types were very broad. Building upon Mintzberg's work, we designed a research project aimed at better understanding managers' information systems by including all sources and all media and relating all of those inputs to the four decisional roles.

The model in Figure 4–1 is the basis for the study:

- The *upper* box represents the *sources* of information, both internal and external. These sources can be organizations or individuals.
- The *middle* area of the model represents the *media* that funnel information to the manager. The media are either written or oral, and Mintzberg's five types have been expanded to eleven.
- The *lower* box shows the information being used in the four *decisional roles.*

STUDYING FIVE SYSTEMS

Five senior executives consented to participate in the project by permitting us to take a detailed look at their information systems. The executives included Peter Hennessey III, president of a life insurance company; Bob Camp, president and CEO of a retail chain; John Easton, corporate officer and vice-president of tax for a diversified energy company; Bill Guthrie, corporate officer and vice-president of finance for an oil field services company; and Jody Grant, chairman and CEO of a bank. All firms are located in the Southwest.

Prior to initial interviews, we gave each executive a copy of an article that summarized Mintzberg's management role concept.[2] The purpose was to provide a starting point for the discussions. During the interviews, the executives talked about their management philosophies and gave examples of information use in each of the decisional roles.

Forms were left with the executives and their secretaries to use in logging the executives' incoming information transactions for a two-week period. The executives logged business meals, social activity, and observational tours. The secretaries logged transactions that they could observe: telephone calls, letters, memos, meetings, reports, and periodicals. During the two-week period, a total of 1,454 transactions were logged.

INFORMATION VOLUME

How many pieces of information reach a senior executive each day? Is the number rather stable, or does it fluctuate widely? Is an executive's information system taxed to its limits? These are key questions relating to an important dimension of an information system—the volume of information that it handles.

Varying Volume Levels

The executives received an average of 29 transactions per day. (A transaction is any unit of the logged media, such as a memo or a meeting.) The daily averages ranged from a high of 41 for Camp, the retail CEO, to a low of 14 for Guthrie, the president of finance.

Fluctuations were the greatest for Easton, the vice-president of tax. On the high day he was 52 percent above average, and he was 39 percent below on the low day. Fluctuations were the least, ranging from 21 percent above to 39 percent below, for Hennessey, the insurance president. Hennessey's low fluctuations may have been caused by the fact that he has had more time to build his information system than the other executives. He has been a president longer, and he had the benefit of an orientation period of several years before assuming the responsibilities. It seems logical that the more an executive knows about his or her information system, the better it can be managed. This increased knowledge comes, in part, from time on the job.

Occasionally, an executive's information system will become overloaded. The executive can let some of the excess slide over to the next day, delegate some to a secretary or staff assistant, or devote extra time to handling the backlog. Hennessey sets aside a block of "quiet time" to work on nothing but the information. He will often come to his office early in the morning before any other employees arrive.

None of the executives showed concern lest their information systems become overloaded. All encouraged inputs by maintaining a high visibility within their firms, and, to a lesser extent, outside. The executives are willing to accept high volumes of information.

INFORMATION VALUE

How much value do executives assign to the information that they receive? What factors influence the value? Can information be managed so that all of the items with little or no value can be filtered out? These are important questions that relate to another dimension of an information system—the *value* of the information it produces.

The executives assigned a value ranging from 0 (no value) to 10 (maximum value) to each of the logged transactions. In assigning this value, the executives had to anticipate what use, if any, would be made of each item. As with the volumes, there was a variation from one executive to the next.

Bank CEO Grant assigned the highest percentage of high values (8, 9, or 10). Thirty-nine percent of his transactions fell in this category. Vice-presidents Easton and Guthrie, on the other hand, regarded only 9 percent and 3 percent, respectively, as having high value. The two vice-presidents also had the largest percentage of low-value transactions (0, 1, or 2). Easton assigned a low value to 53 percent of his transactions, and Guthrie was close behind at 39 percent. Insurance president Hennessey and retail CEO Camp viewed most of their transactions as having medium value (3 through 7). Hennessey viewed 75 percent of his transactions in this manner. Camp followed with 73 percent.

Since in this study vice-presidents logged the lowest values, it could be conjectured that the information of *all* vice-presidents is not so pure as that reaching presidents. A vice-president may filter out much of the impure information as it is routed up to the president. However, the small sample size of the study makes it impossible to reach such a conclusion. For this reason the subject of information value is best addressed by considering the factors relating to a particular executive's system rather than using averages of several systems. The averages provide only general guidelines and must be used with care.

The major finding of the value analysis is that these top executives receive much information that they regard as having little or no value. This condition seems to dispel the notion that an upper-level manager can design a system to filter out all of the impurities. Even at the top management level there is a need to sift through many low-value transactions to find those containing material of real importance.

SOURCES OF INFORMATION

Each transaction was coded to identify its source. Figure 4–2 reflects the findings. Each source is identified by a rectangle containing two numbers:

- The one *above* the diagonal is the percentage of overall volume.
- The one *below* is the average value.

The source representing the largest volume is the external environment, with 43 percent. Internally, the executives obtained 5 percent of their information from levels above them in the hierarchy, and 38 percent from below. Hennessey was the only president obtaining more than 1 percent from upper levels. He obtained 3 percent from his father, the board chairman. Because of their lower rank, the vice-presidents had an opportunity to gather more upper-level information, and they did. Easton's percentage was 5, and Guthrie's was 11.

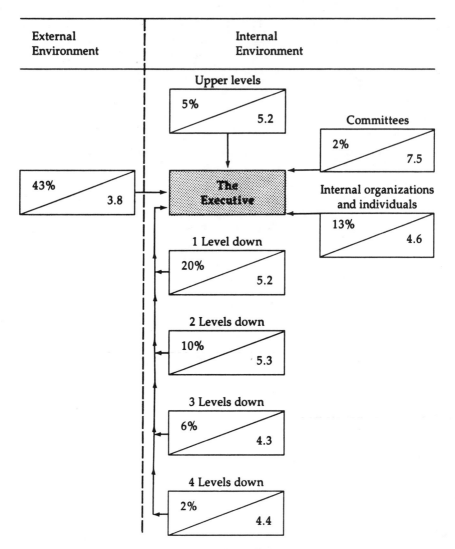

Figures may not total 100 percent because of rounding.

In each rectangle, the number *above* the diagonal is the percentage of overall volume for that source. The number *below* the diagonal is the average value, from 0 (no value) to 10 (maximum value), assigned the transaction.

Figure 4-2. *Sources for Executive Information*

The figure shows that a lesser amount of information was gathered at each lower level. That characteristic held true for all executives. The executives differed, however, in the depth of their networks. Retail CEO Camp, bank CEO Grant, and tax vice-president Easton obtained much information from three and four levels down, but life insurance president Hennessey and financial vice-president Guthrie preferred to look only to the two levels immediately below.

Only 2 percent of the inputs came from committees, and only 13 percent came from internal organizations (such as the accounting department) and individuals (such as the manager of stockholder relations) who perform a support function for the entire firm.

An analysis of the sources in terms of their average value reveals a different picture. The source with the highest volume—the external environment—produced the lowest average value, and the source with the lowest volume—committees—produced the highest value. That inverse relationship did not hold for all of the sources. The two levels immediately below the executives produced 30 percent of the volume, yet provided information value that was exceeded only by committees.

Even though the executives varied in the levels of their values, the presidents all assigned high values to their committees and lower values to inputs from outside their firms. Grant, however, assigned a high value to inputs from persons outside his bank, and Hennessey did the same for organizations outside his insurance company.

INFORMATION MEDIA

Based on the logs, how was the media pie sliced? Figure 4–3 shows that written media accounted for 61 percent of the transaction volume, with letters and memos used as the vehicles 39 percent of the time. The only oral medium handling a large volume (21 percent) was the telephone. Clearly the executives had built information systems to communicate information primarily in written form.

Figure 4–3 also reveals that the executives favored informal systems. An informal system is one that is not specified in a procedure and is enacted as the situation demands. The only formal systems are scheduled meetings and the two types of reports—computer and noncomputer. These media accounted for only 17 percent of the inputs.

The preference for oral information was reflected as well in the assigned values. Figure 4–4 shows that the top four media, based on average value, are oral. The most highly valued medium was scheduled meetings; the next most valued was unscheduled meetings. Tours and social activity also outranked all written media. Memos were the top-ranked written medium, higher than both computer and noncomputer

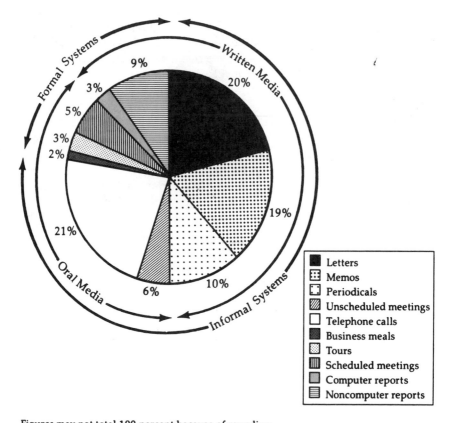

Figures may not total 100 percent because of rounding.

Figure 4-3. *The Media Pie: Volume of Various Media*

reports. Telephone calls and business meals, although oral, ranked quite low. The average value of the information gleaned from periodicals was the lowest of all the media.

There was considerable variation in how the executives ranked the media, but all executives preferred the oral media. Looking at the top four preferences for all five executives, oral media outnumbered written media by a ratio of 2 to 1.

Scheduled Meetings and Tours

It is easy to understand why scheduled meetings rank so high. A particular type of recurring problem or opportunity has been identified and a group of persons selected to best address it. The group assembles in surroundings that facilitate communication, and the participants are

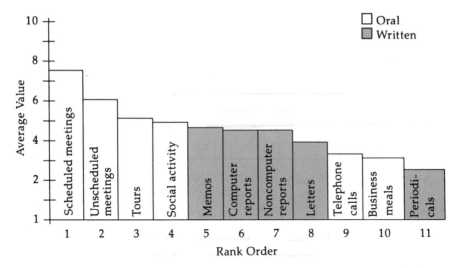

Figure 4-4. *Ranking the Media by Their Value to the Executive*

usually well prepared. It also is common for several other media to be reviewed during a meeting.

We recognized earlier that the small sample size makes it impossible to draw any conclusions relative to managerial level. That precaution applies here as well, but the study reveals an aspect of executive behavior that merits additional research.

The three presidents in our study made greater use of scheduled meetings than did the two vice-presidents, who showed special preference for tours. A tour takes the executive out of his or her office for the purpose of gathering information. It can be a stroll down the hall or a visit to a contact outside the firm. Perhaps the presidents liked the control they have over scheduled meetings, whereas the vice-presidents liked the features of the tour that enabled them to obtain good information with little wasted time. Guthrie spoke of his controller being "just down the hall," and Easton appreciated the greater ease of cutting off a conversation in the other person's office. One might assume that the responsibilities at the top level would make that person less mobile than managers on the lower level; the executives in our study seemed to demonstrate the validity of that assumption.

Memos and Reports

Memos are timely and focused, characteristics that make them the most favored written medium. Very often an executive will tell subordinates, "Put that in a memo," to help them crystallize their thinking. Memos can also distill information gathered by other media, such as periodicals or reports.

The executives valued memos slightly higher than both computer and noncomputer reports, which they valued about equally. However, noncomputer reports outnumbered computer reports three to one. Insurance president Hennessey pointed out that noncomputer reports are often reviewed in his scheduled meetings but that computer reports seldom are. Someone usually rewrites a computer report, putting it into a noncomputer form.

Financial vice-president Guthrie and retail CEO Camp indicated a greater reliance on computer-produced information. Guthrie described how he detected an $800,000 scam in foreign operations by analyzing computer reports. Camp explained how he has begun to redesign his computer reports, working closely with his computer specialist. He has added a new report that identifies his "dogs"—slow-moving items. Prior to a store tour, he reviews this report so that he can ask store personnel for their explanations. He uses a computer report to increase the value of information gathered on a tour.

The executives' computer reports were sent to them either from their computer departments or from managers on lower levels. The reports received from the managers were valued much higher (6.3) than those from the departments (4.4). The reports from the managers are more informal and are sent because they bear on some topic of current interest.

AN "INFORMATION CHAIN"

The study brought to light an "information chain," a technique that executives might use to gather information for decision making. On several occasions the executives described how information from one medium is related to another. Hennessey's use of noncomputer reports in scheduled meetings and Camp's use of computer reports prior to tours are examples.

Managers on all levels make use of multiple media during the problem-solving process, but it seems unlikely that the media are selected at random. Rather, the media may form a type of *information chain.* Certain media are used first to identify and define problems, and other media build upon the initial information to form the basis for decision making.

For example, a president sees an article in a periodical revealing that a competitor is moving into the firm's trade area. A telephone call is placed to the sales manager to get an appraisal of the situation. The president asks the sales manager to look into the matter and put the findings in a memo. Upon receiving the memo, the president calls a special meeting to discuss possible strategies.

In this scenario the values of the media (as shown in Figure 4–4) increase with each link of the chain. The chain concept may help to explain the low values assigned to telephone calls. The telephone is often used early in the chain to signal problems and opportunities. At that point the manager might hesitate to assign a high value, not knowing what the eventual outcome of the signal will be. As the decision process unfolds, other media convey explanations and solutions, and their high value is more easily seen. The highest value would be perceived for those media used immediately prior to and during the time that the decision is made.

The media used during the early portions of the chain would be those offering a "broadcast" capability—such as periodicals, computer and noncomputer reports, and telephone calls. Media used subsequently to shed additional light on the problem permit more concentrated focus—memos and the face-to-face tours and meetings. Variations in the choice of media at specific points in the chain would be expected from manager to manager, based on individual preferences.

The chain concept helps explain the willingness of the executives to utilize "low-value" sources and media. The executives recognize the ability of the sources and media to function during early stages of the chain. All of the links of the chain must be present if the system is to support the entire decision process.

INFORMATION AND DECISIONAL ROLES

According to Mintzberg, managers use their information in four decisional roles: resource allocator, disturbance handler, entrepreneur, and negotiator.

- *Resource allocation* is somewhat short-term in nature, such as annual budgetary planning.
- A *disturbance* is something that happens unexpectedly and demands immediate attention, but it might take weeks or months to resolve.
- *Entrepreneurial activity* is more long-term and strategic in nature, as improvements are made in the unit to increase its performance level.
- *Negotiations* involve the manager in some type of dispute, either internal or external to the organization.

Each transaction of the five executives in the study was coded with the decisional role where the information would most likely be used. In terms of volume, most (42 percent) of the transactions were intended to be used in handling disturbances. Slightly fewer (32 percent) were intended for making entrepreneurial improvements. Resource allocation accounted for a sizable volume (at 17 percent), but negotiating (at 3 percent) did not. Six percent of the transactions could not be associated with any of the roles.

The executives' information systems were geared primarily to support disturbance handling and entrepreneurial activity and, to a lesser extent, resource allocation. The executives valued their information most when it could be associated with one of these three decisional roles. The average value of information to be used in the entrepreneurial role was 4.8, followed by 4.7 for resource allocation and 4.6 for disturbance handling. When it was to be used in negotiating, the information was not valued so highly (3.8), and it was given a very low value (1.1) when its use in a particular decisional role was not apparent.

1. *Entrepreneurial activity.* Although 69 percent of the entrepreneurial transactions originated externally, they were given a lower value than those coming from within. Most of the inputs were written—letters, periodicals, memos, and noncomputer reports. Noncomputer reports were valued more highly than computer reports. Although smaller in number, oral transactions were given the highest value. Telephone information was valued more highly for this decisional role than for any other, and more than half of the highly valued scheduled meetings were related to making improvements.

2. *Resource allocation.* Most of these transactions were generated internally, and were valued much more highly than inputs coming from the outside. Computer reports were valued more highly than noncomputer reports, which may indicate that the decisional role may influence what type of report is preferred. A considerable number of the unscheduled meetings and observational tours were devoted to gathering information to be used in allocating resource. The executives valued the information gathered on tours most highly when this information was to be used in resource allocation.

3. *Disturbance handling.* When handling disturbances, the executives used mostly internal information, which was valued more highly than external information. Most of the internal information came from support organizations and the three levels below. Most of the transactions utilized written media such as letters, memos, and noncomputer reports, but oral media such as telephone calls, unscheduled meetings, and tours were given the highest value.

4. *Negotiating.* Most of the negotiating information came either from persons outside the firm or from the three levels immediately below, but there was no clear preference. There was also no preference for a particular medium. Eighty percent of the transactions

were letters, memos, and telephone calls. Little negotiating information was gathered face-to-face—only one scheduled meeting, four unscheduled meetings, and one tour were earmarked for this role. However, this information was valued very highly.

5. *Information and decisional roles.* The executives preferred to use certain kinds of information in certain situations.[3] When making improvements, they preferred internal information over external, and for either source they preferred oral media over written. When allocating resources, they preferred internal information, but medium had no influence on the value. When handling disturbances, the executives preferred internal information, and they preferred that these internal sources communicate verbally. When negotiating, they found that neither the source nor the medium had any influence on the value.

These relationships have significant design implications. Information systems for executives must contain strong internal networks of oral information to support decisions that handle disturbances and make entrepreneurial improvements. In no decisional role is there a clear preference for written media as currently constructed. If written media such as computer reports are to play a more important role in the executive's information system, they must be revised to provide the information that the executive needs. Executives in this study perceived computer reports to be more valuable in allocating resources than in making improvements. If the information requirements for each role can be identified, then the media best communicating that information can be utilized.

IMPLICATIONS FOR MANAGEMENT INFORMATION SYSTEMS

While it is neither possible nor prudent to eliminate all low-value transactions, managers should strive to increase the value of all transactions. In order to do this they must have a good idea of where they get their best information. Information management, therefore, is a two-step process:

1. Inventorying information sources and media; and then
2. Implementing strategies designed to effect improvements.

- *Inventory sources and media.* A manager's perceptions of information sources and media are likely to be distorted to some extent. They need to be sharpened with a more formal record.

    A secretary can help by keeping a record of observed transactions—meetings, reports, memos, letters, telephone calls, and periodicals. Perhaps some of these records are already being kept in the form of an appointments calendar. The manager can keep a log of transactions that occur away from the office—tours, business meals, and social activities. Each day a value should be assigned to each logged entry. This may be all the recordkeeping that is necessary. A review of the logs will give managers a good understanding of their information sources and media. For a more sophisticated analysis, a staff assistant can enter the data into a computer and produce various tabulations.

When managers have a good idea of who is supplying them with good information and which media do the best communication job, they can begin to manage their information. The managers in our study made the following suggestions.

• *Stimulate inputs from high-value sources.* Special attention should be given to high-value sources, giving them every opportunity to communicate. Bank CEO Grant values especially information from his committees and gives much thought to ways to stimulate their inputs. To make all of the members feel that they have an equal say, Grant selected a round table for the conference room where the committees meet.

Retail president Camp values highly the inputs that he gets from lower levels. Through his behavior he conveys his readiness to communicate. He encourages any manager or secretary to call him on the phone, and he frequently writes to persons as far as four levels down. When he attends company meetings, he takes notes. He says, "I think it's good for them to see, and it helps me remember what to do with their input."

This strategy of stimulating high-value sources applies equally well outside the company. Insurance company president Hennessey carefully selects external organizations with members who may be able to help him when the need arises. He often will ask one of his external contacts to help him focus on a problem, appreciating the fresh approach that someone outside the insurance industry can provide.

• *Take advantage of information opportunities.* All managers do not prefer to seek out information opportunities; some prefer a less aggressive approach. Regardless of style, when an opportunity presents itself, the manager should take advantage of it.

While attending a Harvard retailing seminar, Camp had the choice of working on a case assignment or going out for an evening cup of coffee with four other presidents of large chains. He accepted the coffee invitation, and the discussion focused on bonus plans. He said, "You couldn't buy that information from a consultant at any price."

The other managers cited examples of tactics they have developed to make the most of information opportunities. When Grant wants to engage in a serious conversation with a visitor, he sits next to that person on the sofa in his office. When a visitor has materials to be reviewed, Hennessey will invite that person to spread them out on a large table. Vice-president of finance Guthrie purposely positions his desk next to the wall so that he must drop whatever he is working on to turn around and give his visitor his full attention.

- *Tailor the system to fit individual needs.* One message was clear: There is no best approach to constructing an information system. Methods that play key roles in one executive's system were not emphasized in others. Managers can get their information in many ways.

  Camp's predecessor disdained the tour. To avoid contact with his employees, he entered his office through a private entrance. Camp takes the opposite approach. He uses the building's front door to come in contact with as many people as possible. Recognizing the value variety, Camp observed, "There is more than one way to get to the bank."

- *Use technology to improve information quality.* The computer has the potential for playing a more important role in a manager's information system than the study revealed. Hennessey has the strongest computer background, having once been a COBOL programmer. Therefore, it is no accident that he is the biggest computer user. The more that a manager knows about computers, the better support the computer can provide. In Hennessey's case, he has elected to put computer power in the hands of lower-level management rather than rely on personal use. This is a sound strategy. The lower levels can screen the corporate data base for items to be passed upward through the full spectrum of communication media. When the computer resource is distributed throughout the organization in the form of terminals or personal computers in the managers' offices, the computer acquires the qualities of the informal system preferred by managers.

  The computer can also be used to expedite the flow of informal information. Office automation may be the real key to increased computer use. Applications such as computer conferences, electronic calendars, and word processing can increase the value of information communicated in meetings, on tours, and in memos. Yet these office automation applications are typically viewed as clerical transactions, a view that ignores their potential in decision support systems. Hennessey's firm has excelled in recognizing the potential support computers can provide. All of his managers have had the opportunity to attend a special word-processing course offered by a local college. Since the data were gathered, Hennessey has obtained a terminal for his office and has become a heavy user of electronic calendaring and electronic mail.

Realistically, however, the computer will never replace the face-to-face media. In commenting on the limitations of the computer, Camp said, "It won't know what a raised eyebrow looks like and what a fake smile looks like." Instead of replacing other media, the electronic technology should be used to make the other media even better and to offer entirely new communication opportunities.

Managers know their own information systems better than anyone else does. They should continue to use those sources and media that have worked best for them in the past. But their perceptions of where their best information comes from are not perfect.

Based on our study, we advise:

- Take an inventory, and then take a close look at each source and medium—each one can be improved.
- Don't be blind to new opportunities.
- Look at new technologies (such as office automation) as ways to improve your computer support.

Information systems do not come about by chance. They are built over a period of time with very little formal direction. Systems developed by managers have helped them to get where they now are in the organization. By considering their sources and media, managers can increase the effectiveness of these important links that lead from problem signals to solutions.

REFERENCES

1. See Henry Mintzberg, *The Nature of Managerial Work* (New York: Harper & Row, 1973).

2. See Henry Mintzberg, "The Manager's Job: Folklore and Fact," *Harvard Business Review*, July-August 1975: 49–61.

3. The analysis of variance (ANOVA) technique was used to determine the significance of the relationship between source and media on the one hand,

and information value on the other. All of the source and media preferences quoted are significant at the .0003 level or better. The influences of source and media on value could have occurred by chance no more than 3 times in 10,000. It can therefore be stated with a great degree of certainty that the value of the information was influenced by the source and the medium.

QUESTIONS

1. Discuss how the authors placed this study in the context of Mintzberg's *The Nature of Managerial Work*. Include the ten managerial roles and the five general media that Mintzberg mentioned.
2. What is an "information chain"?
3. Discuss the implications of this study for all computer-based information systems.
4. McLeod and Jones state that executives have many information sources. Where do computer-based information sources (for example, EISs) fit among all possible executive information sources in terms of volume? Value? Why is this the case? How has technology improved this situation since this article was published in 1986?

5

User Expectations—The CEO's Perspective

George L. Ball

I have tried to put down some thoughts on information, and on your job. Incidentally, I don't want to be held to accuracy.

I will make one statement that is deadly accurate, however, concerning the world of technology and information as it is viewed by CEOs. To us, information is the bane of consumer-oriented service industries. It removes uncertainty, eliminates opportunities to create alibis, and permits customers to find out what we are doing wrong. We do not like information. It lifts the veils of obfuscation that permit overpricing, and it destroys barriers to competition.

CEOs of companies like mine do not like technology. We are appalled by the improved flow of information that it produces. We despair of ever again enjoying adequate profit margins, now that clients in our businesses can peek underneath our rather barren tents of talent. Although I say that with tongue in cheek, I think that, in one way, the availability of information has changed things permanently. We can no longer hoodwink people simply because they don't know things. Our business—the financial service business—is probably one of the first either to benefit or to be altered by that. Unfortunately, we can't turn the clock back. Since an informed consumer is our worst customer, our only hope for maintaining profits and profit margins is to harness technology so that we do things better, smarter, and faster.

What CEOs are looking for at the outset is something that I think is quite different from what is usually expected of people in your jobs. The

Previously published in *Information Times*, a newspaper of the Information Industry Association, April 1987. Used with permission.

availability of data is no longer an issue: when you turn on the morning news, there are shows that give you information that only stock exchange floor boxers or investment bankers could get for days or weeks after the fact. Now you can get it the next day or even the same day, sitting in the middle of Belgium in a hotel.

What is it, then, that CEOs want? I start by professing a substantial lack of knowledge in technology, and I'm probably not atypical. I have gone to computer schools and spent a couple of weeks at IBM, read the manuals, have a PC at home, use it in my office, but am not knowledgeable at a level of sophistication that would make me anything but a little bit dangerous. That is probably your typical CEO.

The thing that we want first and foremost is information that will give us a relatively enduring preemptive strategic advantage. Preemptive—so that others can't come after it real fast. Strategic—not just a tactical advantage—but ways to win whole campaigns, not just battles. We want to capture entire fronts, and be able to hold them.

There are several notions embedded in that desire. First, technology has to make information simple. You've got to give us less. We get too many reports that are too long and contain so much data that we can't use them. Indeed, one can't find anything because there is so much of it. Now, you might well say, "That is really not my job. My job is to get information to the CEO." But I don't believe that is correct anymore.

I believe that the role of the Chief Information Officer has gone well beyond that of being merely a provider of information. You have to be diligent, even ruthless, in keeping reports and other information products within specific bounds. You now have an active responsibility to see that we get less. To see that the less we get is the right less, not the wrong less. You will be the one to make that judgement, and in making it, you will have to "tier" information, as well as streamline it.

You'll notice that much of the information that flows through an organization contains the detail from the base level all the way up to the top. That isn't terribly valuable, nor is it terribly smart. We need reports that contain less detail as they go higher and higher in the chain of command. A 250-page report should be pared down to two pages by the time it reaches the CEO—since too much information is sometimes as useless as no information at all.

Within only a few organizations are there top level people who have been assigned the task, as either a full or part-time duty, to edit, to tailor, and to suggest. These people are quite knowledgeable about the business units in which they operate. They do not accept what the user says as gospel. Applying their knowledge of the business, they try to craft or create information flows that are different.

So instead of being user-responsive, you are to some extent user-influential. CEOs want that now. Here, I'm not talking about the technology.

Technology itself is not of primary concern to us. The output from the technology and its usefulness are what we really care about.

Finally in this little litany, but maybe most important, is for yourselves to meet with top management, in various business units, and talk about what sort of information will let the company develop preemptive, enduring competitive strategies. A business unit manager may not be able to describe the type of information that will let him (or her) get out and conquer. If not, then he is not strong enough to use any information to the company's absolute maximum ability. But if that manager can articulate or define the kind of information needed, he should be approached formally, informally, and in a variety of generally irregular sessions, rather than once every two weeks when you meet from 11 to 12 o'clock.

Our firms need things that will shock people away from their normal thought patterns, and put them into a creative mode. You have to take the initiative to force them away from their customary ways of thinking about things. That role is not a comfortable one for most Chief Information Officers, nor is it what you have been asked to do, or even permitted to do, in the past. But I would submit that most CEOs today want you to do something that is more active, in terms of jarring the organization out of its customary traps. The CEO now views technology and information flow as being at least equal with the CFOs or the CEOs flow, even though that is not yet widely recognized.

Next, help us on the intelligence front in new and more effective ways than currently exist. Companies have enterprise planning units; they have competitive intelligence reports; they have business development units analyzing the competition. There are shortcomings to that methodology. It works far too slowly. By the time you get data, it is virtually useless. There are common textual databases that, because of the lead time, are completely unhelpful. There is no point in knowing the umpire's proclivities when he has already called the third strike. You've got to know beforehand.

For example, at Prudential-Bache, we were getting underwriting standards from the common sources six months after the fact. By the time we knew we'd slipped from fourth to twelfth, we could have slipped from twelfth to twentieth. It was basically useless information. A junior level individual in our underwriting department found a database that was available at, I think, Dow Jones. It costs us almost nothing and gives us the information the next week. So instead of being six to seven months behind that fact; we are three to four days behind, with the ability to find out which one of our competitors is stealing the margins on us. At least we can react almost immediately. So we need information, quickly.

Again, I would say the CIO should have people looking for nonconventional sources of intelligent information, which are more and more readily available.

Collaboration with competitors may be necessary to derive collective data quickly enough so everyone can use it. The fact that your competitors may have the same access to information doesn't make it less useful. If you get it to me or my counterparts quickly, the fact that other CEOs of other business units or different companies may have it doesn't render it useless. I just have to use it more skillfully to play the shot better. So collaborate with competitors to develop quick databases that are relatively accurate when they do not exist elsewhere.

In the case of the mutual insurance industry, a lot of the data on new premiums and business accountability was coming out about a year and a half after the fact. We have now, however, tightened that up to about every six months. That's two or three times better than a year ago, because people reached out to gather collective data that was useful. I would say that the CIO should not wait for management to push, but you push management to see what things like that may be necessary. Clearly, I am advocating an aggressive posture for the CIO, one that is not reactive, but quite bold.

One thing you might try, which is apt to be controversial, is to help us to leverage our winners. Our winners can be people who sell the most; they can be the most productive businesses; they can be the product lines where we are getting the greatest return; or the businesses where the ROE or the ROS is the greatest. You have to help us identify our winners. When we establish new business activities, we need you, together with the CFO, to determine the measures by which that business will be gauged, to determine how often and how quickly. We also need CIOs to develop a set of impartial measures by which all businesses can be judged, so that we no longer use the measures suggested by the businesses themselves.

It is interesting, as technology has developed, what various businesses will do to define and set forth, with instrumentation by you, a series of self-serving yardsticks. Because of that, many business units are essentially deceiving management by looking good where they really aren't. I may be the best redheaded, lefthanded Chief Executive Officer in the securities business, and also the only one. But if that is the measure set forth because I suggested it, and that is what gets into the monthly or daily or annual report coming out in the information system, then we lose. I think that the CIO has to oversee and direct the integrity of this process. He does not bypass the CFO, but works with him, in selecting the best measure of performance and getting it into the information architecture. I think that the CIO has to have either primary or co-responsibility for the particular type of business unit evaluation.

The COO, the CFO, and the CIO are now, I think, co-equals with many shared and many strictly defined responsibilities. That idea has not yet reached most Chairmen, Presidents, or Chief Administrative Officers. You are still viewed in the main as being the provider or service, and

Con-Ed of data flows, rather than as one who judges, who interprets, who evaluates and directs those particular flows.

There are some perhaps more obvious needs that seem to me the least in the hierarchy of things. First is the need to have the right technologies clearly defined and in place. We want you to simplify the definition of the systems, to create a clear picture of the architecture that exists. We need a rudimentary idea of what it can and can't do, of what makes it work.

Secondly, keep the information system reliable. Make sure, if at all possible, that it works almost all the time. The irksome wish of a CEO is to have something developed that's so good that the business units become highly dependent on it. When they are deprived of it, they scream like banshees. We have something called the Branch Office Support System, which did not exist three or four years ago. Our stockbrokers love it. It has done wonders for their productivity; they think it's the greatest thing in the world. When it goes down for even a minute, you ought to hear the phones ring—my phone, my Regional Director's phone—it doesn't matter. We have created a generation of dependent people, and if we take away their support system, they can't tolerate it.

So whatever you do, keep it simple so we can understand it, try to keep it reliable, and make it global. Too much is being written about the globalization of the marketplaces. Clearly, every manufacturing, every service, every financial business today is global. Technology has created that. It has let the genie out of the box, and the genie is not going to be stuffed back. Rather than making a big to-do about it, let's all simply accept the fact that internationalization is fascinating, and to most people it is still foreign. They will domesticate it sooner rather than later, however. The architecture that develops, therefore, has to be the same in Japan or in Bangladesh as it is in Dallas or Detroit. We don't care where on earth it is, but it has to be the same equipment working in the same way, just as quickly and with the same response time.

If you possibly can, make it adaptable. There are few things that rile CEOs more than being told about computers that aren't compatible with one another, about languages that require some sort of impossible bridge, or about line capabilities that mean something similarly impossible. Or, we've got PCs here, and minis there, and the architecture will not permit any sort of interactive response. Make sure that it all works together.

If you can create adaptable architecture of one sort or another, we will happily trade off being on the cutting edge of technology, with being on the reliable edge. It may seem strange, but being right out on the extreme of what technology can do today is not as important to us as having "staying power."

One thing I would suggest to all of you, however you want to do it, make sure that the CEO grants you total power to approve any purchases, any outside data bases. Anything of an informational and technological basis has to go to you at least for your "ok." You really ought to operate in that sort of environment, you ought to have that type of control.

I guess what I am describing here is a new partnership that is sought by CEOs between themselves and you. No longer is it enough for you simply to deliver the information. You are not asked to be in the business of creation, interpretation and judgement. And again, the judgement is the tough part. Instead of being an impartial observer, you will be the person who decides what is right or wrong, and that is going to make your relationship with various user departments more difficult than before, with a real potential for acrimony. You will be more powerful and less of a servant, more a D'Artagnan, a kind of musketeer yourself. What CEOs are looking for are musketeers to play with their D'Artagnans. The whole area of information is no longer in any way a team counting on MIS. It is management direction. You must help us to use the information you acquire from disparate sources. Assign some of your brightest people and you yourselves push organizations to codify data, to seek new types of data, to use data strategically, and to use it in the execution of business plans. That is a revolution. Whether it is a quiet or a noisy one, I am really not sure, but I think that in a well-positioned company that wants to be ahead today and tomorrow, it can happen and it can happen now.

QUESTIONS

1. Ball states that information for the CEO should have certain characteristics. What are they? How do EISs provide information with these characteristics?

2. Ball notes that EIS support team personnel should have particular skills. What are they and why is it important that they have these skills to be able to support the EIS?

3. How can the EIS support team personnel influence the users of the EIS?

4. What does Ball mean by "intelligence" information? Can an EIS provide this type of information? If so, how?

5. What are the characteristics of EIS hardware and software that Ball says are necessary for a successful system?

PART *III*

DEVELOPING AN EIS

Developing an executive information system (EIS) is a potentially high-risk undertaking because it has demanding requirements. The nature of executives and their work means that an EIS must be so easy to use that it is "user intuitive" and requires little or no training to use. Also, an EIS must be flexible enough to adapt to rapidly changing executive information needs. The riskiness of the EIS development process and the relative recency of EIS have led to many articles concerning EIS development. Part III contains 14 articles that provide a varied, yet encompassing view of EIS development.

Frameworks can provide an orderly way of examining a complex subject and the interrelationships among its components. EIS development is complex and Hugh Watson, Kelly Rainer, and Chang Koh present a framework for studying the process in "Executive Information Systems: A Framework for Development and a Survey of Current Practices." They use data from 50 firms with an EIS to discuss various aspects of EIS development.

Craig Barrow, in "Implementing an Executive Information System: Seven Steps for Success," notes that EISs must support nontechnical users, are more dynamic than traditional information systems, and that no two EISs are alike. He presents seven steps that firms should take to successfully implement an EIS.

In their article, "Is Your EIS Meeting the Need?," Gary Gulden and Douglas Ewers address two major reasons why an EIS might not be successful—a lack of clear purpose from the sponsoring executive and a failure to incorporate the EIS into the management processes of the organization. They note that EIS can impact an organization in four areas: (1) simplification of information access, (2) motivation of management performance, (3) expansion of insight and (4) understanding and acceleration of communication. The authors argue that firms must know which area(s) their EIS will address to successfully implement such a system.

Most organizations have had operational transaction processing systems and management information systems for many years. Fewer firms have added decision-support systems and still fewer have implemented executive information systems. In "A Path Framework for Executive Information Systems," Ido Millet, Charles Mawhinney, and Ernest Kallman present a two-by-two information systems grid. One dimension of the grid is composed of batch and on-line systems and the other dimension is high and low information focus and integration. The authors call the four cells MIS (low and batch), query (low and on-line), batch EIS (high and batch), and on-line EIS (high and on-line). They discuss the paths that 46 organizations took through the cells of the grid toward the development of batch EIS or on-line EIS. From these paths, they draw implications for organizational investment and change.

Linda Volonino and Hugh Watson present a six-step process that organizations can follow when creating an EIS in "The Strategic Business Objectives Method for Guiding Executive Information Systems Development." They illustrate their proposed process using a case study based on Fisher-Price's experience. This process is a top-down approach, meaning that the EIS is designed to support organizational strategic objectives as stated by top management.

Possibly the most critical element of EIS development is the process of obtaining executive information requirements. An organized approach to this process must be taken because simply asking an executive what he or she wants from an EIS can lead to disjointed, unrelated, and/or incomplete information specification. Hugh Watson and Mark Frolick, in "Determining Information Requirements for an Executive Information System," discuss methods for eliciting executive information requirements, which include participation in strategic planning sessions, formal critical success factor sessions, informal discussions with executives, tracking executive activity, discussions with executive support personnel, examinations of noncomputer-generated information, attendance at meetings, software tracking of EIS usage, collaborative work-system sessions, and examinations of computer-generated information.

George Houdeshel describes two phases in the process of obtaining executive information requirements in "Selecting Information for an EIS: Experiences at Lockheed-Georgia." The initial phase is to work with information that is immediately available. The sustaining-enhancing phase is to develop a rapport with executive users that will result in a continuous enhancement of EIS information contents. He draws insights about the two phases by drawing on his experience as the EIS project director at Lockheed-Georgia.

At present, four major vendors in the EIS software market are Pilot (Commander EIS), Comshare (Command Center), Execucom (Executive Edge), and IBM (Executive Decisions). These firms supply full-featured EIS software. There are also many other firms that offer EIS software, but these products may not have all the features the "big four" have. This wide variety of software products suggests that selecting EIS software is not a trivial task. Hugh Watson, Betty-Anne Hesse, Carolyn Copperwaite, and Vaughn deVos in "Selecting EIS Software: The Western Mining Corporation Experience," use a case study to describe a multi-stage process for choosing EIS software. The authors suggest a checklist for software feature analysis and capability review.

Experienced EIS developers and users can provide insights into what features and characteristics an EIS should have. Alan Paller and Richard Laska asked people what they like or dislike about their systems, and what features they would like to see added to those systems. What they learned is discussed in "What Users Want Today."

Eileen Carlson describes the confusion that results from the variety of EIS software on the market in her article, "What Color Is Your EIS?" She notes that companies can build an EIS in various ways: they can use in-house tools, they can build a customized front end to a DSS, they can use vendor EIS software that is not full capability, or they can use full-featured vendor EIS software. She states that firms often do not choose full-featured vendor EIS software because of its high cost.

Successfully developing an EIS means that the system should continue to be successful over time In "Avoiding Hidden EIS Pitfalls," Hugh Watson uses a case study to describe five problems that may occur some time after an EIS becomes operational. He discusses possible solutions to each problem and also offers insights into designing an EIS that meets user needs initially and into the future.

Linda Volonino and Stephen Robinson illustrate the high-risk nature of EIS development in "EIS Experiences at Marine Midland Bank, N.A." They examine possible reasons contributing to a decline in executive usage of the bank's EIS and present guidelines to improve the potential for successful EIS development and on-going operation.

David DeLong and John Rockart discuss eight factors critical to successful implementation of EIS in "Identifying the Attributes of Successful Executive Support System Implementation." They derived these factors from interviews in 30 companies who had attempted to implement EIS. They illustrate the eight factors using a case study of a firm that had failed in its implementation of an EIS.

David Armstrong describes the EIS implementation at a division of Rockwell International in "How Rockwell Launched Its EIS" and "The People Factor in EIS Success." The first article discusses top management's objectives for the EIS. It also examines the prototype Rockwell developed, the information systems department's role, and the software selection process. The second article stresses that EIS success is not a function of technology alone, but depends on people as well. Armstrong describes the roles of the steering committee, the data providers, the data keepers, the EIS developers, and the project coordinator. He also discusses EIS data management and the EIS application development process. Armstrong draws interesting insights about the ways that the EIS is changing the executive culture at this division of Rockwell.

6

Executive Information Systems: A Framework for Development and a Survey of Current Practices

Hugh J. Watson
R. Kelly Rainer
Chang E. Koh

INTRODUCTION

The target audience for computer support in organizations has evolved over the years. Clerical workers were the first to be impacted as transaction processing systems were automated in the 1950s and 1960s. At about the same time, engineers gained access to computers and started what is now recognized as end-user computing. Management information systems (MIS) appeared with much fanfare in the 1960s. While some envisioned them as "central nervous systems" for organizations, in practice they largely expanded the reporting system for lower-level managers. Office automation began two decades ago with the introduction of word processors for secretaries and continues to expand today as a growing variety of support becomes available for office workers. In the 1970s, decision support systems (DSS) provided assistance for specific decision-making tasks. While DSSs can be developed for and used by personnel throughout the organization, they are most commonly employed by staff and middle and lower managers. Among

Previously published in *MIS Quarterly,* Volume 15, Number 1, March 1991. Copyright 1991 by the Society for Information Management and the Management Information Systems Research Center at the University of Minnesota. Used with permission.

the latest developments are expert systems, which capture the expertise of highly trained, experienced professionals in specific problem domains.

As the evolution of computer support for organizational personnel is considered, one group is conspicuously missing: the senior executives of a firm. They have not been omitted by design, and in fact, previous advances were originally thought to potentially serve them (e.g., MIS and DSS), but for a variety of reasons, little support has been provided. This lack of support is rapidly changing, however, as executive information systems (EIS) or executive support systems (ESS) are being developed in a growing number of firms (Main, 1989). International Data Corporation, a market research firm, predicts that the U.S. market for EIS is growing at a compound annual rate of nearly 40 percent and that expenditures for EIS software development, including the purchase of software, custom consulting, and in-house software development, will grow to $350 million in 1992 (Alexander, 1989).

Even though EISs support an important clientele and are becoming prevalent, little research has been done about them. The available EIS literature is case study or anecdotal in nature. In order to learn more about current EIS practices, we studied 50 firms that either have an EIS or are well along in developing one. The findings are presented in the context of a framework that can be used to understand and guide EIS development efforts.

The results of this study should be of interest to practitioners who already have an EIS or are planning to develop one. The findings provide benchmarks against which individual company experiences can be compared. The results also should stimulate academicians to do further research. Specific research questions raised by this research are presented later.

The next section defines an EIS, lists EIS characteristics, and distinguishes between EIS and ESS. This is followed by discussion of the failure of previous efforts to support executives. Next, an EIS development framework is introduced and the research methodology of the study is described. Then, the findings of the survey are discussed in the context of the framework. Finally, conclusions are drawn from the study.

EIS DEFINITION AND CHARACTERISTICS

Researchers have used a variety of definitions for EIS (Paller and Laska, 1990; Turban and Watson, 1989). For our purposes, an EIS is defined as a computerized system that provides executives with easy access to internal and external information that is relevant to their critical success factors. While a definition is useful, a richer understanding is provided by describing the characteristics of EIS. Research (Burkan, 1988; Friend, 1986; Kogan, 1986; Zmud, 1986) shows that most executive information systems:

- Are tailored to individual executive users;
- Extract, filter, compress, and track critical data;
- Provide online status access, trend analysis, exception reporting, and "drill-down" (drill-down allows the user to access supporting detail or data that underlie summarized data);
- Access and integrate a broad range of internal and external data;
- Are user-friendly and require minimal or no training to use;
- Are used directly by executives without intermediaries;
- Present graphical, tabular, and/or textual information.

The EIS and ESS terms are sometimes used interchangeably. The term "executive support system," however, usually refers to a system with a broader set of capabilities than an EIS (Rockart and DeLong, 1988). Whereas the EIS term connotes providing information, the ESS term implies other support capabilities in addition to information. Consequently, we find it useful to conceptualize an ESS as including the following capabilities:

- Support for electronic communications (e.g., e-mail, computer conferencing, and word processing);
- Data analysis capabilities (e.g., spreadsheets, query languages, and decision support systems);
- Organizing tools (e.g., electronic calendars, automated rolodex, and tickler files).

These additional capabilities are typically made available as options on a system's main menu or by the ability to "hot key" the workstation into a PC mode of operation.

The distinctions between an EIS and an ESS are not particularly important for our purposes other than to recognize that an ESS influences and increases system requirements. For example, many systems include e-mail; hence, e-mail software and a keyboard must be available. The materials provided here apply equally well to EIS or ESS, even though the EIS term is used throughout.

WHY PREVIOUS EFFORTS FAILED

There are many reasons why previous efforts to bring computer support to senior executives have failed. Understanding these reasons is important because they provide insights into what problems must be overcome if an EIS is to be successful.

One of the difficulties involves the executives themselves. Many of today's senior executives missed the computer revolution. Consequently, they may feel uncomfortable using computers, have poor keyboarding skills, or believe that "real" executives do not use computers.

Another difficulty involves the nature of executive work. Previous studies provide a better understanding of what senior executives do and insights into how computer support must be delivered (Isenberg, 1984; Kotter, 1982; Mintzberg, 1975). Executives' busy schedules and travel requirements are not amenable to long training sessions, do not permit much uninterrupted time for system use, and do not allow a system to be employed on a daily basis (Albala, 1988). The result is that senior executives are unlikely to employ systems that require considerable training and regular use to be learned and remembered. Because senior executives have ready access to staff personnel to fulfill their requests for information, any system must prove to be more responsive than a human (Rockart and DeLong, 1988).

Another problem in providing computer support includes technology that is difficult to use, at least from most executives' perspective. Powerful workstations, improved micro-to-mainframe software, high-quality color graphics, and touch-screens are just some of the technological developments that now make it possible to deliver appealing systems to senior executives.

Finally, many previous systems have contained little information of value to senior executives, which is a problem related to a lack of understanding of executive work. This lack was exacerbated by systems designers who often possessed excellent technical knowledge but little business knowledge (Reck and Hall, 1986). This condition is improving as organizations recognize that business skills and the ability to interact with executives are critical.

Three broad guidelines for developing a successful EIS can be gleaned from these failures. First, the EIS must meet the information needs of senior executives. Second, in order to do this, the EIS must be developed by personnel with both business and technical skills. Finally, the EIS must be so easy to use that it might be considered to be "intuitive" or "user seductive." Even though it is challenging to implement an EIS that meets executive information needs and is extremely easy to use, a number of EISs has achieved these objectives (Applegate and Osborn, 1988; Houdeshel and Watson, 1987).

AN EIS DEVELOPMENT FRAMEWORK

According to Sprague (1980), a *development framework* is "helpful in organizing a complex subject, identifying the relationships between the parts, and revealing the areas in which further developments will be required" (p. 6). It guides practitioners in developing systems and provides insights for academicians in identifying where research needs to be performed. Gorry and Scott Morton's (1971) framework for MIS and Sprague's (1980) for DSS are two of the best known and most useful frameworks. Turban and Schaeffer (1987) suggest the need for an EIS development framework. This article provides such a framework based on the EIS literature, our experiences in developing EIS, and discussions with vendors, consultants, and EIS staff members.

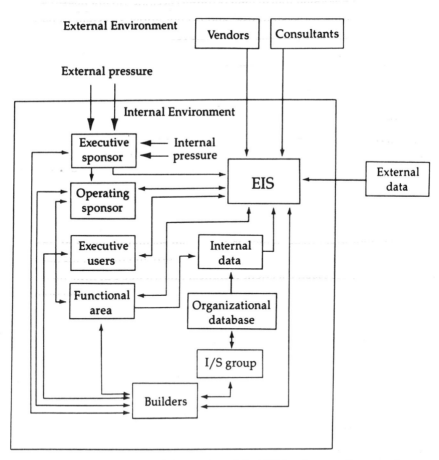

Figure 6-1. *Structural Perspective of the EIS Development Framework*

The EIS development framework introduced here is illustrated by the structural perspective depicted in Figure 6–1. With this perspective, there are key elements and interactions among the elements that are important when developing an EIS. The elements include executives, functional area personnel (e.g., line managers, staff personnel, and data suppliers), information systems personnel, vendors, data, and information technology. The interactions are in the form of pressures, human interactions, and data flows.

The development of an EIS is a dynamic process that places the key elements and interactions in motion. In order for this to be successful, an appropriate development process must be used. This consideration is another important part of the framework.

From the users' perspective, the dialog with the system is of fundamental importance. It includes what must be known in order to use the system, how to direct the system's actions, and how the output is presented by the system (Bennett, 1977). The dialog is another important part of the framework.

Table 6–1. *Aspects of the EIS Development Framework*

Structural	Development Process
Personnel	External and internal pressures
EIS initiator	Cost/benefit analysis
Executive sponsor	Costs
Operating sponsor	Development costs
EIS builder/support staff	Annual operating costs
EIS users	Development time
Functional area personnel	Development methodology
IS personnel	Hardware
Data	Software
Internal	Spread
External	Evolution
	Information provided
User-System Dialog	EIS capabilities
Knowledge Base	
Training	
User documentation	
System user	
Action Language	
User-system interface	
System response time	
Presentation Language	
Multiple information formats	
Color	

In summary, the EIS development framework includes a structural perspective, the development process, and the user-system dialog. There are a number of aspects associated with each. Those that are explored in this research are identified in Table 6–1.

THE STUDY

The research study was begun in the spring of 1988 to investigate current EIS practices. The authors mailed a multi-part questionnaire to a large sample of geographically dispersed firms. The first part of the questionnaire defined an executive information system. The definition is important because EISs are the most recent computer-based information system to evolve, and, therefore, a precise definition of EIS is not universally accepted among academicians and practitioners. The second part of the questionnaire gathered demographic data on each organization. Finally, the questionnaire sought data concerning the development, operation, support, and capabilities of the EIS in the organization. Suggested changes made after two pretests were incorporated into the final survey instrument.

The survey population was chosen from three groups. The first group attended either the DSS-87 to DSS-88 conferences. One hundred and eighty-five questionnaires were sent to this group. Questionnaires were not sent to attendees from educational institutions or consulting firms. The second group, all of whom received questionnaires, consisted of the 100 firms identified by a *Computerworld* survey as having invested the most effectively in information systems. The authors believed that organizations that are leaders in the use of information systems (IS) are likely candidates to have an EIS. The third group consisted of 19 firms known by the authors to have an EIS but were not included into the first two groups. Each firm was carefully checked to ensure that the firm was not included in more than one group. Because 18 firms appeared more than once, a total of 286 questionnaires were mailed. The survey was not a random sample. Because most firms had not developed an EIS at this point in time, a frame was used that maximized the likelihood of contacting firms with an EIS.

Initially, the authors received 72 usable responses, with 30 of the firms indicating that they had an EIS, and 42 indicating that they did not. Five weeks after the first mailing, another questionnaire was mailed to nonrespondents. This follow-up resulted in responses from 20 additional firms with an EIS and 20 with none. The profile of responses from the second group corresponded closely with the profile of the initial responses. A total of 112 usable responses was received for a response rate of 39.1 percent. The number of companies with an EIS was 50, which provides the "n" on which percentages are based when describing current practices in this article. In some cases, the respondents did not answer every question. In such instances, the percentages calculated are based on the number of responses received.

FINDINGS AND DISCUSSION

Demographics

Organizations in this survey represent a variety of industries located in widely dispersed geographic areas (see Figure 6–2). Their total corporate assets average $5.37 billion, with only three firms reporting total assets of less than $1 billion. Forty-eight respondents listed their positions in their firms (see Figure 6–2). The largest number of respondents are IS managers, followed by executives and IS staff members. The respondents averaged 18.74 years of work experience, 13.78 years of IS work experience, and 2.77 years of EIS experience.

Forty-seven firms (94 percent) had an operational EIS, and three firms (6 percent) were far enough along in developing one that they were able to partially answer the questions on the survey. The latter three firms all indicated that they would have an operational EIS in less than one year.

While some EISs date back to the late 1970s (Houdeshel and Watson, 1987), most of them are recent. The survey findings support this statement as 40 firms (80 percent) indicated that their EISs were less than three years old. The average age of an EIS in this survey is two years.

A Structural Perspective

Personnel. Thirty-four firms (68 percent) indicated that a company executive(s) served as the *initiator* of the development of the EIS. Survey respondents were allowed to define the term "executive" in the context of their own organizations. Information systems personnel initiated EIS development in 14 firms (28 percent). Finally, the information center in one firm (2 percent) initiated EIS development.

The finding that IS personnel initiated EIS development in 14 firms is somewhat surprising because the literature indicates that executives initiate EIS development (Houdeshel and Watson, 1987; Stecklow, 1989). However, 11 of these 14 firms (79 percent) had EISs that were less than two years old. Of the 34 firms with EIS initiated by executives, 19 (56 percent) had EISs that were less than two years old. These numbers suggest that executives motivated EIS development when these systems first evolved. Few IS departments had the confidence of management and/or the risk-taking propensity to push for an EIS. However, as the number of EIS success stories has grown, more IS departments are taking

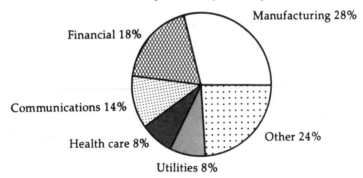

Respondents by Industry

Manufacturing 28%

Financial 18%

Communications 14%

Health care 8%

Utilities 8%

Other 24%

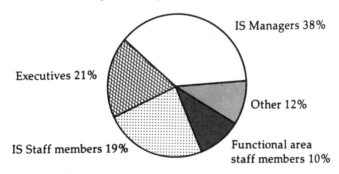

Respondents by Position in the Firm

IS Managers 38%

Executives 21%

Other 12%

IS Staff members 19%

Functional area staff members 10%

Figure 6-2. *Respondents by Location, Industry, and Position*

the lead in advocating EIS development by keeping abreast of technological developments and communicating the potential benefits of the technology to senior executives (Volonino and Drinkard, 1989).

EIS development is spurred by a highly placed senior executive who serves as the system's *executive sponsor* (Barrow, 1990; Rockart and De-Long, 1988). This person is typically the president or a vice president of the company. Rockart and DeLong (1988) suggest that three major responsibilities of the executive sponsor include making the initial request for the system; staying on top of the system's development and providing direction and feedback about proposed applications; and communicating strong and continuing interest to those with a stake in the system, such as key staff groups and line managers supplying data.

In this study, 42 firms (84 percent) reported having executive sponsors for their EISs. Interestingly, 62 percent of the executive sponsors hold positions other than CEO or president (see Table 6–2). A partial explanation for this finding relates to the scope of the EIS. While it is not explored in this survey, the authors are familiar with a number of EISs that serve a functional area rather than the entire organization. In these situations, it is logical that the executive sponsor would be the vice president from the functional area served.

The executive sponsor typically assigns an *operating sponsor* to manage the day-to-day development of the EIS (Rockart and DeLong, 1988). The operating sponsor is often a senior executive who has an interest in having an EIS for his or her own purposes. An information systems project manager may serve as the operating sponsor. The operation sponsor works with executives, specialized staff, functional area personnel, IS personnel, and vendors in creating the EIS.

Forty-five firms (90 percent) reported having an operating sponsor, and 42 firms listed the operating sponsor's position. The operating sponsor held a variety of positions, the most prevalent being the manager or director of IS (42 percent of firms) (see Table 6–3). This finding

Table 6-2. *Positions Held by Executive Sponsors*

Position	Percent of Firms
Chief executive officer	21
President	17
Chief financial officer	14
Vice president	42
Controller	6

Table 6-3. *Positions Held by Operating Sponsors*

Position	Percent of Firms
Manager or director of IS	50
Manager or director of functional areas	14
Vice president	12
Analyst	10
Staff	7
Consultant	7

is different from what might be expected because the literature suggests that the operating sponsor is typically a senior executive (Rockart and DeLong, 1988).

The *EIS builder/support staff* is responsible for creating and maintaining the EIS (Paller and Laska, 1990; Rockart and DeLong, 1988). The staff may be either newly created or an existing organizational unit given a new charge. For example, a unit that provides specialized information and presentation materials to senior management can be given EIS responsibilities (Houdeshel and Watson, 1987). It is likely that an existing group will require help with technical matters. This lack of technical skills is not the case when IS personnel are responsible for the EIS, but IS personnel are often judged to be out of sync with the needs of senior management or too busy with other activities. Consultants and vendors can also be involved, especially during initial development.

All firms in this survey had EIS builder/support teams, with 37 firms (74 percent) indicating that their group consisted of five or fewer full-time people. The average size of the team was four people. Table 6–4 shows that the four categories of personnel most commonly found on the EIS team are end-user support personnel (58 percent of firms), systems analysts (54 percent), programmers (44 percent), and executive staff support personnel (40 percent). Only seven firms (14 percent) reported using vendor personnel when developing their EIS.

The builder/support team should include personnel with a mixture of business and technical skills because the team must work closely with many different people in the firm (e.g., executives, the IS department, and functional area personnel) (Reck and Hall, 1986; Rockart and DeLong, 1988). The business skills typically come from people who have experience in the company. The technical skills often come from IS personnel, either by virtue of being assigned to the staff or given specific responsibilities for supporting EIS activities (see the dotted-line relationship in Figure 6–1).

Respondents were asked to rank the top five skills in order of importance. Five points were awarded to the most important skill, four points to the second most important skill, and so on. The ability to work well with executives was found to be the most necessary skill for a development team member, followed by knowledge of the business and interpersonal skills (see Table 6–5). Technical skills ranked only fourth.

While it was not explored in the survey, it is worth noting that the EIS builder/support group can have a variety of organizational structures. One approach is to have a centralized group that reports to IS or a functional area. Another approach is to have a small, centralized group with functional area personnel working on a part-time basis performing tasks such as identifying information requirements and supplying data. These tasks are in addition to other job responsibilities. This arrangement

Table 6-4. *EIS Development Team Members*

Category	Percent of Firms
End-user support personnel	58
Systems analysts	54
Programmers	44
Executive staff	40
Executive	22
Vendor personnel	14
Others	14

Table 6-5. *Important Skills for the EIS Development Team*

Skill	Total Points
Ability to work well with executives	161
Knowledge of the business	143
Interpersonal skills	141
Technical skills	133
Ability to organize data	115
Other	12

matches up well with the skills that the support group needs in order to work effectively with executives.

The executive sponsor, operating sponsor, and EIS staff identify the users of the EIS. This group is usually small initially and expands over time. A key to the success of the EIS is identifying the system and information requirements of the executive users (Stecklow, 1989). A variety of methods can be used, including participation in strategic planning sessions, formal CSF sessions, informal discussions, monitoring executive activities, discussions with staff support personnel, software tracking of system usage, and others (Watson and Frolick, 1988).

Functional area personnel are an important source of data for the EIS, and an implementation strategy should be pursued that encourages their cooperation and support for the system. Before implementation of an EIS, much of the needed data are already being gathered but often only for the executives of the functional area in which the data originate. Two of the major organizational resistances to EIS are staff personnel who feel threatened by the possibility of a diminished role in supplying information to executives and subordinate line managers who fear that their operations will be too visible to top management (Argyris, 1971; Carroll, 1988; Rockart and DeLong, 1988).

Information systems personnel may not lead the EIS project, but their support, cooperation, and assistance are critical (Leibs, 1989). Helping select and install hardware and software, providing maintenance, trouble-shooting problems, and providing access to machine-resident data are some of the support responsibilities that fall to IS personnel. In organizations where IS personnel has the attention and confidence to top management, they may be able to create an interest in the creation of an EIS (Volonino and Drinkard, 1989). This task is accomplished by demonstrating what an EIS is and the kind of information it provides. Possible demonstration strategies include showing a potential executive sponsor an EIS in another company; arranging a vendor-provided demonstration, ideally using company data important to the executive; or prototyping an EIS in-house.

DATA

Data play a critical role in an EIS because they are the basis for the information provided (Houdeshel and Watson, 1987; Rockart and DeLong, 1988). The data can come from internal or external sources and can be hard or soft. The EIS can require that new data be collected and stored. Much of the *internal data* is extracted from existing organizational databases that are used by transaction processing systems and functional area applications. This tends to be hard data. The use of this hard data in an EIS is not as straightforward as it might seem, however, because of different reporting and updating cycles, functional area feelings of data ownership, and multiple, incompatible databases (e.g., inconsistent data definitions). Other internal data come from human sources and often are soft in nature and are critical to understanding complex problems (Mintzberg, 1975; Zmud, 1986). Included can be news, rumors, opinions, ideas, predictions, explanations, and plans. Collecting, analyzing, and entering these data to an EIS tends to be very labor-intensive but adds considerably to the richness of the information provided.

Firms in the survey listed a variety of internal data sources. The corporate database is a common source of internal data for most (82 percent) of the firms. Other internal data sources include the functional areas of the firm (62 percent), documents (38 percent), and humans (34 percent). These data indicate the richness and variety of data sources that can be used by an EIS. Further, the data illustrate the extensive data access requirements associated with and EIS.

External data are also important to an EIS (Runge, 1988). Like internal data, they can be hard or soft and can come from existing databases or require special collection efforts. Data sources include external databases (e.g., Dow Jones News Retrieval), published data, customers, and suppliers. External data sources primarily noted in this survey include news services (56 percent of firms), stock markets (46 percent), and trade/industry data (34 percent).

The Development Process

The executive sponsor's interest in the development of an EIS can be the consequence of external and internal pressures (Gulden and Ewers, 1989; Houdeshel and Watson, 1987; Rockart and DeLong, 1988). The *external pressures* come from the firm's external environment and can include environmental turbulence (e.g., rapidly changing costs of raw materials), increased competition, and increased government regulations. *Internal pressures* include the need for new, better, or more timely information; having to manage organizations that are increasingly complex and difficult to run; and the need for more efficient reporting systems.

The study asked respondents to rank order the three most important external pressures and the three most important internal pressures. Three points were awarded to the most important pressure in each category, two points to the second most important pressure, and one point to the third most important pressure.

The most critical external pressure is an increasingly competitive environment. Other critical external pressures, in descending order, include the rapidly changing external environment and the need to be more proactive in dealing with the external environment (see Table 6-6).

The survey findings for internal pressures (see Table 6-6) reveal that respondents consider the need for timely information to be most critical. Other internal pressures include the need for improved communication, the need for access to operational data, and the need for rapid status updates. An interesting finding is that respondents place the need for more accurate information as the least critical internal pressure. This seems to indicate that EIS users already consider the information they receive to be accurate.

Table 6-6. *Pressures Leading to EIS Development*

	Total Points
External Pressures	
Increasingly competitive environment	113
Rapidly changing external enviromnent	59
Need to be more proactive in dealing with external environment	46
Need to access external databases	25
Increasing government regulations	15
Other	8
Internal Pressures	
Need for timely information	61
Need for improved communication	39
Need for access to operational data	35
Need for rapid status updates on different business units	34
Need for increased effectiveness	27
Need to be able to identify historical trends	27
Need for increased efficiency	25
Need for access to corporate database	25
Other	17
Need for more accurate information	15

Many researchers observe that *cost/benefit analyses* are difficult to perform on EIS because of the difficulty in quantifying many of the benefits (Houdeshel and Watson, 1987; Moad, 1988; Rockart and DeLong, 1988; Rockart and Treacy, 1982). These researchers suggest that there is simply an intuitive feeling that the system will justify its costs. After the system becomes operational, specific benefits and cost savings may be identifiable (Wallis, 1989). Forty-four firms answered this questionnaire item. Their responses support these assertions; forty-two respondents (95 percent) indicate that their firms assessed potential benefits of their EIS through intuitive feelings about improved decision making. Only two firms (5 percent) assessed hard dollar benefits.

Costs

Even though most firms do not measure hard dollar benefits, many firms do consider the costs involved before undertaking EIS development. Most firms estimate software costs (79 percent), hardware costs (68 percent), and personnel costs (68 percent). Fewer firms (32 percent) estimate training costs, perhaps because training costs are anticipated to be minimal.

In conjunction with data on firms that estimated EIS costs before development, this study gathered data on actual EIS development costs and operational costs. *Development costs* are those costs incurred creating the first version of the EIS. Thirty-three firms provided development costs for their EIS. The firms averaged $128,000 on software, $129,000 on hardware, $90,000 on personnel, and $18,000 on training. These firms also supplied *annual EIS operating costs,* which were found to average $117,000 on personnel, $46,000 on software, $29,000 on hardware, and $16,000 on training. These numbers suggest that an EIS is expensive and, consequently, may be limited to larger firms with considerable financial resources.

Of note is that annual operating costs for personnel appear to be higher than personnel development costs. A possible explanation for this finding is that companies may need additional people to handle increases in the number of users, screens, and system capabilities.

The *time to develop* the initial version of an EIS is important. As with other systems that support decision making, the first version of an EIS should be developed quickly and presented to users for their reactions (Moad, 1988; Runge, 1989). Forty-six firms (92 percent) developed their EIS using an *iterative, prototyping methodology* and four firms (8 percent) used a formal systems development life cycle approach.

The *hardware* and especially the *software* used in developing the first version may or may not be what are used in later versions. At one extreme, a few screens can be designed using existing software to run on workstations already in place (Rinaldi and Jastrzembski, 1986).

Information for the screens can be entered manually. This approach minimizes development time and cost. At the other extreme, a commercial EIS package can be purchased and installed. The EIS builders use the package to create the initial screens and to supply them with information. This approach minimizes the difficulties of moving to later versions if the EIS proves to be successful.

There are several hardware configurations possible with an EIS (Paller and Laska, 1990; Rockart and DeLong, 1988). Forty-eight companies indicated the hardware configuration used for their EIS. Forty firms (83 percent) use a mainframe approach. The mainframe approach includes 18 firms (37 percent) that employ a shared mainframe, 17 firms (35 percent) that use a PC network connected to a mainframe, and five firms (11 percent) that employ a dedicated mainframe. Eight firms (17 percent) use a PC network with a file server for their hardware configuration. More vendors have been offering local area network-based EIS products (e.g., Lightship from Pilot) since this study was conducted.

The availability of commercial software has contributed considerably to the growth of EIS. Products from vendors such as Comshare (Commander EIS), Pilot (Command Center), IBM (Executive Decisions), and EXECUCOM (Executive Edge) facilitate the development and maintenance of an EIS. These products support ease of use (e.g., mouse or touch screen operation), access to data, screen design and maintenance, interfaces to other software (e.g., Lotus 1-2-3), and other system requirements.

An EIS can be developed using in-house developed software, vendor-supplied software, or some combination of the two (Paller and Laska, 1990; Rockart and DeLong, 1988). Twelve firms (24 percent) developed their EIS using custom-built, in-house software; 12 firms (24 percent) used vendor-supplied software; and 26 firms (52 percent) used a combination of in-house and vendor software. Of the 38 firms that employ at least some vendor-supplied software, nine firms (24 percent) use Pilot's Command Center, seven firms (18 percent) use Comshare's Commander EIS, five firms (12 percent) use Interactive Image's EASEL, and the remaining 17 firms (46 percent) use a wide variety of other vendor software. These results are not surprising; Pilot and Comshare are generally recognized to be the two leading vendors of EIS software.

Over time an EIS evolves in terms of the number of users, the number of screens, the content and format of the screens, and EIS capabilities (Houdeshel and Watson, 1987; Rockart and DeLong, 1988). In some cases the EIS may be "pushed" on users, but a more desirable approach is to allow "demand pull" to occur. The latter normally occurs as subordinates learn that their superiors have access to certain information and they "want to see what their bosses are looking at." Still, some executives may legitimately have little interest in using the EIS because it contains little information relevant to them, or they have well-established alternative sources of information.

Executive information systems usually spread over time. *Spread* refers to the increase in the number of users who have access to the EIS (Rockart and DeLong, 1988). It can be argued that an EIS that does not spread is likely to fail (Friend, 1990). The survey question about spread referred only to the number of users over time and did not specify that the users be executives. Therefore, the users could include executives, executive staff, and other organizational personnel. This study found that the EIS supported an average of 7.75 users initially, with a steadily increasing number of users over time, as can be seen in Figure 6–3. The "n"s shown in Figure 6–3 are the number of respondents who provided data for the various points in time.

Evolution refers to additional capabilities and information provided by an EIS over time (Rockart and DeLong, 1988). This study gathered data on the number of screens available to users over time. An average of 55.8 screens were available initially, and the number of available screens increased in each time period (see Figure 6–3). This increase implies that users usually want more information as time passes and they become familiar with the system.

Even though the data show that the number of screens consistently increases, outdated screens must be deleted and other screens modified. Adding, modifying, and deleting screens is an important responsibility of the EIS support staff. Software tracking of system use is very helpful in identifying screens that may need to be changed. Screen content and format can change over time. As an example of this change, screens may become denser in content as users become more familiar with them (Houdeshel and Watson, 1987). Information that was spread over several screens may be placed on a single screen, which can result in format changes.

To be most effective in supporting executives, an EIS must *provide information* from many areas (Houdeshel and Watson, 1987; Rockart and DeLong, 1988). It can supply information about the industry in which the firm competes, company information, work unit information, and information that may be of interest to only a single executive. The information can span subsidiaries, divisions, functional areas, and departments.

The surveyed firms reported that their EISs provided information by strategic business unit (88 percent), functional area (86 percent), key performance indicator (71 percent), product (67 percent), and location (53 percent). These percentages demonstrate that EISs are able to supply information for various perspectives, thus allowing users flexibility in the information they can access.

An EIS can have a variety of *capabilities* (Friend, 1986; Kogan, 1986). Eighty-eight percent of the firms in this study state that their EIS

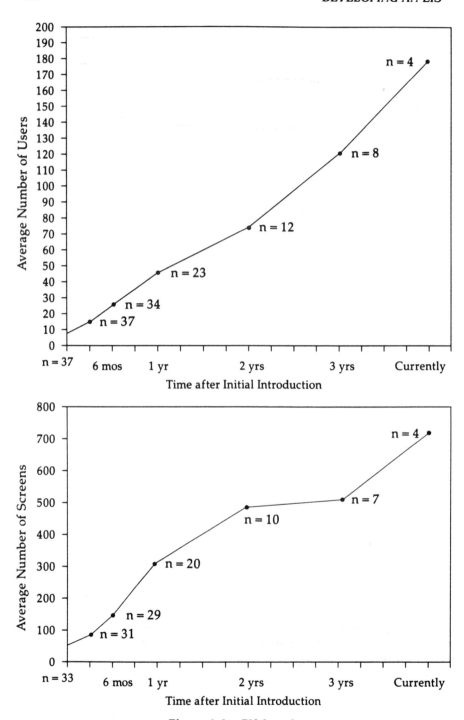

Figure 6-3. *EIS Spread*

provides access to current status information about the company. Other capabilities provided in a majority of firms are electronic mail, external news access, and access to other external databases (see Table 6–7).

Executives may want to access to the EIS while at home (Wallis, 1989). Executives who are traveling may also want to access the EIS. This offsite, use creates special communications, security, and support responsibilities. This is just one example of a system requirement that can evolve over time.

The Dialog

From the executive's perspective, the dialog with the EIS is the most important component of the system (Zmud, 1986). As was pointed out previously, because of the nature of executives and executive work, the system should be quite user-friendly. It should avoid elaborate logon procedures. Movement among EIS components should be seamless (e.g., e-mail might be a main menu option and not require a separate user ID). The system should provide context-dependent online help. Menus and a keyword index for locating screens should be included to help the executive find information. Sequence or command files should be created that allow executives to page through regularly viewed screens. The inclusion of a "drill-down" capability allows executives to go into more detail when an exceptional situation is encountered. The screens can provide the names and telephone numbers of people who can discuss the information presented.

Training on the use of the EIS should be one-on-one. Any system that requires more than a few minutes of training probably does not satisfy ease-of-use requirements (Carroll, 1988). *User documentation* should not be necessary for a well-designed EIS. If documentation is provided, it should be kept to a single page.

The *system user* of the EIS may be the executive, or it may be operated by an intermediary (Rockart and DeLong, 1988). Forty-eight respondents answered this item on the questionnaire. Forty-three firms (89 percent)

Table 6–7. *Capabilites Available on the EIS*

Capability	Percent of Firms
Access to current status	88
Electronic mail	65
Other external database	57
External news access	56
Word processing	43
Spreadsheet	37
Automated filing	22
Other	14

report that their executives use the EIS directly, and five firms (11 percent) report that intermediaries operate the system.

In keeping with the fact that an EIS must be highly user-friendly, the *user interface* and *response time* of the EIS are critical (Houdeshel and Watson, 1987; Rockart and DeLong, 1988). Ninety-two percent of the EISs employ a keyboard interface, one-half a mouse, and one-fourth a touch screen. These percentages indicate that there are multiple interfaces available on many of the EISs in this sample. The mean response time of the EISs in this survey was 2.8 seconds, with 42 firms (84 percent) reporting average response times of less than five seconds.

The EIS can provide a variety of capabilities for selecting screens. Keystrokes can be employed to move through menus or to identify particular screens. Even though some executives are adverse to using keyboards, this typically is not a major problem if the required skills are not too great. A keyboardless system can be provided by using a mouse or a touch screen. Most vendor-supplied software offer these methods of system operation as options. Icons are commonly used to make the system more intuitive.

Screens should include graphical, tabular, and textual presentation of information. Most supplied software provides a large variety of screen design capabilities. Standards should be established for any terms used, color codes, and graphic designs (Smith and Mosier, 1984; Tullis, 1981). These standards help to avoid misunderstandings and reduce the amount of mental processing required to interpret information.

Executive information systems should be able to present information to the user in *multiple formats* (e.g., graphical, tabular, and textual) (Friend, 1988; Houdeshel and Watson, 1987; Rockart and DeLong, 1988). Ninety percent of the EISs in this study have graphical formats available, 90 percent use textual formats, and 88 percent employ tabular formats. These percentages suggest that many EISs present information in multiple formats.

Executive information systems make extensive use of *color* in presenting information (Friend, 1988; Houdeshel and Watson, 1987; Rockart and DeLong, 1988). Out of 47 respondents who answered this question, 39 EISs (83 percent) in this study employ color displays and eight (17 percent) do not.

CONCLUSION

This study has presented a framework for the development of executive information systems and data related to this framework from 50 organizations. In most cases, the data support the "conventional wisdom" found in the literature:

- EISs are a recent development.
- EIS development is typically driven by a senior executive.
- An EIS has an executive sponsor, and this person is normally a CEO or a vice president.
- The development of an EIS is approved with little formal cost/benefit analysis.
- EIS development groups include a variety of personnel with a mixture of business and technical skills.
- An EIS obtains data from multiple internal and external sources.
- An EIS provides broadly based information.
- Pilot's Command Center and Comshare's Commander EIS are the two most popular vendor products for creating an EIS.
- The initial version of an EIS is developed quickly.
- Most EISs are mainframe-based.
- An EIS is created using an iterative, prototyping development methodology.
- The number of users and the number of screens of an EIS increase over time.
- Nearly all EISs are used directly by executives without intermediaries.
- An EIS presents information in graphical, textual, and tabular formats.
- Most EISs use color in presenting information.

The study also provides insights about areas where little is previously reported:

- The increasingly competitive environment and the need for timely information are the main external and internal pressures that lead to the development of an EIS.
- On average, the total costs of developing an EIS are $365,000, and the annual costs to maintain one are $208,000. It should be noted that the firms in this study are large, and smaller companies might develop more limited, and therefore less expensive, EIS due to cost considerations.
- The average size of an EIS development group is four people.
- On average, about one-fourth of the EISs are created using in-house developed software, one-half with vendor supplied plus in-house software, and one-fourth with only vendor-supplied software.

- On average, it takes 4.9 months to develop the initial version of an EIS.
- On average, 92 percent of all EISs employ a keyboard interface, one-half a mouse, and one-fourth a touch screen.

And finally, there were a few surprising findings:

- In some firms, EIS development is initiated by IS, and this seems to be a growing trend.
- A vice president is most often the executive sponsor for an EIS.
- An IS manager or director is most often the operating sponsor for an EIS.

While this and other studies provide information about EIS, there is much that still needs to be learned. After reading the MIS literature, one is surprised by how little academic research has been conducted on EIS. Most of the literature only provides glowing descriptions of specific EISs and how they are being used. In conducting this research, a variety of interesting and important EIS research questions surfaced.

- Is the organizational position and level of commitment of the executive sponsor related to EIS success?
- What considerations are most important when selecting an operating sponsor?
- How can the benefits of an EIS be assessed in advance?
- How does the software used in building an EIS affect the development process and system success?
- What level of staffing and organization structure are best for the EIS builder/support staff?
- What methods can be most effectively used to identify executives' information requirements?
- What are the major EIS data management problems and their solutions?
- What impact does the inclusion of soft data have on EIS success?
- What are the major problems associated with EIS "spread" and its evolution?
- How can EIS functionality be increased while maintaining ease-of-use?
- What emerging technologies (e.g., voice, optical disc) can be effectively used with EIS?
- What are the most effective screen presentation formats for an EIS?

Currently, the technology for EIS is evolving rapidly, and future systems are likely to be different from those that are in use today. A number of interesting and promising changes that can be anticipated include:

- Better integration with other applications. For example, better support can be provided by integrating EIS with decision support systems, group decision support systems, and expert systems. A DSS can provide analysis capabilities when problems are identified using an EIS; an EIS can be used to provide information in a decision room setting; and an expert system can be created to help guide executives in using the EIS effectively.

- Better commercial EIS software. Some of the advances to expect include better interfaces to organizational data and other organizational systems, enhanced capabilities for monitoring system usage, industry-specific template screens, and expanded sets of builders' tools (e.g., icons for use in screen development).

- Better executive-system interfaces. While keyboards are required for e-mail and most decision support applications, mouse and touchscreens are attractive alternatives for other types of system use. Animation is likely to be increasingly used to "add life" to information. Television may be available in a window. Voice may be used to direct the system.

An EIS is a high-risk system, and many failures have occurred (Watson and Glover, 1989). By following the EIS development framework, however, the likelihood of having a failure should be reduced. Over time, as more experience is gained, better products emerge, and more research findings are available, the chances for having an EIS success should grow.

REFERENCES

Albala, M. "Getting to the Pulse of the Company," *Personal Computing* (12:10), October 1988, pp. 196–198.

Alexander, M. "Executive Information Systems Catch On," *Computerworld*, February 27, 1989, p. 31.

Applegate, L.M. and Osborn, C.S. "Phillips 66 Company: Executive Information Systems," Harvard Case (9-189-006), Harvard Business School, Boston, MA, December 1988.

Argyris, C. "Management Information Systems: The Challenge to Rationality and Emotionality," *Management Science* (17:6), June 1971, pp. B275–292.

Barrow, C. "Implementing an Executive Information System: Seven Steps for Success," *Journal of Information Systems Management* (7:2), Spring 1990, pp. 41–46.

Bennett, J. "User-Oriented Graphics Systems for Decision Support in Unstructured Tasks," in *User-Oriented Design of Interactive Graphics Systems,*" S. Treu (ed.), Association for Computing Machinery, New York, NY, 1977.

Burkan, W.C. "Making EIS Work," *DSS 88 Transactions,* The Institute of Management Sciences, Providence, RI, 1988, pp. 121–136.

Carroll, P.B. "Computerphobe Managers," *The Wall Street Journal,* June 20, 1988. p. 21.

Computerworld. "The Premier 100," Special Supplement, September 12, 1988, p. 9.

Friend, D. "Executive Information Systems: Successes, Failures, Insights, and Misconceptions," *DSS 86 Transactions,* The Institute of Management Sciences, Providence, RI, 1986, pp. 35–40.

Friend, D. "EIS and the Collapse of the Information Pyramid," *Information Center* (6:3), March 1990, pp. 22–28.

Gorry, G.A. and Scott Morton, M.S. "A Framework for Management Information Systems," *Sloan Management Review* (13:1), Fall 1971, pp. 51–70.

Gulden, G.K. and Ewers, D.E. "Is Your ESS Meeting the Need?" *Computerworld,* July 10, 1989, pp. 85–91.

Houdeshel, G. and Watson, H.J. "The Management Information and Decision Support (MIDS) System at Lockheed-Georgia," *MIS Quarterly* (11:1), March 1987, pp. 127–140.

Isenberg, D.J. "How Senior Managers Think," *Harvard Business Review* (62:6), November-December 1984, pp. 81–90.

Kogan, J. "Information for Motivation: A Key to Executive Information Systems That Translate Strategy into Results for Management," *DSS 86 Transactions,* The Institute of Management Sciences, Providence, RI, 1986, pp. 6–13.

Kotter, J.P. "What Effective General Managers Really Do," *Harvard Business Review* (60:6), November-December 1982, pp. 156–157.

Leibs, S. "EIS: It's All Down Hill From Here," *Information Week,* May 1989, pp. 44–46.

Main, J. "At Last, Software CEOs Can Use," *Fortune* (119:6), March 13, 1989, pp. 77–83.

Mintzberg, H. "The Manager's Job: Folklore and Fact," *Harvard Business Review* (53:4), July-August 1975, pp. 49–61.

Moad, J. "The Latest Challenge for IS Is in the Executive Suite," *Datamation,* May 15, 1988, p. 43.

Paller, A. and Laska, R. *The EIS Book,* Dow Jones-Irwin, Homewood, IL, 1990.

Reck, R.H. and Hall, J.R. "Executive Information Systems: An Overview of Development," *Journal of Information Systems Management* (3:4), Fall 1986, pp. 25–30.

Rinaldi, D. and Jastrzembski, T. "Executive Information Systems: Put Strategic Data at Your CEO's Fingertips," *Computerworld,* October 27, 1986, pp. 37–50.

Rockart, J.F. and Treacy, M.E. "The CEO Goes On-Line," *Harvard Business Review* (60:1), January-February 1982, pp. 84–88.

Rockart, J.F. and DeLong, D.W. *Executive Support Systems: The Emergence of Top Management Computer Use,* Dow Jones-Irwin, Homewood, IL, 1988.

Runge, L. "On the Executive's Desk," *Information Center* (4:6), June 1988, pp. 34–38.

Smith, S.L. and Mosier, J.N. "Design Guidelines for User-System Interface," Software Report (ESD-TR-84-190), The MITRE Corporation, Bedford, MA, September 1984.

Sprague, R.H. "A Framework for the Development of Decision Support Systems," *MIS Quarterly* (4:4), December 1980, pp. 1–26.

Stecklow, S. "The New Executive Information Systems," *Lotus,* April 1989, pp. 51–55.

Tullis, T.S. "An Evaluation of Alphanumeric, Graphic, and Color Information Displays," *Human Factors* (23:5), October 1981, pp. 541–550.

Turban, E. and Schaeffer, D.M. "A Comparative Study of Executive Information Systems," *DSS 87 Transactions,* The Institute of Management Sciences, Providence, RI, 1987, pp. 139–148.

Turban, E. and Watson, H.J. "Integrating Expert Systems, Executive Information Systems, and Decision Support Systems," *DSS 89 Transactions,* The Institute of Management Sciences, Providence, RI, 1989, pp. 74–82.

Volonino, L. and Drinkard, G. "Integrating EIS into the Strategic Plan: A Case Study of Fisher-Price," *DSS 89 Transactions,* The Institute of Management Sciences, Providence, RI, 1989, pp. 37–45.

Wallis, L. "Power Computing at the Top," *Across the Board* (26:1–2), January-February 1989, pp. 42–51.

Watson, H.J. and Frolick, M. "Determining Information Requirements for an Executive Information System," unpublished working paper, Department of Management, University of Georgia, Athens, GA, 1988.

Watson, H. and Glover, H. "Common and Avoidable Causes of EIS Failure," *Computerworld,* December 4, 1989, pp. 90–91.

Zmud, R.W. "Supporting Senior Executives Through Decision Support Technologies: A Review and Directions for Future Research," in *Decisions Support Systems: A Decade in Perspective,* E.R. McLean and H.G. Sol (eds.), Elsevier Science Publishers B.V., North-Holland, Amsterdam, 1986, pp. 87–101.

QUESTIONS

1. Differentiate between EIS and ESS. Are the two likely to remain distinct? Are the two distinct at all?

2. Why have TPS, MIS, and DSS not provided effective computer support for executives?

3. Why is it more difficult to provide computer support for executives than for other knowledge workers or managers?

4. Discuss the findings from the 50 organizations with EIS in regard to:

   (a) those that provide insights where little has been reported;

   (b) those that reveal surprising new findings.

7

Implementing an Executive Information System: Seven Steps for Success

Craig Barrow

Successful implementation of an executive information system (EIS) is not an easy job for any organization. But, of the many factors to consider, the success or failure of an EIS ultimately depends on how well the implementation process is managed in terms of both the technology and the users.

An EIS differs from other information systems in ways that require a different approach to its planning and implementation. First, the users—senior level executives—are not usually computer literate and do not have the time or inclination to become so. Thus, an EIS must address their needs in a manner that requires minimal training. Second, an EIS is more dynamic than a traditional information system. Because it is constantly responding to new user demands, an EIS must be flexible enough to change and expand as its users' corporate needs do.

A sophisticated tool, an EIS increases the number of users who can benefit from information delivered by the system, providing access for those executives who are computer savvy and those who are not. By automating complex data access paths to a variety of existing data sources, the system integrates internal and external information resources to derive information appropriate for managerial applications. Usually, the EIS links data from diverse sources to provide information in a new perspective. A successful EIS creates quality reports and charts

Previously pubished in *Journal of Information Systems Management*, Volume 7, Number 2, Spring 1990. Used with permission. Copyright 1990 Comshare, Inc.

that eliminate the need of combining information from various systems and inputting it into another system to produce a separate report.

Because no two executive information systems are exactly alike, neither are the methods for implementing them. However, the following seven steps can help MIS managers successfully implement an EIS.

FIND AN EXECUTIVE CHAMPION

One of the most important factors for success is to obtain an executive champion (i.e., a sponsor) for the system. This person does not need extensive technical knowledge, such as a director of information systems might. However, the executive champion should be a high-level executive who possesses decision making power within the organization and who understands and supports the EIS project. The champion should be considered a peer within the executive ranks; someone who can influence his or her constituents.

This person may be the CFO, the controller, or any executive who works closely with the executive users for whom the EIS is being designed. This champion must know what the senior executives want and need, their work styles, and what information their current systems are providing. MIS managers should ensure that this person is easily and frequently accessible to them.

Usually, the executive champion is someone who is forward-looking and has heard of the many benefits of executive information systems and, as a result, wants the MIS department to develop a better way to make more useful information available to solve executives' business problems in a timely manner. Often, an organization has invested a significant amount of money in its information systems; the champion wants to get better use out of that technology and investment. He or she is looking for a solution that will have a significant impact on the organization's direction or bottom line. Supporting the implementation of an EIS offers the champion that solution, as well as enhanced stature within the organization as an aggressive thinker.

The executive champion is involved in planning, reviewing prototypes and implementation plans, and promoting the completed system. Then, a user of the EIS, the champion becomes an active participant in suggesting modifications and expansions to the system as it continuously evolves to meet growing executive needs.

A Successful Champion

The EIS at the Quaker Oats Company in Chicago started nearly five years ago with a request from the chairman of the board. The project was directed by the vice-president of corporate planning. The success of this system is mostly due to the fact that Quaker had strong executive backing and direction from the very beginning.

Initially, Quaker's data was located in many diverse places throughout the organization. Gradually, working through several phases of implementation, Quaker was able to locate all its important data and incorporate it into a common EIS.

Quaker's current system makes it easy for executives to obtain timely data quickly, and in whatever form they need to make their decisions. For example, users can obtain daily sales figures and access Dow Jones financial data and other information essential for strategic decision making. Quaker's EIS is mostly used for financial analysis and planning, and the chairman of the board remains one of its most frequent users and supporters. With senior management reviewing ideas, plans, and prototypes, the MIS manager can have the vital input necessary to develop and implement a productive executive information system.

MAINTAIN SIMPLICITY

A second key to successful implementation of an EIS is keeping the system extremely simple and relevant to the executive users' sophistication level and needs, but without sacrificing system capability for more technical users. MIS managers should remember that the executives should use the EIS with a minimum amount of training, but their staff should also use the EIS for advanced applications.

For example, the EIS should have a simple way of allowing executives to navigate through the system to access their desired information. With a mouse or touch screen, the executives do not even have to use a keyboard to access complex data. At the same time, the EIS also needs a mechanism that allows more sophisticated users to access other applications such as Lotus 1-2-3 or Excel for spreadsheets and forecasting, word processing, dBase for data base management, and electronic mail.

A Simple EIS

Grumman Data Systems in Woodbury CT provides a suitable example of an EIS that is simple to use yet accommodates varying levels of computer knowledge within its user base. Grumman uses the EIS as the principal vehicle to deliver current and consistent data on the market and other competitive activities to its senior management.

The system was designed with simplicity in mind. The EIS project team realized that senior executives' acceptance and use of the system would depend on its ease of use. Therefore, Grumman's EIS provides touch screens, mouse input, and menu-driven systems with no technical terminology. It is completely self-instructive.

Users receive just 20 minutes of training with the system before they begin to use it. At the end of that short session, the executive users are comfortable with the computer technology and know that they can quickly get whatever information they need from the system—whether it's financial data, marketing information, or a market-by-market analysis of the past five years. They also have enough confidence that the system is providing current information.

Since the EIS has been installed at Grumman, vice-presidents, assistant vice-presidents, directors, and middle managers all look at the same data but at different levels of detail. The highest level executives are primarily interested in the "big picture" in order to identify problem areas or trends. Directors and managers, however, must delve further into the data and examine spreadsheets, for example, to identify the causes of problems and factors influencing business trends. This more detailed picture allows them to incorporate this information into their daily activities. More advanced applications provide access to this type of data.

Grumman's project manager noted that the key to the system's success is the total integration of detail data combined into the highest level of summary. It is a system all users find valuable because it provides the type of information different executives and managers need, in the format that they want, and in an easily accessible manner.

USE MIS EXPERTISE

A vital point in developing and implementing the EIS is for MIS managers to include their staff in the EIS project from day one. They should use their technical software experts who can make building the EIS an easier task. These experts not only know how to access information from diverse data bases and other sources, but also how to integrate it. MIS managers should also ensure that their other MIS staff members understand how the EIS will make their jobs function even more strategically to the business, and that executives who have the capability of getting their own MIS-based answers will be more productive than ever before, which affects the organization's overall success.

In a sense, creating an EIS allows the MIS department to do more of what it has always done, but in a more visible role because of the close contact with senior executives. The MIS staff must work closely with the executives, guiding them and responding to their information systems needs and desires. Both MIS and executive users become active participants in the evolution of an EIS. As the executives continue to want more features and functions as they become more familiar with what an EIS offers, the MIS staff must create new ways to access and package information to meet the executives' needs.

Here, the executive champion and other executive users play a role in shaping the EIS as they identify their needs and specify the types of presentation they seek. Custom icons, logos, or graphic applications developed to highlight a unique area of the organization are examples of how the EIS can be tailored to the specific organization and user.

ENSURE FEASIBILITY OF DATA AVAILABILITY

Another factor that contributes to an EIS' success—data availability—can also be one of the most time-consuming elements of an EIS implementation. Although MIS managers are expected to be experts on anticipating all the executives' information needs, they are expected to know how to satisfy these executives by understanding where the data is and how to access it, even if it is in different departmental or external systems.

MIS managers should consider these questions. How are they going to access the data the executives consider important? And, how do they distinguish between important and unimportant data? Feedback from executives can help them make this distinction.

It is important to have a simple interface that is powerful enough to integrate information from various sources. For example, an executive may want to determine whether new machinery or technology has improved productivity. The executive must access information from production and combine it with information on staffing and work time, as well as with sales data. Through the EIS, MIS managers can integrate data from the production floor, personnel records, and general ledger and deliver the type of information that the executive can really use. However, if data on the number of hours each employee spends in the production operation is not available on that department's computer, the information will have to be obtained elsewhere and input into the EIS.

In short, MIS managers should identify achievable goals for data they know is available when first creating a prototype of the initial system. MIS managers should not promise more than they can deliver, or they will set themselves—and the EIS—up for failure before the system's merits can be demonstrated.

Twenty years ago, the MIS department promised executives immediate access to every bit of data they identified as important and pertinent to their jobs. Of course, this was an impossible order to fill. MIS managers must be careful to first verify the feasibility of obtaining various types of information before they commit to incorporating it into the EIS. This way, MIS managers can manage executive expectations of what the system will do. The EIS should include historic and futuristic information as well as information from both external and internal systems.

As for which data is and is not important enough to be included in the system, MIS managers should realize that the EIS must supply at least the same amount of information the executives are currently receiving through written communications and at least one new element of strategic information. From there, MIS managers should ask the executive users and their support staffs to determine what additional information would be useful but has been absent from their traditional reports.

Some typical interview questions MIS managers might ask executives include:

- What are your objectives and how do these relate to your information needs?
- Are there types of information that pass only verbally between managers but should be incorporated into the organization's decisions and information resources?
- Should this information be included in a formal report or chart?
- What types of information gathering tasks are assigned to support staffs?
- Is there overlap in different parts of the organization in terms of information resources and needs?
- How does information from different sources and departments need to be integrated?
- Can some of these tasks be centralized and processed automatically?
- What information do you wish you had but currently lack?
- What future needs do you anticipate?

MIS managers should remember the EIS is evolutionary and grows from user input. The system requires cooperation among executives, information providers (e.g., the controller), and MIS managers to integrate new information technology, changing information needs, and new sources of information.

DEVELOP A SMALL BUT SIGNIFICANT PROTOTYPE

Designing an EIS requires a different approach than most MIS managers are accustomed to. Rather than waiting to get all the details perfectly aligned, MIS managers should start with a small but tangible element that can be incorporated into a prototype. This prototype need not be perfect but should be an example they can use to garner the executives' interest.

MIS managers should remember that most executives are extremely busy and will not be willing (or able) to devote a lot of time to assisting in the development of the EIS. As a result, MIS managers have to use the executives' time efficiently.

Traditional systems development involves a needs analysis, flowcharts, and detailed specifications which MIS managers usually want to complete before they present their system to users to review. This long process will not work with an EIS because it is a dynamic system rather than a static one. A traditional system that analyzes current needs may not accommodate the executives' needs next year or even next month. An EIS, however, will have the capability to satisfy executives' needs as they change.

Rather than designing and formalizing a completed system, MIS managers should identify a business issue within the organization that can be addressed using information from different sources. Then, they should develop a small prototype that demonstrates what an EIS can do for the organization.

Before developing the prototype, MIS managers should try to get some idea of the types of new information that might be useful for the executives. Often, the executives' support staffs can be a good resource for the executives' needs and interests. Once the prototype is completed, the executives will be able to describe what they like and dislike about the EIS, and what other types of information they would like to see incorporated into the EIS.

For example, an executive at a manufacturing company had been trying to determine whether the plant was operating efficiently. Using an EIS prototype, the MIS manager accessed and integrated data from various sources and provided valuable information on productivity and efficiency at the plant, which the executive had previously been unable to obtain. That aroused the executive's interest; the executive became a key sponsor (i.e., the champion) of the company's EIS, helping to develop and maintain the system.

MIS managers do not have to develop these systems from scratch. Packaged EIS software allows them to quickly develop a prototype and deliver the desired information using a simple interface. At the same time, the software should make the systems prototype more effective and interesting for these executive users, by offering such features as access to financial and competitive data, color graphs, and personalized exceptions (e.g., variants from plans or budgets) and by incorporating touch screens, mouses, and other features that do not require computer training. Depending on which software package MIS managers select, they should be able to build their EIS from the prototype without discarding the prototype and beginning again on the real system.

COMMUNICATE TO OVERCOME RESISTANCE

Theoretically, the executives will be receptive to answering questions and providing feedback on their needs. After all, the EIS is a tool to help them do their jobs better. Realistically, however, MIS managers may experience resistance from higher-level executives who are uncomfortable facing a computer screen, lack an understanding of what the EIS can do and how they can benefit from it, or simply do not have extra time to think about such a system.

To overcome these negative feelings, MIS managers should make the executives feel that they own the system and that they are active participants in its creation and growth. MIS managers should not simply design the EIS and present it to the executives. Instead, the executives should be involved on an ongoing basis as the EIS is developed.

MIS managers should educate the executives by showing them how the system can help them access and monitor critical business information. MIS managers should not waste time talking about what the system does; they should show executives how the EIS can make them perform better in their own areas, using specific examples to which executives can relate.

In addition, the executive champion has a key role in fostering acceptance of the system. As a peer within the executive ranks and a leader within the organization, the executive champion's endorsement of the EIS should command respect and interest among the other executives. And, because the champion believes that the EIS is a valuable strategic tool for the organization, he or she is a strong advocate for its implementation.

Once the system is implemented, communication becomes less of a problem as the EIS tends to sell itself within the organization. The more executives see what the EIS can offer, the more features and functions they will want from it. Inevitably, a successful EIS will grow within the organization; MIS managers must plan for this growth.

PLAN FOR THE FUTURE

As they move into the final stages of releasing the completed executive information system, MIS managers should ask themselves, "Where will the system go from here?" Up to this point, they may have addressed only basic information needs. But what happens next?

MIS managers should not think of an EIS as exclusively designed for senior executives. In fact, an EIS is a management direction tool that can be used by many levels of knowledgeable workers within the management and executive departments. MIS managers should not think small when planning an EIS, or they will get caught unprepared.

Preparing for growth is critical because six executive EIS users can quickly expand into 60 users. As more people within the organization realize the system's capabilities, the more they will want to use the system. Senior executives will want their vice-presidents and directors to have access to the EIS. Executive support staffs will also become more productive when they access the system.

It is essential that MIS managers have a good infrastructure that will support this growth. They should select software that enables the EIS to grow efficiently and accommodates the technical factors that will best service the organization. MIS managers should think about the growth before it happens, determining the types of applications that will be added next and how they will be implemented. MIS managers should also think about which employees are likely to become users of the system and in what logical sequence. They should ensure that the software capabilities and MIS support staff are in place as well.

Depending on the organization, this growth can be both hierarchal or lateral. With hierarchal growth, use of the EIS usually spreads from the top down in an organization. First, the top corporate staff begins to use the system, then senior executives from financial, marketing, personnel, and other departments access the EIS and finally, their executive support staffs.

In lateral growth, use of the EIS is likely to start in one division of the organization, then move to another division. Within each division, users may access their system for various types of data in marketing, sales, production, and finance.

As MIS managers set performance and benefit goals for the future of the EIS, they should remember these goals will always change. MIS managers will find that over time, the EIS will be in increasing demand to meet the growing needs of more users. Financial, production, marketing, sales, and personnel executives are likely to become user candidates as the EIS expands. MIS managers should therefore determine who will be the support person for these new areas of growth, whether it be an MIS or executive functional support staff member.

CONCLUSION

A successful EIS is not a process-oriented system that performs in a limited fashion. Thus, MIS managers will have plenty of opportunities to be creative, and to continue to respond professionally and successfully to future executive information needs.

MIS managers should remember to rely on their own skills and talents when implementing an executive information system. In addition, by following these seven steps, MIS managers can help ensure that the implementation of an EIS is a successful experience for their organizations.

QUESTIONS

1. What does the following statement mean: ". . . EIS are more dynamic than other computer-based information systems?"

2. What is meant by: ". . . no two EIS are exactly alike?"

3. Why do EIS require a different approach to implementation than other computer-based information systems?

4. List and briefly discuss the seven steps for successful EIS implementation. Are there other steps that should be included? What might they be? Justify each step you include.

5. What does the author mean by a "simple EIS"?

6. What does the author mean by a "small but significant prototype"?

8

Is Your ESS
Meeting the Need?

Gary K. Gulden
Douglas E. Ewers

Lately, there has been an outbreak of publicity on executive support systems (ESS). The slick vision that has been conjured up is one of a highly customized computer system that empowers a top executive to view crucial information unfiltered by management layers, to communicate and coordinate in lightning speed with anyone in the organization, to analyze business scenarios as never before and, like a master puppeteer, to control and shape important decisions made in the far reaches of the corporation.

While this may sound like hype, there is actually some substance to these scenarios. ESSs delivered by information systems have proved crucial to executives making major changes in business direction (such as shifting from a product to a market focus), organizational structure (especially flattening the organization) and eliminating staff functions and ·organizational communications patterns (as in moving to global product sourcing).

However, the majority of ESS efforts we encounter in the field today are on a course toward disappointment—destined to fall short of their potential impact. Why? Most often, it is because the ESS does not meet the need it was requested to fill.

Previously published in *Computerworld*, Volume 23, Number 28, July 10, 1989. Gary Gulden is an Executive Vice President and Doug Ewers is a Vice President of CSC Index, an international management consulting firm specializing in business reengineering. Used with permission.

OBSTACLES TO EFFECTIVE ESSs

While the benefits of executive support systems may be obvious, they tend to hide the difficulties inherent in building them. The most powerful ESSs in use today are not generic information and office automation utilities; rather, they are highly customized solutions for executives or executive teams with specific business needs and desired effects on their minds.

Therefore, successful ESSs cannot be designed with any one view in mind of how executives work or the kinds of information they need. IS organizations that follow this assumption and rely soley on the commercially available software packages labeled "executive support" or "executive information systems" will fall short. These products may be a strong starting point or platform for building a custom ESS, but for most executives, they are incomplete on their own.

There are two major reasons why most ESSs deliver less than they promise—or fail to deliver at all. First is the lack of clarity on the part of the sponsoring executive as to the purpose of the ESS. Second is the failure of IS to incorporate the system into the management processes of the organization.

Disappointments arise most often because the executive sponsor's fundamental purpose for the ESS is vague or left up to the IS staff to determine. Keep in mind that there is a range of basic executive motivations for implementing an ESS:

- To gain computer literacy.
- To "send a signal" to subordinates.
- To boost work efficiency.
- To improve insights.
- To facilitate business change, either through strategic redirection or reorganization.
- To solve specific problems relating to either decision making or control.

Note that it is surprisingly easy for senior executives to articulate what is behind their requests for ESSs once these options are spelled out as above. But unless IS holds an explicit conversation with executives about motivations, they will almost always remain fuzzy to the system designers.

Making clear distinctions among the various motivations is very important because different motivations generally call for substantially different design and implementation approaches. A general-purpose reporting, information retrieval and office automation system that is developed with minimal executive involvement might be adequate if the motivation was merely computer literacy. However, the same approach would be a miserable failure if the basic motivation was to support a strategic redirection or reorganization of the business.

In addition, it is common for eventual users of the system to have several motivations but to articulate only one at first: "I want our ESS to be a learning experience first, but then I intend to use it to help drive a fundamental change in the way we do our business." Being aware up front of this direction or potential evolution is critical to avoid executive disappointment later on.

Consider, for example, the chief executive officer of a large energy firm who ordered that an executive support system be installed in the offices and homes of his management committee executives. His expressed rationale at the time was that the senior executive group needed to begin to move into the 20th century. The system provided electronic access to management reports already available in hard copy, electronic mail, calendaring, word processing, spreadsheets and an electronic news service.

Use of the new system was fairly active for a week or so, then it fell into disuse by all but the CEO, who was quite disappointed. When asked what his purpose was for creating the system, he said, "Well, what I really wanted was for the management committee members to start looking at the business in new ways and to think more strategically." Clearly, a lead-the-horses-to-the-water approach did not work.

In contrast, a group of managers at Eastman Kodak Co. quickly became active users of a customized IS that helped them implement a new business strategy. In this case, the motivation for the system was made clear by the group executive: A reorganization aimed at cutting manufacturing costs and boosting product quality required the adroit coordination of manufacturing facilities on a global basis. Manufacturing managers now needed information in a form that never existed before, and it was clear from the outset that there was no way for this strategic move to be executed quickly and well enough in the absence of executive support tools.

SUPPORT OR CHANGE?

Achieving clarity is certainly crucial (see Figure 8–1). The diagram spells out four primary areas of potential impact that an ESS can deliver. Where on this picture is the intended emphasis of your company's ESS? Different areas of emphasis call for different design and implementation strategies. The four primary areas—simplification, acceleration, expansion and motivation—form the basis for building most executive support systems.

Just Your Type. Based on Need, There Are Four Kinds of Executive Support Systems; the North-South Axis Represents Support-Only Systems, and the East-West Axis Shows Change-Oriented Systems

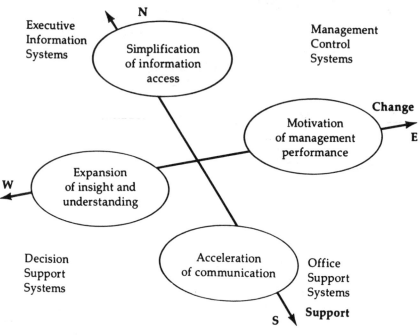

Source: Index Group, Inc.

Figure 8–1. *Four Kinds of Executive Support Systems*

Simplification addresses the need to quickly and easily maintain one's feel for the business. This type of ESS provides flexible access to, and formatting of, the wide array of operating data typically contained in the piles of printed monthly management reports.

The complaint that managers receive too many voluminous reports does not mean that the reports are all useless; however, it may mean that managers spend two or three hours going through the reports each month just to extract the relatively small amount of data they really need.

Some managers say that the information they receive is too superficial or incomplete. They want to be able to see what is behind the numbers that interest them. Others are frustrated that it is so hard to see trends and gain insights from lists of numbers, and they need a more graphic, visual representation. If you hear this type of complaint, you are hearing the need for simplification.

Many of the executive information system software packages excel in this area. They provide the visual representation some managers need to spot trends, and many of them allow users to "drill down" to greater levels of detail in which they are interested. Furthermore, off-the-shelf packages address the specific need being felt here: the delivery of the information. Simplification has more to do with the format, depth, frequency and presentation of information than with how it is used.

The downside of the commercial packages is that they do not necessarily address the other three dimensions of ESSs, and too often, they are used as a catch-all solution. They should not be purchased as a substitute for spending time determining the user's real requirements.

Acceleration refers to the way electronic messaging, voice mail, calendaring, word processing and other office support systems can accelerate the flow of communications. That may not sound like an ESS executive support system to some in information systems, but consider the following:

A manager receives monthly reports on paper and frequently has questions about some of the data he sees. He pulls out a few pages, scribbles his questions on them and gives them to the person in charge of that area for clarification. The problem is, he distributes so many questions that he has no reasonable way of keeping track of whether he has received an answer. Further, the delay that occurs before he receives an answer often makes the answer irrelevant.

An ESS with a messaging capability, or the option of writing notes on the same screen you are reviewing, addresses this problem. The manager does not have to tear up his reports or give away pages he may need. He knows his message will be read the next time the recipient logs on, with no telephone tag. He can also see what he has asked them and when the response is received.

Another feature of acceleration is that it removes time and location as constraints. For example, at the beginning of the personal computer revolution, a leading floppy-disk supplier's management team was trying to cope with the transition from a company growing at a 30% annual rate to one growing at 300%.

HIGH DEMAND

Prior to the explosion in demand for its product, printed management reports and the weekly management committee meeting in the headquarters conference room allowed the senior executives to feel in control of their business.

Once the growth hit, though, everyone was on the road setting up manufacturing and distribution centers around the world. The printed reports piled up, the conference room was nearly empty during the management committee meeting, and the valuable face-to-face exchanges that once took place in those meetings could not take place.

An ESS was developed to provide electronic access from anywhere in the world to the previously printed management report information.

The reporting system was built around a core of E-mail and office automation applications, so the executives could annotate and share the reports with one another and resume their "face-to-face" conversations electronically, regardless of their location.

Simplification and acceleration make up the North-South diagonal of Figure 8–1. This is called the "support" axis because these functions support the routine information- and communications-handling tasks of management. They make managers more efficient without necessarily changing the way they manage.

ESSs THAT CREATE CHANGE

The East-West axis of the figure has a different flavor; it is the "change" continuum. It makes managers more effective by allowing them to change the way they manage.

For this reason, developing this type of ESS requires much more up-front analysis of the business priorities and management processes than the "support" line does.

The East-West diagonal consists of expansion and motivation. Expansion refers to the way a properly constructed ESS can broaden the executive's understanding and insight into the business. The system does not focus on the delivery of data but on defining the data and how it is used. Typically, this type of system provides the most value when there is a targeted business problem or specific area to tackle.

This was the case several years ago at a manufacturing company. Its manufacturing process, which involved creating a line of inexpensive consumer goods, was efficient but not low-cost, and product quality had deteriorated relative to the imports with which they competed. The question was, where in the massive plant should it invest to gain the greatest competitive impact?

The company needed to understand exactly what the consumers wanted most—that is, it wanted to let the customers define "quality"—and then it planned to pursue that target throughout every step of the design, engineering and manufacturing process.

Maintaining the integrity of the original customer request meant tracking all the links between the departments, many of which had never talked to one another before.

This business problem required an automated, ESS-type solution because of the vast amounts of detailed information the executives needed to track.

However, the automation also created the need for many more interactions between departments that were previously unaccustomed to interacting. Furthermore, it allowed the original consumer requirement to be spelled out in much greater detail, so compromises did not creep in unnoticed.

MOTIVATION

The fourth type of executive need, motivation, refers to ESSs as a key ingredient in a management control system. Here, the system is used to change the focus of attention and behavior of executives in a management team.

For example, motivation was the name of the game for Du Pont Co.'s medical products business a few years ago. The group's new chief operating officer was leading a transition from a product orientation to a market orientation. Where once there were business units organized by product, he put into place business units that focused on specific health care markets whose needs spanned the full line of Du Pont's product offerings—and beyond.

The management teams of these new business units needed to radically change the way they looked at and understood their marketplaces. Their performance was also being measured by new standards such as customer segment, market penetration and profitability.

Here, ESSs employing the principles of modeling, analysis and management control were initiated to drive and support the needed change in the thinking and behavior of the management teams. Unlike some ESSs, these systems do not show measures of product profitability. The only profitability they look at is market segment profitability: How well is the company doing in individual places in the market? In addition, these ESSs show detailed information pertaining to less tangible measures such as how salespeople are doing following up leads.

ESSs such as Du Pont's are not being used to invent new processes but to implement them. They allow executives to use information to follow through on initiatives they have begun. The ESSs might consist of a combination of planning and performance measurement data that is then used to determine the rewards, recognition and compensation of employees. In that sense, they are directly linked to motivating employees. Clearly, this type of system is not used for just communicating but for a behavioral change.

A major insurance company, for example, found that its geographically scattered independent agents were ill-equipped to sell the growing number of insurance products and financial services the company was beginning to offer. Executives knew they needed to change how the agents sold the complete product line and how they were supported and managed by the company.

Through an ESS, executives determined that segmenting the agents by geographic areas was no longer useful. Instead, they noticed the agents fell into three groups according to their performance levels and earnings. One group, the star performers, already produced high volume and earned high incomes. The second group had real development potential. Achievers already, these agents would go much further with additional training and support. The third group, nicknamed the "steady part-timers," always seemed to do just enough work to earn themselves a modest income and no more.

Clearly, the insurance company could gain the most by managing the steady part-timers in a laissez-faire manner and concentrating attention on the other two groups. The system allowed them to segment the agents by their own performance expectations because it provided the information required to measure and categorize them.

In some cases, an ESS of this type can go a step further and allow executives to analyze profitability, pushing their sales forces toward the most profitable products rather than rewarding them on straight-dollar volume without regard to profit. Again, by their nature, motivation-oriented ESSs require a great deal of analysis before implementation because they involve changing the behavior of people and the management processes by which work gets done.

The preceding illustrations strongly underscore the importance of clarity of purpose if you want to develop ESSs that make a difference. An East-West system would not have helped managers in the floppy-disk company stay in touch, and a North-South system would have failed to achieve the change in thinking and action needed by Du Pont. Unfortunately, this kind of mismatch occurs all too often in the ESS efforts under way in many companies.

DON'T FORGET THE CONTEXT

Beyond clarity of purpose, the second major success factor is integrating the ESS into the management processes already in place in your corporation. A weekly operations review meeting is a management process. So is a master manufacturing schedule session, a pricing committee meeting, a quarterly budget update, the capital appropriation process or the incentive compensation plan. Some management processes are less formal, such as setting goals with a subordinate.

Management processes that are poorly informed are next to worthless, and, by the same token, ESSs that are disconnected from the basic management mechanisms of the business are of very limited value.

In fact, it is the connection with management processes that normally provides the executive with a solid reason to learn and keep using an ESS in the first place.

The senior executive who initiates an ESS without an eye to how it will support or change management processes—or the IS staff that allows this connection to be ignored—runs a serious risk of ending up with a system that will fail to achieve its potential. Ultimately, it is the executive sponsor who must take the lead here. But IS can't take a back seat, either.

For example, executive support systems at Xerox Corp. were fairly benign and unevenly used until the CEO, the chief of staff and the director of ESS decided to completely reengineer the corporation's planning process around the capabilities of the existing ESS. This single act, which required the executives to make active use of the ESS to produce and negotiate their annual and long-range plans, raised the stakes on the ESS and turned it from an information/communication utility service into an essential management tool.

ESSs are becoming key tools in the executive arsenal. In this era of corporate reorganization, mergers and acquisitions, turbulent markets and increasing competition, managers now more than ever need more effective ways to understand their markets and their competition and to guide their operations and their people.

However, building these systems requires pushing hard to get the intended user's business problems, information needs and management processes to rise to the surface. Only when the executive support system takes all of those factors into account, actually inducing change rather than merely supporting it, can the executive fully tap the power of information and information technology.

QUESTIONS

1. What is a generic ESS? Is it doomed to failure? Justify your answer.

2. List and discuss the four kinds of ESS.

3. If your firm is an old, well-established organization that needs modernization, which type of ESS would be optimal? Explain your choice.

9

A Path Framework for Executive Information Systems

Ido Millet
Charles H. Mawhinney
Ernest A. Kallman

Executive information systems (EIS) are clearly becoming a more significant member in the information systems portfolio of contemporary organizations. Friend (1988) claims that executive information systems have been installed on the desks of senior executives in nearly 25 percent of the largest U.S. companies. In terms of the value of software sales (although the figures differ among sources), U.S. companies sold $22 to $30 million worth of EIS software during 1987, $60 to $120 million in 1989 and will sell a projected $115 to $240 million in 1992 (*Computerworld Focus,* 1987, Kolodziej, 1989). Even at the low end of these ranges, the figures represent a significantly high level of acceptance of both the software and the potential for EIS. This level of expenditure is further increased by adding the cost of in-house EIS development. In-house development adds costs in two ways. First, a large number of firms, perhaps as many as 25 percent will develop their own EIS without employing outside software. And second, those using outside software will, in most instances, supplement the packages with in-house enhancements (Ryan, 1989).

Much of the literature on executive information systems focuses on two significant and not necessarily exclusive areas: (1) prescriptive

Ido Millet, C.H. Mawhinney, and E.A. Kallman, "A Path Framework for Executive Information Systems," Transactions of the Eleventh International Conference on Decision Support Systems, 1991. Used with permission.

suggestions for their design and implementation (Armstrong, 1980; Barrow, 1990; DeLong, 1988; Jones & McLeod, 1986; McLeod & Jones, 1986; Reck & Hall, 1986; Rockart & DeLong, 1988; Watson, 1990), and (2) descriptive explanations of how EIS work, often with case examples of specific installations (Jordan, 1988; McNurlin, 1987; Rinaldi & Jastrzembski, 1986; *Computerworld* Executive Report, 1986; Tobias, 1988). This paper adds a new perspective by drawing attention to the importance of timing and coordinating EIS development so that it is appropriately matched with the organization's level of "decision-making maturity" and technical capabilities.

The major theme of this paper is that provisions for executive information proceed through stages of technological and organizational capabilities. The transition from the traditional MIS stage to an online EIS stage requires a shift along two dimensions: (1) a move from batch to interactive online environment, and (2) an increase in information integration and focus. Each of these transitions requires significant technological and organizational changes, and hence, attempting to effect both transitions simultaneously may be ill-advised. It is important to consciously choose and manage an appropriate transition path according to organizational contingencies.

The first part of this paper defines and compares the EIS and MIS concepts. Previous literature and descriptive data from EIS experts suggest that the EIS and MIS concepts are quite similar in capabilities and in goals. EIS depend on MIS capabilities and may be viewed as an integrative front-end to the MIS, focused and specialized for use by executives.

The second part of this paper presents a path framework for the transition from batch MIS reporting to online EIS. The framework can be helpful in managing investments in MIS and EIS, and in conducting future research.

The third part of this paper reports some preliminary findings about the actual paths taken by 46 organizations.

The fourth part of this paper describes the relative advantages of different paths and shares some views concerning limitations of online EIS and advantages of batch EIS.

The discussion is based on a combination of: (a) previous literature, (b) personal experience with EIS, (c) a previous study of EIS experts (Millet & Mawhinney, 1990), and (d) pilot questionnaires administered to 46 graduate business students.

DISTINGUISHING MIS FROM EIS

There is a lack of a universally accepted definition and agreement on terminology in relation to the MIS and EIS concepts. The terms are not clearly and uniformly defined in the literature, and are often used synonymously (Rockart & DeLong, 1988). Although numerous frameworks have been proposed in the literature (Chervany, Dickson & Kozar, 1972; Gorry & Scott Morton, 1971; Ives, Hamilton & Davis, 1980; Lucas, 1973; Mason & Mitroff, 1973; Mock, 1973), they have lacked empirical validation (Kirs, 1989) and thus have not produced generally accepted definitions for MIS and EIS. This poses a problem for both researchers and practitioners as they attempt to understand and implement such systems. In the following sections both MIS and EIS are defined and distinguished in a way that will provide a useful foundation for later discussions (see Table 9–1).

The MIS Concept

MIS is defined as a system that provides managers at various organizational levels with detailed and summarized information from operational databases about the operation and performance of the organization (Sprague, 1980). The operational databases are typically created by transaction processing systems (TPS) which were developed to support various business functions (Newmann and Hadass, 1980). An MIS is, in effect, a layer on top of the transaction processing system. Thus the characteristics of the TPS limit the capabilities of the MIS. TPS are relatively inflexible and use mostly internal data sources resulting in MIS whose primary purpose is internal monitoring of past activities (Newmann and Hadass, 1980). A TPS is often developed in a piecemeal and independent fashion in an attempt to support a particular organizational function. This results in MIS which lack data integration across functional areas. This lack of integration becomes a severe limitation when

Table 9-1. *MIS and EIS: A Comparison*

System	Primary Purpose	Primary Users	Primary Output	Primary Operations	Time Orientation	Example
MIS	Internal monitoring	Managers & executives	Pre-defined periodic reports	Summarize information	Past	Sales report
EIS	Internal & external monitoring	Executives	Pre-defined customized periodic or ad-hoc reports, presentations & queries	Integrate present, track CSF	Past & present	Market share tracking

attempting to satisfy the needs of top-management for comprehensive, organization-wide information.

The most common and basic MIS is one which periodically summarizes data from the operational databases and reports it periodically to various levels of management (Sprague, 1980; Friend, 1986). More sophisticated MIS may provide descriptive statistics and exception reports. Such systems can provide information to all three levels of management described in the Anthony model (Anthony, 1965). In this reporting mode, higher levels of management tend to receive higher levels of aggregation and to use longer reporting cycles. In some MIS environments this passive mode is augmented with an active (query) mode that allows users to interrogate the database in an ad hoc fashion (Raho and Belohlov, 1982). In general though, MIS are limited to supplying information through pre-defined batch reports with low levels of focus and integration)

The EIS Concept

Early researchers discussed the need for, and characteristics of, information systems to support executive decision making (Anthony, 1965; Gorry & Scott Morton, 1971; Mason & Mitroff, 1973). But the term Executive Information System was not used until Rockart and Treacy introduced it in 1982, and only since that time has much of the hardware and software been developed to facilitate EIS implementation. Executive information systems integrate and focus data, enabling executives to monitor and access internal and external information of specific importance to them via effective presentation formats. Further, an online EIS allows executives to interact directly with the data via a user-friendly interface on an executive work station.

Both MIS and batch EIS systems typically monitor organizational performance on a monthly basis. Online EIS on the other hand, allow executives to monitor performance on a weekly, daily, or even near real-time basis. Such high-frequency monitoring systems have recently been the marketing emphasis of one major EIS vendor (Friend, 1990).

Rockart (1979) described five different approaches upon which an information system could be built: (1) the null approach, (2) the by-product approach, (3) the key indicator system, (4) the total study process, and (5) critical success factors (CSF). The impetus for EIS comes from a combination of the by-product, key indicator, and CSF approaches. In the by-product approach, management information is extracted from, and is limited to, the data that is already available in transaction processing system. Key indicators are a set of criteria whose achievement levels are reported to management in toto or on an exception basis, i.e., only those performing outside an acceptable range are included. "Critical success factors . . . are . . . the limited number of areas in which results, if they are satisfactory, will ensure successful competitive performance for the organization" (Rockart, 1979). Performance in each area is constantly measured and that information made available to management. Though much of the data required for all three approaches is potentially available from the MIS, the MIS delivery system is typically inadequate to provide the information in a meaningful, integrated, focused, timely and needs-oriented format. That is the task of the EIS (Rockart & DeLong, 1988).

James Martin (1989) supports this position as follows:

> Executive information systems are specifically designed to help executives gain insights and track critical success factors. The focus of an EIS is to aid a decision maker in assimilating information quickly and identifying problems or opportunities, not as an aid in problem analysis or resolution. In many corporations, well-developed EIS have replaced the traditional periodic executive summary reports.

Figure 9–1 clarifies the relationship between EIS and other information subsystems. The EIS is a monitoring system that draws information from MIS data bases and from external data sources for use by executives.

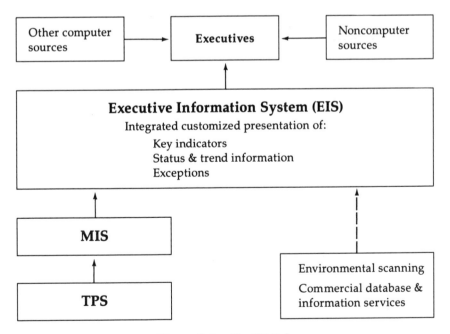

Figure 9–1. *The EIS Role*

Whereas the MIS does not provide integrated access to data files, the EIS does provide the missing integration through database extraction capability. However, the bulk of EIS data needs are met through the underlying MIS. This is confirmed by EIS vendors who indicated that indeed 90 percent of the EIS data is internal (Millet & Mawhinney, 1990).

In addition to the common databases, EIS and MIS are similar in many other respects. As indicated in Table 9–1, both MIS and EIS monitor past performance, are used by executives, and make extensive use of predefined reports. Further, 98 percent of EIS functionality could have been delivered via MIS capabilities, 94 percent of EIS implementations were significantly motivated by trying to give executives MIS information with a better format and/or interface, and 90 percent of EIS implementations were significantly motivated by trying to provide executives with integrated, combined, and unified MIS information (Millet & Mawhinney, 1990).

Another aspect of EIS is the way that executives employ them in decision making. Executives rely extensively on other (subordinate) managers and professionals to provide input for decision making with the computerized information system as an important and powerful supplement, but not the primary focus. More often than not, the other managers and professionals are the ones who interact directly with the computerized system.

Those cases where the executive does interact with the computer are characterized by requests for status reports rather than by analysis activity (Moore, 1986). This supports the view of EIS as a monitoring oriented system. The EIS vendors interviewed indicated that 81 percent of EIS are used predominantly for monitoring purposes.

Obviously, actual systems may not always map neatly into this framework. For example, EIS with many users may take on more of the characteristics of either MIS or decision support system (DSS).* It is estimated that installed EIS average 40 users, only 28 percent of which are executives (Millet & Mawhinney, 1990). The adding of users to an EIS reduces the ability to customize reports and increases the instances of periodic report distribution, thus lending the system an MIS flavor. On the other hand, when staff analysts or even executives demand analysis and modeling capabilities, the system may acquire a DSS flavor. In one reported case, a system that was called an EIS was in reality a combined MIS/DSS with 2,000 users (Millet & Mawhinney, 1990).

Many executives want to move beyond the limitations of MIS. They want integrated information from across functional areas as well as from external sources. They need more focus on their individual areas of responsibility through the use of key performance indicators and critical

---

* A DSS is a system designed to deal with specific decision problems based on algorithms or models (Sprague, 1980).

success factors. They want more exception reporting to alleviate the information overload that traditional reports create. Yet executives also want the option to access deeper levels of detail and to plot historical trends through a user-friendly online interface. In addition, they require effective information presentation capabilities or formats, typically through customized graphics. The system that holds the promise of fulfilling these needs is an Executive Information System (Friend, 1986). With this distinction between MIS and EIS in mind, an explanation of the possible development paths is now appropriate.

AN EIS FRAMEWORK

The above discussion presents EIS and MIS as similar in concept and in practice. EIS evolve from the MIS foundation to answer managers' needs for integrated, focused and accessible information. Figure 9–2 presents a two-dimensional framework for EIS development. The "focus and integration" dimension deals with the system's ability to provide information about specific performance measures across the broad range of typical business functions, as described in the previous section. The "mode of operation" dimension is commonly used to characterize information systems by distinguishing between "batch" and "online" systems (Davis & Olson, 1985; Laudon & Laudon, 1988). Batch systems rely extensively on periodic reporting whereas online systems permit the interactive ad hoc retrieval of information. These two dimensions result in four different types of information systems: MIS, Query, Batch-EIS, and Online-EIS.

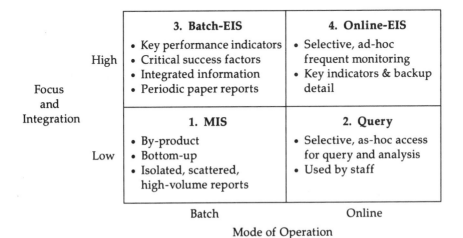

Figure 9-2. *An EIS Framework*

The typical starting point is an MIS where information is provided through a traditional information system. As described in the previous section, such a system is characterized by sundry batch reports with little integration across functional areas and little focus on specific performance measures. By-product data from transaction processing systems is summarized and "pushed" up for periodic review by managers.

As the organization progresses toward advanced stages of EIS development, the previous MIS capabilities are typically not abandoned but rather supplemented. A transition along the mode of operation dimension from a batch to an online environment, without additional integration and focus, would move an organization from an MIS to a Query system. This type of system usually results in an emphasis on access to raw data for analysis by staff personnel rather than on performance monitoring by executives.

A transition along the integration and focus dimension instead would move an organization from an MIS to a Batch-EIS. This type of system provides managers with periodic reports that integrate data from various functional systems and from external sources. These systems provide periodic monitoring of critical success factors. Typically, such systems include graphs and tables that present status data and trend lines for key performance indicators. For example, executives may track performance indicators relating to the number of new customers, service levels, sales, profitability and financial ratios, capacity utilization, and quality of operations.

The Online-EIS represents the most advanced stage. The transition from an MIS to an Online-EIS requires a shift along two dimensions: (1) a move from a batch to an interactive online environment, and (2) an increase in information integration and focus. Such a system provides for interactive and flexible monitoring of key performance indicators on an ad hoc basis to identify problems within the organization. It also provides the ability to "drill down" to the backup detail at lower levels to determine underlying causes.

There are numerous paths an information system might follow as it evolves from an MIS into an Online-EIS. The simplest paths are illustrated in Figure 9–3. Two possible paths would involve transitions along one dimension at a time, following either a Via Query Path or a Via Batch Path. However, it may be possible for a system to evolve simultaneously along both dimensions following a Direct Path. It is also possible to move from Query to Batch-EIS or vice-versa, as illustrated in Figure 9–4. In such cases the functionality of the second dimension is being added, but without sufficient links between the online capabilities and the EIS information to qualify as Online-EIS.

The Type 4 Online-EIS has been portrayed here as the eventual steady state. This does not preclude the possibility that an organization might

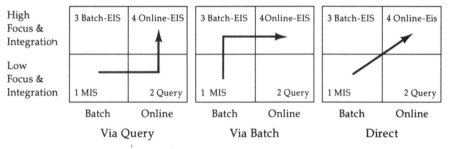

Figure 9–3. *Simple Path Alternatives*

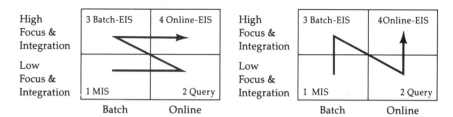

Figure 9–4. *Other Path Alternatives*

achieve Online-EIS capabilities, but will then move along one or both dimensions to add other types of reporting to its portfolio. For example, a query system can be added for use by staff professionals.

THE PILOT STUDY

In order to verify the face validity of the model and to explore its usefulness, a pilot study was conducted using 46 part-time graduate business students who were familiar with the history of the information systems in the organizations for which they worked. These organizations represent diverse industry segments including: service, hi-tech, finance, manufacturing, health care, government, and retail.

The questionnaire asked the students to specify the transition paths taken by their organizations. Since this was only a pilot test administered to a small convenience sample, the results serve merely as interesting preliminary evidence. However, the reactions and responses from the students indicated that the framework was clear and meaningful to them. Further, these preliminary results do support the conceptual value of the path framework.

Table 9–2 shows the frequency distribution for the paths of evolution followed by the respondents' information systems. This distribution

Table 9–2.   *Frequency Distribution of Paths of EIS Evolution*

Path	Frequency
1-2-3	14
1-2	8
1-3-4	5
1-3	4
1-2-3-4	3
1-2-4	3
1-3-2	3
1-3-2-4	2
1-3-4-2	2
1	1
1-2-4-3	1

provides several important insights. First, all of these systems did indeed begin with a Type 1 (MIS) system as the starting point. Second, fully one-third of these organizations had achieved a Type 4 (Online-EIS) system at the time of the survey, although three of them proceeded to add capabilities characteristic of Type 2 or Type 3. Third, in each of the three cases where an organization moved out of the Type 4 system, it moved to the opposite type of system from the one it passed through

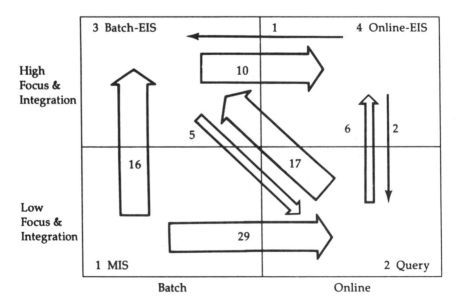

Figure 9–5.   *Path Flows of 46 Organizations*

when entering Type 4. Finally, and perhaps most surprising, none of these organizations went directly from a Type 1 to a Type 4 system.

Figure 9–5 presents another view of the data. It depicts the transition frequencies between the pairs of cells in the framework. The widths of the arrows represent the relative frequencies. This figure provides some additional insights. First, although there is apparently considerable activity between most pairs of cells, there is none at all between Type 1 and Type 4 systems. Second, there is considerable bi-directional activity between most pairs of cells. Third, once an organization moves out of a Type 1 system it apparently does not ever go back to a Type 1 system. Fourth, although the dominant path out of a Type 1 system was to a Type 2 system, more than half of the organizations selecting that path then moved to a Type 3 system. Indeed, the dominant path into a Type 4 system was from a Type 3 system rather than from a Type 2 system.

SUCCESSFUL PATHS TO EIS

The above results suggest there are several paths to an Online EIS which organizations have successfully followed. The results also indicate that there is at least one path which should probably be avoided.

The Via Batch-EIS Path

Most of the organizations in the survey took the path through a Batch-EIS, which suggests this may be the most successful route to Online-EIS. Quite possibly the technological capabilities and the organizational maturity required for integration and focus call for an incubation period at the Batch-EIS stage. This is where the information sources, the critical success factors, and the key performance indicators are developed in an evolutionary manner. Such a process allows organizations to maintain flexibility and to ease the organization into a period of enhanced executive monitoring. The path through the Batch-EIS stage also allows executives to become familiar with available data, presentation formats, and their own information needs.

Another explanation for favoring the path through the Batch-EIS is that only recently have the technology and scope of possible services reached the critical mass for introducing Online-EIS. These technologies and services include EIS data management, processing, and interfaces; electronic mail; and external online databases and news services.

The Via Query Path

The survey results suggest that many organizations first extend their MIS capabilities by adding online query capabilities rather than intensifying focus and integration. However, it would appear that such organizations then have a difficult time adding the focus and integration necessary to move directly from that stage to Online-EIS. Instead, a majority proceed to Batch-EIS before moving on to Online-EIS, indicating the possible need for the incubation period described above. Another possible reason for such a move is that after the Query system is implemented its use is resisted by managers suffering from "technophobia."

In those organizations that go directly from Query to Online-EIS, it is possible an executive who is familiar with the technology pushed the organization along this path. Such an executive may have enjoyed working directly with the online Query system and then became a champion for the Online-EIS cause. This provides the much needed management support for the development, but might also result in premature Online-EIS. Such systems may be built at high expense to serve the needs of one executive. When the executive changes position or leaves the company, such a system may be scrapped (David Friend, 1990).

The Direct Path

The Direct Path from an MIS to an Online-EIS might be a tempting strategy. It could possibly be accomplished much faster than any other, and perhaps with the expenditure of less resources. However, none of the organizations in the sample chose this route, which suggests that the Direct Path is not very practical. In general, making incremental changes is usually the preferred organizational approach (Quinn, 1978). Attempting to make two transitions simultaneously compounds the difficulty of implementing a new system and would thus increase the risk of failure.

Limitations of Online-EIS

Online-EIS has thus far been presented as an ideal. However, three of the organizations in the sample that implemented such systems then moved to either a Batch-EIS or a Query system. This suggests that Online-EIS may suffer from some limitations.

The Online-EIS might indeed suffer from some interesting limitations. These limitations include lower flexibility, difficulty in sharing information, and detrimental effects on decision quality and time orientation. Online-EIS are less flexible due to the elaborate structure and design behind them. For example, if the EIS provides six graphs on one screen for six major sales territories, a conversion to eight territories might require substantial modifications. Sharing screen information with other managers may also be problematic if they have no screens or if hardcopy is not available.

Online-EIS typically provide access to deep levels of backup detail. Supplying executives with detailed data without analysis and without recommendations might lead to premature decisions and to deterioration of top-level decision making quality. Furthermore, too much executive involvement with "micro-management" might prove disruptive to staff and line work.

Online-EIS might bias the organization's agenda and time orientation. Executives will spend more of their time, and the time of subordinates, on information and issues presented by the EIS. It may also result in an increased orientation toward the short term in reaction to the tighter and more frequent feedback supplied by the EIS. This seems undesirable in view of common claims that American executives are already biased toward the short term (Kerr, 1975; Gordon, 1983; Iaccoca, 1984; Webber, 1980; Silver, 1988).

A more subtle source of agenda and time horizon bias might be found in defensive chain reactions throughout the organization. Lower-level managers recognize very quickly when executives constantly monitor certain dimensions of their performance. These managers often shift their agenda and shorten their time horizon at the expense of overall organizational performance. Consider, for example, a case mentioned by Rockart and DeLong (1988) where a system was developed for the chairman of a firm to track the response time of departments to his correspondence. The system is credited with reducing the average response time from 15 to less than 5 days. This "achievement" might have had the hidden, but dire, consequences of generating disruptive work patterns throughout the organization as respondents reply to memos rather than perform higher priority tasks.

There is another potential danger that may be associated with Online-EIS. Previous literature (Forrester, 1968; Roberts, 1978; Rasmussen & Mosekilde, 1988) suggests that managerial systems may demonstrate oscillations or even chaotic behavior under certain conditions of external disturbance and internal feedback and adjustment. Similar concerns were recently expressed in relation to database technology:

> Information feedback that is too rapid and not controlled properly is very destabilizing for a system, causing its behavior to oscillate wildly . . . we may inadvertently destabilize large organizations by forcing them to react too quickly to changes. (Chapnic, 1989)

Online-EIS might throw organizations into oscillations or even chaotic behavior in cases where executives overreact to the supplied information by making adjustments which are too frequent and too strong.

Advantages of Batch-EIS

While ad hoc reporting and query capabilities would appear to be beneficial for most managerial processes, there are some advantages to periodic reporting cycles. Periodic EIS reporting provides consistent information on a regular basis which is reviewed simultaneously by all managers. This synchronization facilitates discussion and management processes. Note that the introduction of Online-EIS might disrupt such reporting cycles and cause a loss or lack of synchronization in some managerial processes.

A periodic review of all performance indicators also permits managers to make decisions and prioritize issues with a more global perspective. This has the added benefit of clearly communicating priorities to subordinates and reducing confusion. With Online-EIS, the executive might neglect to review some performance dimensions, and might be tempted to react to information on a "last come first served" basis. The periodic mode can thus minimize disruptions due to scattered executive inquiries that might be typical of the Online-EIS mode.

A periodic distribution of hard copy reports on key performance indicators to various levels of management has several advantages over an interactive mode. The hard copy format of Batch-EIS reporting facilitates hand written annotation, distribution, and communication with peers and subordinates. The distribution of the report to various levels of management increases motivation due to increased performance feedback.

These positive effects of periodic reporting were observed in a batch performance monitoring system for a complex logistics system and for a large commercial bank. The bank system, for example, is currently tracking more than 300 performance indicators on a monthly and quarterly basis and involves five management levels in the organization (Radding, 1990).

The above limitations of Online-EIS can be avoided to a large extent by preceding and balancing them with Batch-EIS. Indeed, even after a transition to an Online-EIS, some organizations maintain some periodic reporting under a batch mode only. This view is reinforced by a study of EIS experts that estimated 83 percent of EIS usage was via standard reports, and that 84 percent of these standard reports were used periodically (Millet & Mawhinney, 1990). Note that the actual distribution of such periodic reports may be done on paper as well as electronically. The periodic reporting noted in that study may have been the result of the periodic nature of updates to the information database feeding the EIS. Still, further research may indicate that the use of periodic reports is at least partially motivated by the above considerations. In general, the use of batch and online EIS should be matched to organizational maturity and to reporting needs and capabilities.

CONCLUSIONS AND RECOMMENDATIONS

This paper has attempted to provide useful definitions for the concepts of MIS and EIS which demonstrate the overlap and dependencies between these two types of information systems. A path approach to EIS development based upon a two-dimensional framework has been proposed. A pilot study has demonstrated that the framework and path approach are indeed meaningful and do provide a basis for describing the evolution of EIS.

The purpose of this paper was to clarify the options and factors that should be taken into consideration when contemplating an investment in an EIS. It is obvious from the pilot study that organizations follow a multitude of paths in the evolution of EIS. While Online-EIS are technically more advanced, Batch-EIS seems to offer some interesting organizational and technological advantages. The evidence from the pilot study suggests that an organization should seriously consider the Via Batch Path and first enhance its MIS by increasing its integration and focus. Even organizations which already have a Query system in place should consider a shift to Batch-EIS prior to Online-EIS.

Movement along either dimension in the framework requires significant technological and organizational changes and risks. Such a transition is not minor. Managers need to understand and plan this process. Attempting to effect both transitions simultaneously may be ill-advised. Managers should be warned that certain political forces may push for a premature transition from MIS to Online-EIS. An executive may request such an investment after viewing an Online-EIS at another organization or after a demonstration by an EIS vendor. Alternatively, the MIS department may see such a project as an exciting technological adventure that can provide higher development budgets and increased visibility.

Several limitations of Online-EIS have been described, suggesting that it is not necessarily the best type of EIS for all organizations. However, some of these limitations will diminish as technology improves and becomes more widely available. Recent advances in group decision support system (GDSS) technology are particularly relevant for Online-EIS. Such capabilities include: (1) simultaneous voice/data communication so that physically disperse persons can simultaneously view and discuss a problem, and (2) the ability to make hand-written annotations on an electronic document and forward copies to colleagues.

Much research still needs to be done on the framework, the path approach, and their implications. The questionnaire used in the pilot study needs to be refined and expanded to attempt to determine the rationale for following one path rather than another, and the levels of satisfaction related to each path. A larger group of organizations should be studied, focusing on information managers who have been with their organizations sufficiently long to know the history of their systems.

Further research on the effects of periodic versus non-periodic reporting could yield interesting insights and contingency frameworks that could be useful for EIS implementations as well as for the MIS domain. Future research should provide more empirical evidence on the frequency and efficacy of EIS development paths under various organizational contingencies. EIS research and literature should also investigate the possible organizational liabilities and biases that might be introduced by Online-EIS. The existence and extent of those phenomena should be ascertained and possible mitigating approaches should be devised. Much of this area can be approached via existing theoretical perspectives and previous research in management control, organizational behavior, and MIS.

REFERENCES

Anthony, R. N., *Planning and Control Systems: A Framework for Analysis.* Cambridge, MA: Harvard University Graduate School of Business, 1965.

Armstrong, D., "The People Factor in EIS Success," *Datamation,* April 1, 1990, pp. 73–79.

Barrow, C., "Implementing an Executive Information Systems: Seven Steps for Success," *Journal of Information Systems Management,* Spring 1990, pp. 41–46.

Chapnic, P., "Editor's Buffer," *Database, Programming & Design.* 2(4), (April 1989), pp. 7–8.

Chervany, N. L., Dickson, G. W. & Kozar, K. A., "An Experimental Gaming Framework for Investigating the Influence of Management Information Systems on Decision Effectiveness," MISCR-WP-71-12, University of Minnesota, Minneapolis, (April, 1972).

Davis, G. B. & Olson, M. H. *Management Information Systems: Conceptual Foundations, Structure, and Development,* 2nd ed., New York: McGraw-Hill, 1985.

DeLong, D., "Serving Top Execs: Politics Can Be Deadly," *Computerworld,* July 27, 1988, p. 93.

"EIS Explosion," *Computerworld Focus,* September 9, 1987, p. 13.

Executive Report: Executive Information Systems, *Computerworld,* October 27, 1986, pp. 37–51.

Forrester, J. W., *Industrial Dynamics.* Cambridge, MA: MIT-Press, 1968.

Friend, D., "Executive Information Systems: Successes and Failures, Insights and Misconceptions," *Journal of Information Systems Management,* (Fall 1986), pp. 31–36.

Friend, D., "EIS and the Collapse of the Information Pyramid," *Information Center,* March 1990, 6(3), pp. 22–28.

Gordon, J. R., *A Diagnostic Approach to Organizational Behavior,* Boston: Allyn and Bacon, 1983.

Gorry, G. A. & Scott Morton, M. S., "A Framework for Management Information Systems," *Sloan Management Review,* 13(1), (Fall 1971), pp. 55–70.

Iaccoca, L., *Iaccoca*. New York: Bantam, 1984.

Ives, B., Hamilton, S. & Davis, G. B., "A Framework for Research in Computer-based Management Information Systems," *Management Science*, 26(9), (September 1980), pp. 910–934.

Jones, J. W. & McLeod, R. Jr., "The Structure of Executive Information Systems: An Exploratory Analysis," *Decision Sciences*, V17, 1986, pp. 220–249.

Jordan, M. L., "Executive Information Systems Make Life Easy for the Lucky Few," *Computerworld*, February 29, 1988, pp. 51–58.

Kerr, S., "On the Folly of Rewarding A, While Hoping for B," *Academy of Management Journal*, 18, (1975), pp. 769–783.

Kirs, J. P., Sanders, L. G., Cerveny, R. P. & Robey, D., "An Experimental Validation of the Gorry and Scott Morton Framework," *MIS Quarterly*, (June, 1989), pp. 183–197.

Kolodziej, S., "EIS is a Prestigious 'Strategic Weapon,'" *Software Magazine*, July 1989, pp. 58–60, 62, 64.

Laudon, K. C. & Laudon, J. P., *Management Information Systems: A Contemporary Perspective*, New York: Macmillan, 1988.

Lucas, H. C., Jr., "A Descriptive Model of Information Systems in the Context of the Organization," *Proceedings of the Wharton Conference on Computers in Organizations*. Also in *Data Base*, 5(2), 1973, pp. 27–36.

Martin, J., "DSS Applications Should Shed New Light on a Problem," *PC Week*, 6(17), (May 1, 1989), p. 50.

Mason, R. O. & Mitroff, I. I., "A Program for Research on Management Information Systems," *Management Science*, 19(5), (January 1973), pp. 475–487.

McLeod, R., Jr. & Jones, J. W., "Making Executive Information Systems More Effective," *Business Horizons*, September/October 1986, pp. 29–37.

McNurlin, B. C., "Executive Information Systems," *EDP Analyzer*, April 1987, pp. 1–16.

Millet, I. & Mawhinney, C. H., "EIS versus MIS: A Choice Perspective," *Proceedings of HICCS-23*, 23rd Hawaii International Conference on System Sciences, Kailua-Kona, Hawaii, January 3–6, 1990, pp. 202–209.

Mock, T. J., "A Longitudinal Study of Some Information Structure Alternatives," *Data Base*, 15(2,3,4), (1973), pp. 40–45.

Moore, J. H., "Senior Executive Computer Use, Unpublished Working Paper, Stanford Graduate School of Business, Palo Alto, Calif., (1986).

Newmann, S. & Hadass, M. "DSS and Strategic Decisions," *California Management Review*, Spring 1980, pp. 77–84.

Quinn, J. B., "Strategic Change: 'Logical Incrementalism,'" *Sloan Management Review*, (Fall 1978), pp. 7–21.

Radding, Alan, "Can 1-2-3 Save Fidelity Bank?," *Lotus*, June 1990, pp. 58–61.

Raho, L. E. & Belohlov, J. A., "Discriminating Characteristics of EDP, MIS and DSS Information Interface," *Data Management*, December 1982, pp. 18–22.

Rasmussen, D. R. & Mosekilde, E., "Bifurcations and Chaos in a Generic Management Model," *European Journal of Operations Research,* 35, (1988), pp. 80–88.

Reck, R. H. & Hall, J. R., "Executive Information Systems: An Overview of Development," *Journal of Information Systems Management,* Fall 1986, pp. 25–30.

Rinaldi, D. & Jastrzembski, T., "Executive Information Systems: The Golden Opportunity," *Computerworld Focus,* July 9, 1986, pp. 28–34.

Roberts, E. B., *Managerial Applications of System Dynamics,* Cambridge, MA: MIT-Press, 1978.

Rockart, J. F., "Chief Executives Define Their Own Data Needs," *Harvard Business Review,* (March–April 1979), pp. 81–93.

Rockart, J. F. & DeLong, D. W., *Executive Support Systems, The Emergence of Top Management Computer Use,* Homewood, Illinois: Dow Jones-Irwin, 1988.

Rockart, J. F. & DeLong, D. W., *Executive Support Systems,* Homewood, IL: Dow Jones-Irwin, 1988.

Rockart, J. F. & Treacy, M. E., "The CEO Goes On-Line," *Harvard Business Review,* (January–February 1982).

Ryan, A. J., "Cost of EIS a Big Deal for Most Firms," *Computerworld,* July 24, 1989, p. 46.

Silver, M. S., "User Perceptions of Decision Support System Restrictiveness: an Experiment," *Journal of Management Information Systems,* 5(1), (Summer 1988), pp. 51–65.

Sprague, R. H. Jr., "A Framework for the Development of Decision Support Systems," *MIS Quarterly,* 4, (December 1980), pp. 1–26.

Tobias, A. J., "Today's Executives in a State of Readiness," *Software Magazine,* 8(13), (November 1988), pp. 55–60, 62–66.

Watson, H., "Avoiding Hidden EIS Pitfalls," *Computerworld,* (June 25, 1990), pp. 87–91.

Webber, R. A., *A Guide to Getting Things Done,* New York: Free Press, 1980.

QUESTIONS

1. Briefly discuss the four stages in the authors' EIS development framework.
2. The authors' EIS development framework has two dimensions: mode of operation and focus and integration. Explain both dimensions. Are other dimensions possible? What might they be?
3. Briefly distinguish among MIS, DSS, and EIS.
4. Why don't organizations adopt the direct transition from stage 1 to stage 4?

10

The Strategic Business Objectives Method for Guiding Executive Information Systems Development

Linda Volonino
Hugh J. Watson

INTRODUCTION

Executive information systems (EIS), or executive support systems (ESS) as they are sometimes called, have exploded onto the information systems scene. It was only in 1982 that Rockart and Treacy [13] introduced the EIS term to describe those computer-based systems that a small but noteworthy group of senior executives were using to help carry out their job responsibilities. Since that time, the number of organizations that have developed, are currently developing, or are considering the development of an EIS has grown rapidly. International Data Corporation, a market research firm, estimates that the U.S. market for EIS software development, including the purchase of software, customer consulting, and in-house software development, is growing at a compound annual

Previously published in *Journal of Management Information Systems,* Volume 7, Number 3, N.J. 1990–91. Used with permission.

rate of 40 percent and will reach $350 million in 1992 [1]. Rockart predicts that 25 percent of senior executives will be EIS users by 1993 [8].

Even though the outlook for EIS is bright, they are high-risk systems, surrounded by a myriad of managerial and technical issues that must be resolved. They must appeal to a clientele that has little computer experience or little previous need to be hands-on computer users. Most organizations have not developed, implemented, and operated systems of this type in the past, so they do not have previous development experience to draw upon.

A possible starting point for developing a successful EIS is to learn from other companies' experiences. One of the oldest, most successful systems is the Management Information and Decision Support (MIDS) system at Lockheed-Georgia. Houdeshel and Watson [10] identified the following keys to the success of MIDS: a committed executive sponsor, carefully defined system requirements, a team approach to systems development, an evolutionary development approach, and carefully selected computer hardware and software. Rockart and DeLong [12] studied 30 EIS and identified additional keys to success: an operating sponsor, a clear link to business objectives, management of data problems, management of organizational resistance, and management of spread and evolution.

Much can also be learned by studying why some EIS have failed. Watson and Glover [19] examined 21 EIS failures and identified the following major problem areas: inadequate or inappropriate technology, failure of the system to meet user needs, lack of executive commitment, and executive resistance to technology.

Another perspective can be gained by asking EIS developers what they worry about. This question was asked at EIS '88, a conference dedicated to EIS. Attendees identified the following concerns: getting executives to specify what they want, making sure EIS data are accurate, combining data from multiple sources, having sufficient staff and computer resources to support the EIS, finding a problem big enough for the EIS to have a real impact, making sure executives have enough time to use the system, keeping abreast of executives' changing needs and desires, avoiding political foot-dragging and back-stabbing, dealing with executives' dislike of technology, and deciding what hardware and software to use [16].

Clearly, there are many keys to having an EIS success and avoiding a failure. As important as any, however, is identifying what information to put in the EIS. This issue emerges from the case studies, field studies, and surveys. A related issue is planning the sequencing of the rollout of the various modules that comprise the EIS. It is important to phase in the EIS in a way that sustains executive interest and has a high payoff for the organization.

WHAT IS KNOWN

A critical starting point when developing an EIS is determining what purpose or purposes the system is to serve. Depending on the need(s) motivating EIS development, the system can possess very different information, characteristics, and capabilities.

Guiden and Ewers [9] identify four kinds of systems. One kind of EIS focuses on providing faster, easier access to information. Another stresses improved communications through electronic messaging, voice mail, calendaring, word processing, and other office support systems. Yet another type of EIS might be designed to solve a particular problem and include decision support system capabilities. The final kind of EIS might be designed with motivating performance in mind. The information provided by the system focuses executive attention on areas where it is needed.

Rockart [14] identifies three EIS eras based on the user group that the system is designed to serve. The types reflect an evolutionary shift from limited access toward organization-wide access to corporate information. During the first era, EISs were designed for individual executives. In 1987, there was a noticeable shift to support for teams of executives. The third era, begun in 1989, is characterized by systems that support multiple levels of management. The shift to systems supporting more management levels increases the need to include information about business processes.

The development of an EIS should employ a prototyping/evolutionary methodology. In a survey of 50 firms with EIS, Watson, Rainer, and Koh [20] found that 92 percent of them had used this development approach. Prototyping is required because of the difficulty of specifying in advance what information is needed and how it should be presented [15]. Requirements can be tailored and tested through prototyping and executive use of the system. Employing an evolving development approach enables executives to participate in a learning process and build a sense of ownership with the EIS [18]. Over time, more information can be placed in the system, it can serve more users, and additional features can be included.

A decision must be made about what information to provide in the initial version. A number of options exist and have been used by different organizations. One alternative is to go with the information provided in the prototype that was created to build executive interest in EIS and to demonstrate its feasibility. This information often relates to a current problem that the executive sponsor is facing. A potential problem with this approach is that it does not build a broad base of support for the EIS. As Friend [6] points out, "By addressing individual needs instead of those of the organization, the EIS does not become part of the corporate culture and remains tied to the continuing sponsorship of the executive." Evolution of the EIS should focus on building this support.

Another approach is to focus on key performance data. This information is usually high level and financial in nature, and much of it can be obtained from existing organizational databases. A potential problem with this approach is that it provides only a limited amount of the information that executives need. In particular, it does not address the need for "soft" information, such as plans, rumors, and explanations [11]. Once again, a carefully planned strategy for the design and evolution of the EIS is important.

A third approach is to provide information that is related to helping accomplish the strategic business objectives of the organization. One of Rockart and DeLong's [12] keys to EIS success is that the system should have a clear link to business objectives. Dauphinais [5] states that the information provided should be driven by the mission, objectives, and strategies of the organization. This approach seems especially meritorious because of the potential value provided by the EIS and the opportunity to build a broad base of supportive users.

Watson and Frolick [21] suggests that multiple methods be used when determining executive information requirements for an EIS. Possible methods include participation in strategic planning meetings, formal CSF sessions, formal discussions with executives, tracking executive activity, discussions with executive support personnel, examinations of computer and noncomputer generated information, attendance at meetings, and software tracking of EIS usage.

Multiple methods are needed for several reasons. Information requirements vary from those that are related to the industry and the organization and are shared by all of a firm's executives, to those that are unique to a particular executive's job. Methods such as participation in strategic planning meetings and formal CSF sessions are appropriate for identifying industry- and organization-related information requirements, while informal discussions with executives are useful in identifying unique information requirements.

Some methods are better for identifying initial information requirements for the system, while others are better for the ongoing or evolving requirements. For example, informal CSF sessions may be useful for identifying initial information requirements, but are difficult to use repeatedly because of the broad level of executive participation and the large commitment of executive time required. Informal discussions are better for identifying evolving requirements.

An EIS should contain both hard and soft information [11]. Hard information consists of "facts" and resides somewhere accessible to the user. Soft information includes speculations, impressions, feelings, hearsay, gossip, and so on. They have the potential for affecting the performance of the organization. The credibility of soft information is assigned by the user and is usually based on the user's assessment of its source and how well the information fits into other information known to the user. Special efforts are normally required to collect soft information and to present it in the proper context.

Friend [7] recommends considering how the EIS will stand up over time. It is not uncommon for EIS usage patterns to progress through stages of early euphoria to intermittent access. According to Burkan [4], many EISs give initial impressions of success, but exhibit signs of system failure within six months to a year as usage rates deteriorate. At the outset, users may be enthused by the novelty of the new technology, which can spur a "me-too" syndrome, leading to increased demand for access [18]. Enthusiasm can lead to frustration if executives' expectations cannot be met due to limitations of the system. Without a plan to provide ongoing value to sustain use beyond the novelty stage, system usage will decline.

Key elements of a plan for the spread and evolution of an EIS are known. The system should spread to additional users and this spread is likely to be both hierarchical and lateral [3]. With hierarchical growth, use of the EIS spreads from the top down in the organization. In lateral growth, use of the EIS moves across organizational units. The system is also likely to evolve to include information that is broader in scope, more detailed, closer to real time, and softer. Additional capabilities may be added such as access to external databases, e-mail, or decision support capabilities.

Organizations have handled EIS spread and evolution in a variety of ways. Some organizations have used a "trickle down" the organization chart approach. New EIS users are identified by virtue of their being at the next level down on the organization chart and information is added to the system to meet their needs. Other organizations have taken a more strategic approach. The system is made available to those executives where the need and expected return is the greatest [2]. This approach makes the most business sense, because of the linkage to business objectives.

From the writings on EIS, several guidelines for EIS development emerge. They are:

- Carefully define what purpose or purposes the EIS is to serve
- Use a prototyping/evolutionary development methodology
- The initial version of the EIS should support the strategic business objectives of the organization
- Plan for the evolution of the EIS
- The evolution of the EIS should continue to support strategic business objectives.

There are probably a variety of ways in which these guidelines can be followed by organizations. A particular approach is one we refer to as the strategic business objectives method. It reflects the method used with the successful creation of the EIS at Fisher-Price. It does not attempt to define all of the information that should go into an EIS, but it does identify much of the core information and helps in planning the system's evolution.

STRATEGIC BUSINESS OBJECTIVES METHOD

The strategic business objectives (SBO) method takes a company-wide perspective for EIS development. It focuses on developing a system supportive of strategic business objectives and the information needs of personnel throughout the organization. To achieve this end, corporate needs guide the development and evolution of the EIS. This approach also helps to integrate the EIS into management processes and establishes it as an integral support system.

The SBO method results in an EIS that is less calibrated to the unique information needs of individuals, but better tailored to the strategic goals of the organization. An EIS is developed that can better endure changes in top management and executive sponsors. This ability is critical to continued success, because senior executive turnover is common. An EIS that is closely aligned to a particular sponsor or customized to a transient set of information requirements has a high risk of failure.

The steps in the strategic business objectives method are:

1. the organization's strategic business objectives are identified;
2. the business processes critical to achieving the strategic business objectives are identified;
3. priorities are assigned to the strategic business objectives and, as a consequence, to the critical business process;
4. the information necessary to support the critical business processes is defined;
5. information linkages among business processes are identified; and
6. a plan for a modular EIS development, implementation, and evolution is developed.

Organizations can have a variety of strategic business objectives for achieving economic advantage in the marketplace. Their objective might be producing high-quality products, being the low-cost supplier, providing excellent service, or being a leader in the application of new technology. To assure that resources are obtained and used effectively and efficiently in the accomplishment of the organization's objectives, managers need timely, accurate information to better understand and monitor operations. They also need information on how well the strategic business objectives are being met.

It is necessary for the EIS staff to understand the organization's strategic business objectives, because the design of the EIS is driven by these objectives. Allowing the analysts to sit in on strategic planning sessions is one way to help facilitate the understanding of the objectives. Some firms, however, may not want analysts to attend these sessions. A workable alternative is to have a representative of the strategic planning committee meet with the analysts to communicate the information needed for the design of the EIS.

In order to realize a strategic business objective, the business processes related to the accomplishment of the objective must be identified. These processes may cut across functional areas. For example, if the strategic business objective is to be a high-quality producer, then product design, engineering, purchasing, production, and quality control processes are critical to achieving this objective.

Determining the related business processes is not always easy or straightforward. There are differences of opinion as to what the key related processes are. This is a natural outcome, given the differences in individuals' current position and experiences, limited efforts by most organizations in the past to identify the processes, and the potential ramifications of a process being identified as being critical. Despite the difficulties, the outcome should be a better understanding of what drives the business.

The strategic business objectives and the related critical business processes are prioritized. This prioritizing process leads to a modular, evolutionary development plan. It ensures that the EIS serves the organization's most pressing needs in their order of importance. Next, it is necessary to identify what information about the critical business processes should be included in the EIS. When thinking about these information requirements, it is important to recognize that there will be a wide range of users, all the way from top management to operational personnel. Anyone who has a key role in performing or managing the critical business processes is a likely user of the system. This wide range of users has implications for the scope, source, level of aggregation, time horizon, timeliness, and accuracy of the information provided. A variety of methods can be used to identify information requirements, including informal discussions, examinations of information currently used, and attendance at meetings.

Business processes seldom stand alone; rather, they are related to other processes. At a minimum, different processes share information. For example, an organization's sales force should have access to information about production capabilities and schedules and the availability of items carried in inventory. While these are different systems, information about each is important to the smooth functioning of the other. Identifying these information linkages is important to the design of the EIS.

Even though different processes may need to share information, each may also want to have its own view of it. For example, production personnel may need more detailed information about production schedules than marketing personnel who are interested in the same information, but from a more aggregate, product-availability perspective. In what form to make information available can be as important as what information to include.

The final output from the SBO method is a plan for developing, implementing, and evolving an EIS. The system is developed in modules. The first module is designed to support the organization's most important strategic business objective(s). The information provided supports the planning, analyzing, and controlling of the critical business processes and related processes that are key to achieving the organization's strategic business objectives. The system supports users at a variety of organizational levels. The system evolves by adding modules that support additional strategic business objectives, which results in more users, more screens, and additional capabilities. Each module, however, is a manageable development task for the EIS support staff.

FISHER-PRICE'S CORPORATE HISTORY

Fisher-Price is a major manufacturing, marketing, and distribution company operating in the highly competitive U.S. toy industry, with substantial international business in Canada and Europe.* It has three distinct business groups: Infant, Traditional, and Promotional Products. Within these groups, there are two principle product lines: toys and juvenile products.

During the mid 1980s, Fisher-Price made strategic adjustments to improve its competitiveness and to support company growth. As part of its newly formulated strategy, Fisher-Price's business orientation shifted from being manufacturing driven to being market driven. Rather than being a manufacturing company, it wanted to become a "marketing company that manufactured." This business redefinition required the real-time capture, access, and reporting of internal and market data for planning, analyzing, and monitoring business activities. An emerging management style at Fisher-Price was the desire to understand and monitor all aspects of the business. This interest led to simultaneous changes in the business and information systems plans. Fisher-Price's new plans included bringing computerized support to all levels of management and the sales force.

---

* The Fisher-Price experience was first described in [17].

Prior to the mid 1980s, Fisher-Price was confronted with information and reporting problems that could not be readily remedied with available information systems. Mismanaged data were having operational and strategic consequences. Reporting mechanisms were unsatisfactory, because multiple sources of information created inconsistencies. Tracking and control of purchase orders, production, and shipments were subject to 30-day blindsides due to lack of data timeliness. Little support was provided for the sales force. The clerical staff expended considerable effort collecting, preparing, and routing data and reports. Often the effort was redundant, as senior executives requested the development of similar reports, yet customized to their needs and preferences. These deficiencies led to the consideration of advanced information systems technologies, including EIS, to improve Fisher-Price's competitive and strategic position.

FISHER-PRICE'S EIS

Considerable planning and preparation preceded the development of Fisher-Price's EIS. Executives and analysts met to identify clearly the objectives for the system. The overriding goal was to provide information about the business processes that were necessary to achieve Fisher-Price's new market-driven strategy. In order to achieve this objective, an EIS was needed that differed from those developed in other firms. It had to support a broad base of users from the outset and it had to provide detailed information about business processes. These requirements in turn led to a unique way of thinking about, planning for, and determining the information requirements for the initial and later versions of the EIS.

A number of areas were of importance and were thoroughly covered in discussions between executives and the EIS staff. Analysts learned what drove the business, what business opportunities existed, and what might be done to improve executive productivity. Executives briefed the EIS team on everything of importance to their job responsibilities, what information each business unit needed to have, where the information came from, and how the information was used.

Analysts participated in strategic planning and other meetings in order to better understand the firm's new strategy, how it would be implemented, and the information needed to support it. Attendance at these meetings also helped build an effective working relationship between the executives and the analysts and provided an opportunity for the analysts to learn how, about what, and in which ways managers communicated with one another.

It was found that considerable effort had to go into carefully defining what information to place in the system. For example, saying that information on customer orders was needed was not specific enough. They had to specify exactly what information about customer orders was wanted (e.g., orders that were filled, received, shipped out, or in production).

Based on an understanding of Fisher-Price's strategic objective, the business processes necessary to realize the objective, and the information needed to manage these processes, a plan for the development of the EIS was created. The EIS would be rolled out in modules with the sequencing of their introduction determined by their criticality to achieving the firm's strategic objective. This approach allowed the most important modules to be implemented quickly. Each module was a size that could be easily handled by the EIS staff. New modules were able to draw upon the modules that were already in place. Project management techniques were used to plan the modules and to control their development.

Figure 10–1 shows the modules and the order in which they were developed. EIS development began in 1986 and the last module was completed as scheduled in early 1989. The EIS continues to evolve today.

Fisher-Price's EIS provides online access to timely information that is used for planning, analyzing, and monitoring activities associated with the business. All screens and reports in the system originate from a common database and most have standard formats. The database is updated each night, which provides for current business information each day.

The system is modularized with information logically grouped by topics or "windows." Within each individual window of information is a set of standard screens and reports that can be accessed. Windows are easily found and accessed through the main menu. The EIS is totally

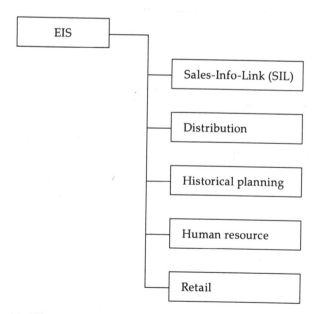

Figure 10–1. *Modules in Fisher-Price's EIS*

menu driven with an online HELP feature that makes it extremely easy to learn and use. Users can obtain instructions, data definitions, and report samples using the HELP feature.

Sales-Info-Link Module

Customer satisfaction is the key to Fisher-Price's new business orientation. Being responsive to customers' needs requires information about customers, products, sales, shipments, and orders. This requirement led to the Sales-Info-Link (SIL) module being developed first.

The SIL module provides critical sales information to management. Managers are provided timely, accurate information about individual products, product categories, business groups, salespersons, and customers for each geographical region. Numerous screens and reports can be generated from the executive windows, product category windows, or customer reporting windows that are options listed on the main menu of the SIL module. Current sales-related information is critical in an industry where dramatic shifts in consumer demand can take place in a matter of days.

Distribution Module

Fisher-Price's competitive position depends upon monitoring the channels of distribution. Aggressive growth prompted the need for responsive system support for the sales force, which had been selling products without information on product availability. Recognizing that the sales force needed significant amounts of product availability and distribution information, the distribution module was developed next.

Another factor contributing to the development of the module was the need for distribution resource planning. The trend toward quick response in the retail trade increased Fisher-Price's need to monitor production closely and coordinate a quick response with distribution. In retailing, quick response means receiving products when they are needed for sale, and it is comparable to manufacturing's just-in-time concept. Neither retailers nor manufacturers want finished goods inventory. Storage limitations at Fisher-Price would be quickly exceeded within a short time without a planned flow of shipments. Coordination of sales, production, and distribution improves market responsiveness and reduces costs.

Historical Planning Module

The historical planning module was added to the EIS to support and monitor short- and long-range planning and forecasting. These activities require information about anticipated changes in tastes and demographics.

Projected sales of each product are stored in the corporate database for comparison with actual sales to date. This information helps research and development planning by indicating when new products are necessary and what types of products are likely to be in demand.

Human Resource Module

The human resource module provides information about employees, their skills, and their potential development. It is used in identifying changes in human resource needs. In addition, there is statistical information regarding salaries, fringe benefits, and recruiting strategies. This information is important to ensure compliance with labor laws.

Retail Module

This module provides information about customers and sales not included in the SIL module. The emphasis here is on retail trade. Consumer behavior information, retail requirements, and competitors' strategies aimed at retailers are included in this module.

Corporate Impact

The EIS was developed to support Fisher-Price's strategic plan. The EIS works remarkably well because it was designed to ensure that executives, managers, and the sales force have the information necessary to perform their jobs. The EIS provides complete, timely information that previously came from numerous sources with significant time delays. Without the EIS, Fisher-Price could not operate as efficiently and effectively. The enhancement in productivity has enabled Fisher-Price to run a growing organization without adding staff.

All information relevant to the strategic operation of Fisher-Price is available through the EIS. Most information is refreshed daily, but certain categories such as shipments have real-time updates. Information is organized in a common way to facilitate comparison and communication among all levels of management. While the EIS is not customized to any individual, easy-to-use menus enable users to single out the information of importance to them.

Successful implementation is attributable to extensive EIS planning and preparation by the EIS staff and users. Fisher-Price's executives can assess current data and projections for identifying trends and receive quick feedback to monitor performance and adjust decision strategies. The EIS provides executives with the information they need to monitor daily operations, address key issues, solve problems, and make strategic decisions. The approach that Fisher-Price used proved to be justifiable economically and feasible to implement. It resulted in a system that is fully accessible by nontechnical users throughout the company.

CONCLUSION

The development of the EIS at Fisher-Price illustrates the use of the strategic business objectives method. "Satisfying the customer" was identified as the primary objective behind the design of the EIS. The business processes necessary to accomplish this objective were identified. Attention focused on forging a better link between marketing and production processes to deliver products that meet rapidly changing customer demands more quickly and effectively. In order to do this, information about customers, sales, orders, shipments, and product availability had to be made available to management and the sales force. This need led to the development of the sales-info-link, distribution, and historical planning modules. The human resource module was added next to meet other corporate information needs. Finally, the retail module was developed to provide information about customers and sales that was not included in the SIL module but is important to marketing efforts.

The EIS at Fisher-Price continues to evolve. At the present time, the finance module is being developed. It was not developed earlier because of the adequacy of existing reporting systems.

The EIS has passed a test associated with many EIS failures: turnover of the executive sponsor. Even though the president and all of the vice presidents at Fisher-Price have changed, the EIS continues to be an integral part of management processes at Fisher-Price.

The SBO method offers a number of strengths and benefits. The design of the EIS is tied to the firm's strategic business objectives. Attention is focused on those business processes crucial to satisfying the strategic business objectives. Information is made available to a broad base of organizational personnel responsible for managing and performing the activities in the critical business processes. This results in a large number of supportive users who make the EIS an integral part of performing their jobs. Because of the attention given to business processes that often cut across functional areas, more attention is given to interdepartmental relationships. A modular, evolutionary plan for the development of the EIS is generated that satisfies the most important organizational information needs first and allows for a manageable development of the EIS.

The SBO method results in a system that meets the key information needs of personnel throughout the organization. It is interesting to note that this was the objective of management information systems (MIS) in the 1960s. By and large, this objective was not achieved for a variety of reasons. Many users, especially executives, were not prepared or trained to be computer users; the technology to build and deliver systems was inadequate; and systems designers typically did not possess the skills or experience to create systems of this type. These conditions are now considerably different. A comprehensive, organization-wide EIS fulfills the hopes for MIS in the 1960s.

The SBO method can be described as a top-down approach. The EIS is designed to support the objectives of the organization as articulated by top management. The processes used to achieve these objectives are identified and information needed to support and monitor these objectives and processes is provided. Access to information is pushed as low in the organization as is needed in order to achieve the firm's objectives.

REFERENCES

1. Alexander, M. Executive information systems catch on. *Computerworld* (February 27, 1989), 31.

2. Applegate, L. Interview with R. G. Wallace, Phillips Oil. Harvard Business School videotape, Cambridge, MA (1989).

3. Barrow, C. Implementing an executive information system: seven steps for success. *Journal of Information Systems Management* (Spring 1990), 41–46.

4. Burkan, W. C. Making EIS work. *Transactions of the Eighth International Conference on Decision Support Systems*, E. Sue Weber, ed. Providence, RI: The Institute of Management Science, June 1988, 121–136.

5. Dauphinais, G. W. The information draught in the executive suite. *Price Waterhouse Review* 1 (1987), 41–47.

6. Friend, D. EIS and the collapse of the information pyramid. *Information Center* (March 1990), 22–28.

7. Friend, D. After the thrill is gone: how to keep your EIS growing. *Transactions of the Tenth International Conference on Decision Support Systems*, L. Volonino, ed. Providence, RI: The Institute of Management Science, May 1990, 4–10.

8. Gelford, S. M. The computer age dawns in the corner office. *Business Week* (June 27, 1988).

9. Guiden, G. K., and Ewers, D. E. Is your ESS meeting the need? *Computerworld* (July 10, 1989), 85–91.

10. Houdeshel, G., and Watson, H. J. The management information and decision support system at Lockheed-Georgia. *MIS Quarterly,* 11, 1 (March 1987), 127–140.

11. Houdeshel, G. Selecting information for an EIS: experiences at Lockheed-Georgia. *Proceedings of the Twenty-Third Annual Hawaii International Conference on System Sciences,* Jay F. Nunamaker, ed. (January 1990), vol. 3, 178–185.

12. Rockart, J. F., and DeLong, D. W. *Executive Support Systems: The Emergence of Top Management Computer Use.* Homewood, IL: Dow Jones-Irwin, 1988.

13. Rockart, J. F., and Treacy, M. E. The CEO goes on-line. *Harvard Business Review*, 60, 1 (January/February 1982), 84–88.

14. Rockart, J. F. Executive support systems: yesterday, today and tomorrow. Plenary speech at DSS-90 Conference, Cambridge, MA (May 1990).

15. Runge, L. On the executive's desk. *Information Center* (June 1988), 34–38.

16. Stecklow, S. The new executive information systems. *Lotus* (April 1989), 51–53.

17. Volonino, L., and Drinkard, G. Integrating EIS into the strategic plan: a case study of Fisher-Price. *Transactions of the Ninth International Conference on Decision Support Systems*, G. R. Widmeyer, ed. Providence, RI: The Institute of Management Sciences, June 1989, 37–45.

18. Volonino, L., and Robinson, S. The experiences of Marine Midland Bank in sustaining an EIS. *Transactions of the Tenth International Conference on Decision Support Systems*, L. Volonino, ed. Providence, RI: The Institute of Management Sciences, May 1990, 164–172.

19. Watson, H. J., and Glover, H. Common and avoidable causes of EIS failure. *Computerworld* (December 4, 1989), 90–91.

20. Watson, H. J.; Rainer, R. K.; and Koh, C. Executive information systems: a framework for development and a survey of current practices. Unpublished working paper, University of Georgia, Athens, GA (1989).

21. Watson, H. J., and Frolick, M. Determining information requirements for executive information systems. *Proceedings of the 1988 INTEC Symposium, Systems Analysis and Design: A Research Strategy*. Atlanta, GA (October 1988).

QUESTIONS

1. Why is EIS development a high-risk process?
2. What are the six steps of the strategic business objectives methodology as applied to EIS development?
3. What are four major problems that can cause an EIS to fail?
4. What are ten main concerns of EIS developers? Can you add others?
5. What are the various methods used to gather or elicit executive information requirements?
6. Discuss the organizational situation at Fisher-Price before and after the introduction of the EIS. Can you generalize about the potential impacts of an EIS on an organization from this case?

11

Determining Information Requirements for an Executive Information System

Hugh J. Watson
Mark Frolick

Management information systems (MIS) in the 1960s and then decision support systems (DSS) in the 1970s were touted for their potential to supply senior executives with the information needed to carry out job responsibilities. While these systems have supplied some information useful to executives, they have not lived up to their proponents' expectations. Recently a new type of computer-based information system (CBIS) has emerged that is making significant contributions to satisfying executives' information needs. These systems are commonly referred to as executive information systems (EIS) or executive support systems (ESS), and the growing number of success stories attests to their potential contribution (Houdeshel and Watson 1987, Rockart and De Long 1988, Sundue 1986).

We define an EIS as a computer-based system under the direct control of an executive that provides the executive with current status information on conditions internal and external to the organization.

EIS characteristics may include:

- The ability to monitor and highlight critical success factors for an individual user's responsibilities (Zmud 1986)

- The ability to extract, filter, and compress a broad range of internal and external information, thus conserving the executive user's time (Friend 1986)
- The ability to call attention to variances from budgets, benchmarks, or expectations as dictated by each user (Burkan 1988)
- Access to:

    —aggregate financial information

    —critical non-accounting data, such as customer satisfaction or staffing levels

    —external data, such as economic indicators and competitive or marketplace information (Friend 1986)
- The ability to combine internal information with external information on the same screen (Zmud 1986)
- The ability to combine graphical, tabular, and textual material on the same screen (Friend 1986)
- Access to public data bases (Kogan 1986)
- Organization and presentation of viewing options in a format meaningful to the individual executive (Burkan 1988)

The executive information systems and executive support systems (ESS) terms are sometimes used interchangeably. However, we view ESS as being broader than EIS with EIS being a subset of ESS. The EIS term makes specific reference to "information," while the ESS term includes "support" and implies a larger set of support capabilities. The additional capabilities in an ESS may include: electronic mail (e.g., e-mail and voice mail), decision support (e.g., electronic spreadsheet), and office support (e.g., word processing). While the distinctions between EIS and ESS are not important for our purposes, we use the EIS term in this article because of our focus on the information provided to executives.

A key EIS design issue is identifying the executive user's information requirements. Only by understanding an executive's information needs can an appropriate system be delivered. Most executives already receive a plethora of information, but this information does not always meet the executive's needs. It may be too old, inaccurate, not concise enough, not interpreted, from the wrong perspective, or presented in an unappealing format.

Determining an executive's information requirements is not an easy task. At EIS '88, a conference on executive information systems, delegates ranked "Getting executives to specify what they want" as their number one worry in implementing an EIS (Stecklow 1989). At EIS '89, attendees were once again asked what their biggest EIS worries were. Their number one concern was the same as before, identifying executives' information requirements (Paller 1990).

Over the past few years, we have interviewed many EIS designers about their successes and failures in identifying executives' information needs. We have also participated in several EIS projects ourselves. Our findings and experiences are that a variety of methods can and should be used to assess executives' information needs. Our purpose is to describe and illustrate a portfolio of methods that can be used by EIS analysts. We begin, however, by considering the general strategies that can be used to determine information requirements and the problems that may be encountered when using these strategies.

STRATEGIES FOR DETERMINING INFORMATION REQUIREMENTS

There are two levels of information requirements that analysts consider: (1) organizational-level information requirements and (2) application-level information requirements.

Organizational-level information requirements are used to define an overall information systems structure for an organization and to specify a portfolio of applications and data bases. Application-level information requirements define and document specific information content for applications and their implementation requirements. An EIS requires the specification of application-level information requirements.

Davis (1982) identifies four strategies for determining information requirements: (1) asking, (2) deriving from an existing information system, (3) synthesis from characteristics of the utilizing system, and (4) discovering from experimentation with an evolving information system. There may be a variety of specific methods that can be used with each strategy. These strategies are applicable at both the organizational and application level.

The best strategies or methods to use are dependent on the characteristics of the environment in which the determination of requirements is conducted (Davis, 1982). The key characteristics are the utilizing system, the information system or application, the users, and the analysts. Depending on these characteristics, a particular strategy may be difficult to use. In regard to EIS, there are a variety of problems that may be encountered.

Asking

With this strategy, the analyst obtains information requirements by asking people about their information needs. The key people to interview are the future users of the systems; in the case of an EIS, the executives of the firm.

Executives are often able to accurately identify only a portion of their information needs. Because executives' jobs are unstructured, dynamic, and broad in scope, some information requirements are almost certain to be unidentified. Adding to the problem are perceptual biases that are inherently associated with human memory and recall abilities (Valusek and Fryback 1985). Because of these weaknesses in humans' information processing abilities, executives may not be able to accurately describe their information requirements.

There can also be problems when the executive and the analyst fail to understand each others limitations (Yadav 1983). The analyst may not know that actual information requirements are likely to differ from what is stated by the executive. The executive, on the other hand, may assume that the analyst can develop a good system even if information needs are not fully specified. These problems can be minimized by using analysts who have an established, successful working relationship with the executives that they support.

The asking strategy also assumes that the analyst has full access to the user. With an EIS, it is unlikely that the analyst will be able to secure as much of the executive's time as desired.

Deriving from an Existing System

Another strategy is to derive information requirements from an existing system or application. This approach is of limited value with most EIS because the EIS is very different from the system it replaces (e.g., a report-oriented MIS). A primary reason for developing the EIS is the inadequacy of an existing system(s). At best, only portions of the old system will be incorporated into the EIS.

Synthesis from Characteristics of the Utilizing System

Information systems provide information to facilitate the operation of systems. These systems are commonly known as object systems. Davis (1982) feels that the most logical and complete method of obtaining information requirements is to develop them from an analyst of the characteristics of object systems. The methods for performing object system analysis include:

- *Normative analysis.* Based on the fundamental similarity of classes of object systems (Davis 1982). Based on these characteristics, the analyst builds a normative set of information requirements.
- *Strategy set formulation.* A method by which information requirements are developed using the strategic objectives of the organization (Davis 1982, King 1978). This approach supports the structuring of information to meet the information needs of the organization.

- *Critical success analysis.* Utilization of significant decisions to derive information requirements. The most commonly used critical success analysis method is the critical success factor method. This method derives information requirements by asking users to identify the factors that are critical to success in performing their jobs (Davis, 1982, Rockart, 1979). This method is discussed in greater detail later.

- *Process analysis.* A method of information requirements determination based on business processes as the basis for information system support (Davis 1982). Business processes are groups of decisions required to manage organizational resources. Business systems planning (BSP) is an example of a process analysis method.

- *Decision analysis.* A method of information requirements determination best suited for well-defined problems. Ackoff (1967) feels that decision analysis follows the following steps:

  (a) Identify and prescribe decision

  (b) Define decision algorithm or decision process

  (c) Define the information needed for the decision process

- *Socio-technical analysis.* Divided into social analysis and technical analysis (Bostrom and Heinen 1977). Social analysis is used to determine information requirements based on the organization's social system. Technical analysis, on the other hand, deals with variances and control loops that require information. This method is best suited for situations that involve many individuals, such as in group decision making.

- *Input-process-output analysis.* A systems approach method, where a system is defined by its inputs, processes, and outputs. This is a top-down approach for determining the information requirements of object systems by dividing the system into subsystems for further detailed analysis (Davis 1982).

Some of these methods are more applicable to EIS than others. Critical success analysis in the form of critical success factors is perhaps the most appropriate. It focuses attention on the information needed for individual and organizational goal accomplishment.

Discovering from Experimentation with an Evolving Information System

This strategy captures an initial set of requirements and implements an information system to satisfy them. As the system is utilized, the information requirements become better understood and later versions of the system satisfy newly discovered requirements (Davis, 1982; Berrisford and Wetherbe, 1979). This method is often referred to as an iterative or evolutionary approach.

Developing information requirements from an evolving system is not possible for the initial version of an EIS because there is no previous version, but it is a highly important strategy for later versions. The long-run success of the EIS depends on developing appropriate methods for discovering additional or changed information requirements from current usage of the EIS.

INFORMATION REQUIREMENTS ELICITATION FOR EIS

It is widely recognized that an EIS should focus on critical success factors (CSFs) (Rockart and DeLong 1988). These are ". . . the limited number of areas with which results, if they are satisfactory, will ensure successful competitive performance of the organization. They are the few key areas where 'things must go right' for the business to flourish . . ." (Rockart 1979, p. 85). The EIS is designed to provide information about these CSFs.

Before exploring the portfolio of methods that can be used to identify the information requirements for an EIS, it is useful to consider some of the subtleties of the CSF concept when applied to the design of an EIS. While the CSF method is often discussed in the literature, the perspective taken here is based on our EIS experiences. It has been well received and proven useful in our work with EIS professionals. As will be seen, CSFs vary in regard to level, calibration, and stability in important ways that have ramifications when developing and maintaining an EIS. They influence whether or not an information requirements elicitation method is likely to be effective in a particular situation.

Critical Success Factor Levels

It is important to recognize that CSFs exist at different levels and have characteristics that vary with the level. There are industry, company, work unit, and individual CSFs. Satisfying CSFs at lower levels (e.g., work unit and individual) contribute to satisfying CSFs at higher levels (e.g., company).

- Industry Level CSFs are relevant to any company within a particular industry and are determined by the characteristics of the industry itself (e.g., total industry sales).
- Company Level CSFs are important to the firm's ability to compete within its industry (e.g., company market share).

- Work unit level CSFs are important to a given workunit within the organization. The workunit may be a division, department, or smaller group (e.g., production costs minimized).
- Individual Level CSFs are important to individual executives in carrying out job responsibilities (e.g., development of a promotion plan on time).

Each organization's executives should be able to access CSF related information at the industry, company, work unit, and individual CSF levels. The organization may choose not to make all of the information in the EIS available to all of the users of the system. For example, some executives may not be able to access information about competitive plans. Functional area executives may not be able to view operational level information outside of their functional area.

As Figure 11–1 indicates, when moving from industry level CSFs to the CSFs of individual executives, an increasing amount of calibration is required; that is, more customization is needed. Industry and company CSFs are likely to be the same for all of an organization's executives; consequently, the same information is relevant to all EIS users. However, at the work unit and especially the individual level, there are information needs that are applicable to only a few or a single executive. As a result, screens customized for single users may be required.

Figure 11–1 also shows that the stability of the CSFs varies with the level. Stability refers to how much the CSFs change over time. Whereas industry CSFs may remain the same for several years, individual CSFs are likely to change because of the dynamic, changing nature of executive work. As executives complete projects and move on to new ones, their information requirements change.

Recognizing these differences in CSFs has important implications when determining the information requirements for an EIS. They also have staffing and software implications that are worthy of mention.

Some information requirements elicitation methods are more appropriate for some purposes than for others. For example, formal CSF

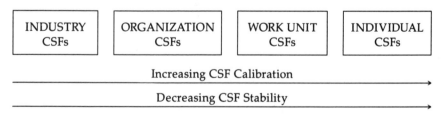

Figure 11-1. *The Calibration Required and Stability of the CSFs Vary with Their Level*

sessions are most useful in identifying industry and organization level CSFs. The asking strategy is especially appropriate for identifying work unit and individual level CSFs.

Identifying and maintaining the information requirements at the work unit and especially the individual level is very labor intensive. The information requirements vary among work units and individuals and change over time. This latter consideration suggests that an EIS developed by a "commando team" will not remain relevant unless an adequately staffed EIS group is assigned the responsibility for maintaining the EIS. It also brings into question the accuracy of many EIS vendors who tell prospective clients that the permanent staffing requirements for an EIS are small. While a small staff may be able to provide useful information on industry and company CSFs, it is less likely to be able to respond to the ongoing information requirements at the work unit and individual levels.

The capabilities of the software chosen for the EIS are important in determining the size of the EIS staff if the objective is to provide information relevant to the CSFs at all levels. Even after the required data for an EIS is identified and collected, it must still be entered and made available to the screens. The ease of doing this varies with the software used because of the variability in system maintenance support provided, which in turn impacts the required size of the EIS staff and the ability to make information available.

Methods for Assessing Information Requirements for EIS

The information requirements assessment methods for EIS can be conceptualized along two dimensions; see Figure 11–2. One dimension deals with the source that the analyst uses to determine the information requirements. These sources are either direct interaction with the executive or indirect interaction with the executive. Indirect interaction typically involves the executive's support staff.

The second dimension deals with the method by which the analyst determines the information requirements. These information requirements can be determined by either a noncomputer-related manner or a computer-related manner. Let us consider the four cells defined by the two dimensions.

Direct, Noncomputer-Related Information Requirements

When determining information requirements for an EIS, an analyst would ideally like to have free access to the executive. It is more likely that the analyst will only be able to obtain a limited amount of the executive's time.

	Noncomputer Related	Computer Related
Direct Executive Interaction	• Participation in strategic planning sessions • Formal CSF sessions • Informal discussions of information needs • Tracking executive activity	• Collaborative work system sessions
Indirect Executive Interaction	• Discussions with support personnel • Examination of noncomputer-generated information • Attendance at meetings	• Software tracking of EIS usage • Examinations of computer-generated information

Figure 11-2. *Methods for Assessing Information Requirements*

Having direct interaction with the executive is not only important for identifying information requirements, but it also heightens the executive's commitment and interest in the EIS. User involvement during system development is widely recognized as an important factor contributing to system success (Ginzberg 1981).

There are several ways that analysts can obtain information requirements when they have direct access to executives: (1) participation in strategic planning sessions; (2) formal CSF sessions; (3) informal discussions of information needs; and (4) tracking executive activity.

• *Participation in strategic planning sessions* can be used to identify industry and company CSFs. Effective strategic planning requires that the industry in which the company competes be well understood and that action plans be developed. Discussions of each of these provide insights about CSFs that need to be monitored.

An interesting example of this interaction is the case in which the initial version of the EIS is developed by a consulting firm. In many instances the opportunity for the EIS consulting engagement results from previous strategic planning consulting with the firm. After participating in the strategic planning process with a company, a consulting firm is in an excellent position to develop an EIS because of its rapport with top management and its understanding of the strategic plans for the company. In this context, this information requirements elicitation method is a by-product of another activity.

- *Formal CSF sessions* are commonly associated with the development of an EIS. Sessions are held in which goals are identified, the CSFs that underlie the goals are discussed, measures of the CSFs are explored, and methods for providing information relevant to the CSFs are discussed (Rockart 1979).

Formal CSF sessions have been conducted in many organizations, some in conjunction with the development of an EIS and some for other purposes. Many positive results are reported (Boynton and Zmud 1984, Munro and Wheeler 1980, Zahedi 1987). It is clearly a useful method for identifying information requirements and belongs in the portfolio of methods used.

Not all organizations have used formal CSF sessions in developing their EIS. The sessions require a formal commitment of time from busy executives who may be skeptical about the project given their previous experiences with computer-based systems. Some organizations that have used formal CSF sessions report mixed results (Burkan 1988). Some executives have difficulty formally thinking about and expressing their CSFs and respond better to the informal approach that is discussed next. Formal CSF sessions are also more appropriate for the initial rather than the ongoing identification of information requirements because of the scheduled commitment of time that is required.

- *Informal discussions of information needs* can also be used. The analyst probes for information requirements by asking about job responsibilities, problems currently being experienced, and commonly used sources of information (Houdeshel 1990). Informal discussions allow the executive to interact with the analyst in a natural way and for a duration that fits within the executive's schedule. Informal discussions are especially valuable in obtaining feedback on the performance of an existing EIS so that later versions can be improved.

- *Tracking executive activity* can be used to better understand how executives spend their days, the work that they perform, who they interact with, and the information they need (Walls 1988). One approach is for the analyst to serve as the executive's "shadow" for several days. The analyst quietly observes the executive at work and at convenient times asks questions about the work performed. This method might uncover, for example, highly valued informal information sources. An alternate, possibly less intrusive, approach is for the executive to maintain a log of daily activities, including what information is needed and its source. A similar method of analysis was used by Mintzberg (1971) in his studies of the nature of managerial work.

Direct, Computer-Related Information Requirements

The potential exists for using computer technology to help identify information requirements. A method that can be used directly with executives (and other organizational personnel as well) involves the use of a collaborative work system.

 • *Collaborative work system (CWS) sessions* are currently a possibility rather than a reality in terms of actual use by organizations. Under a variety of names, including collaborative work systems, group decision support systems, and groupware, computer software is being developed to support group processes. The GroupSystems (also known as PLEXSYS and TeamFocus) software developed at the University of Arizona is a good case in point (Gray and Nunamaker 1989). GroupSystems was initially developed to help analysts develop information requirements but was expanded when it was realized that many other group activities could be supported as well. It includes a large number of tools (e.g., electronic brainstorming, issue analysis, and voting) that can be used to support a variety of group processes. While CWSs have not been used to identify the information requirements for an EIS, it is a natural application and is likely to be used as CWSs become increasingly available.

Indirect, NonComputer-Related Information Requirements

In addition to the executive, other sources can be used to identify information requirements. Methods that do not require direct interaction with the executive are important and appealing because executive time is in short supply. Possible manual methods include: (1) discussions with support personnel, (2) examinations of noncomputer-generated information, and (3) attendance at meetings.

 • *Discussions with support personnel* are a common way of determining information requirements when the analyst is not able to have full access to the executive. Probably the most important person that the analyst can talk to is the executive's secretary. The secretary knows what information is requested on a regular basis, what information was requested recently, what information the executive reads, who the executive talks to, and other information important to requirements determination. Similar information can also be obtained from other staff support personnel.
 • *Examination of noncomputer-generated information* involves studying the noncomputer-related materials that the executive refers to or needs on a regular basis. This category includes newspapers, books, articles, government publications, newsletters, correspondence, and documents. The executive's support staff can help in identifying and obtaining these materials.
 • *Attendance at meetings* helps the analyst understand the information requirements of the executive based on the information the executive needs or uses while in meetings. This method is used by the EIS staff at Lockheed-Georgia (Houdeshel and Watson 1987). The staff members

attend meetings that they think might expand their understanding of the information Lockheed-Georgia's executives need. An interesting side benefit of this practice is that the analyst serves as a resource person during meetings because of the information that the analyst possess by virtue of working intensively with the EIS.

Indirect, Computer-Related Information Requirements

It is also possible to use computer related methods to indirectly understand an executive's information requirements. The possible methods include: (1) software tracking of EIS usage and (2) examination of computer-generated information.

• *Software tracking of EIS usage* is used to help the analyst better understand the information requirements of executives by examining what information is currently accessed. This method assumes of course that the organization already has an EIS in place. It also assumes that the EIS system software has the ability to track executive usage. Some in-house developed systems and a growing number of commercial EIS products (e.g., Command Center from Pilot and Commander EIS from Comshare) have this ability.

The EIS at Lockheed-Georgia is a good example of a system with software tracking capabilities (Houdeshel and Watson 1987). A daily log of system activity shows who accessed what, when, and how. A weekly report lists the previous week's users and the number of displays viewed by each executive. Another weekly report lists how many times each display was accessed. A number of special reports are available on demand.

Consider an example of how software tracking was used to improve the EIS. A review of an executive's use of the system showed that he entered a keyword to the Keyword Index but no match was found. He then used the EIS's menus and ultimately accessed several screens, looking at each screen for a few seconds. Finally, a screen was accessed that the executive examined for several minutes before turning off the system.

In reviewing this session, the EIS analyst came to the following conclusion. When the executive found no match for his keyword, he started browsing through screens that might contain the needed information. The last screen finally met this need. A comparison of the keyword entered with the screen's contents supported this conclusion.

In order to help future users of the EIS, the analyst added the keyword entered by the executive to the Keyword Index and associated with it references to relevant screens. This improvement was made without any direct interaction with the executive.

Knowing which screens are not being used is also important. This information can be used to help decide which screens need to be modified or deleted. At Lockheed-Georgia, 30 to 50 percent of the screens are modified or deleted each year. Cutting through unnecessary information is an important reason for an EIS.

• *Examination of computer-generated information* involves studying what information is currently being received in order to assess its value, and perhaps more importantly, what information is not being provided that would be useful. For example, a report may describe a current situation but not provide sufficient contextual information to allow the situation to be evaluated properly. In other instances, no information may be given to the executive at all.

CONCLUSION

There are a number of potential problems associated with determining the information requirements for an EIS. The executives who are the end users of an EIS are seldom able to articulate all of their information requirements or to give large amounts of time to the analyst. Although it is not a completely satisfactory alternative, support personnel can serve as surrogates for the executive. For the initial version of an EIS, it is not possible to draw heavily on the characteristics of the replaced system. The existing system is likely to have serious deficiencies and the new system needs to be considerably different. The analyst may have problems understanding the utilizing system because of a lack of familiarity with executive work. Consequently, special attention should be given to using analysts with strong business backgrounds, considerable experience, and excellent interpersonal skills. An evolutionary development approach is important because of the difficulty of identifying all of the executive information requirements for the initial version of the system.

One can think of a portfolio of methods for identifying the information requirements for an EIS. Some of the methods such as informal discussions of information needs are the same methods used by analysts with other kinds of computer applications. Other methods such as formal CSF sessions are more unique to EIS. In addition to manual methods, using the computer to assist in identifying information requirements, such as software tracking of EIS usage, is important because of the insights provided and the limited time that most executives have for analysts. For similar reasons, other methods that do not require direct executive—analyst interaction, such as analyst attendance at meetings, are useful.

An organization can choose the information requirements elicitation methods to use from the portfolio of methods given. With the exception of collaborative work system sessions, all of the methods have been used by organizations. The specific methods used will depend on several interrelated factors.

A key consideration is the amount of time that the company's executives are willing to devote to the project. While no company should attempt to develop an EIS without considerable executive participation, some methods such as formal CSF sessions require considerable time from the executive group. Another factor is the extent to which the EIS is intended to provide information relevant to industry, company, work unit, and individual level CSFs. Some methods such as participation in strategic planning sessions are highly appropriate for identifying industry and company level CSFs, and thus, information requirements about them. Other methods such as informal discussions with executives are good for determining individual information needs.

The amount of trust between the analyst and the executive(s) is another important consideration. Some of the methods such as software tracking of EIS usage provide considerable insights into the functioning, thinking, and activities of the firm's executives. Other methods such as participation in strategic planning sessions gives the analyst information about the company's most sensitive plans. Each company has to decide what information to make available to the developers and maintainers of the EIS.

The resources devoted to the EIS is the final factor. All of the methods require some combination of executive, staff, and/or analyst time. Some of the methods require specialized software capabilities. The methods used depend on the resources that are available.

REFERENCES

Ackoff, R.L., "Management Misinformation Systems," *Management Science*, December 1967, pp. 147–156.

Berrisford, T.R. and J.C. Wetherbe, "Heuristic Development: A Redesign of Systems Design," *MIS Quarterly*, March 1979, pp. 11–19.

Bostrom, R.P. and J.S. Heinen, "MIS Problems and Failures: A Socio-Technical Perspective; Part I," *MIS Quarterly*, September 1977, pp. 17–33.

Boynton, Andrew C. and Robert W. Zmud, "An Assessment of Critical Success Factors," *Sloan Management Review*, Summer 1984, pp. 17–27.

Burkan, Wayne C., "Making EIS Work," *DSS 88 Transactions*, Providence, RI., 1988.

Davis, G.B., "Strategies for Information Requirements Determination," *IBM Systems Journal*, 1982, pp. 4–30.

Friend, David, "Helping Corporate Executives Wade Through Data to Find Information," *Data Communications*, September 1986, pp. 283–288.

Ginzberg, Michael J., "Early Diagnosis of MIS Implementation Failure," *Management Science*, April 1981, pp. 459–478.

Gray, Paul and Jay F. Nunamaker, "Group Decision Support Systems," *Decision Support Systems: Putting Theory into Practice,* 2nd edition, (ed.) Ralph H. Sprague, Jr. and Hugh J. Watson, Englewood Cliffs, N.J.: Prentice-Hall, 1989.

Houdeshel, George and Hugh J. Watson, "The Management Information and Decision Support (MIDS) System at Lockheed-Georgia," *MIS Quarterly,* March 1987, pp. 126–140.

Houdeshel, George, "Selecting Information for an EIS: Experiences at Lockheed-Georgia," *Proceedings of the Twenty-Third Annual Hawaii International Conference on System Sciences,* Kailua-Kona, Hawaii, 1990, pp. 178–185.

Kogan, John, "Information for Motivation: A Key to Executive Information Systems That Translate Strategy Into Results for Management," *DSS 86 Transactions,* Providence, RI: The Institute of Management Science.

King, W.R., "Strategic Planning for Management Information Systems," *MIS Quarterly,* March 1978, pp. 27–37.

Mintzberg, Henry, "Managerial Work: Analysis from Observations," *Management Science,* October 1971, pp. B97–B110.

Munro, M.C. and G.B. Davis, "Determining Management Information Needs—A Comparison of Methods," *MIS Quarterly,* June 1977, pp. 55–67.

Munro, M.C. and B.R. Wheeler, "Planning, Critical Success Factors, and Management Information Requirements," *MIS Quarterly,* December 1980, pp. 21–38.

Paller, Alan, *EIS Conference Report,* January 1990, p. 4.

Rockart, John F., "Chief Executives Define Their Own Data Needs," *Harvard Business Review,* March–April 1979, pp. 81–93.

Rockart, John F. and David W. De Long. *Executive Support Systems: The Emergence of Top Management Computer Use.* Dow Jones-Irwin, 1988.

Stecklow, Steve, "The New Executive Information Systems," *Lotus,* April 1989, pp. 51–53.

Sundue, Donald G., "Genrad's On-Line Executives," *DSS 86 Transactions,* Providence, RI, 1986, pp. 14–20.

Valusek, John R. and Dennis G. Fryback, "Information Requirements Determination: Obstacles Within, Among and Between Participants," *Proceedings of the End User Computing Conference,* Minneapolis, MN, 1985.

Walls, Joe, personal conversation, 1989.

Yadav, Surya, B., "Determining an Organization's Information Requirements: A State of the Art Survey," *Data Base,* Spring 1983, pp. 3–20.

Zahedi, Fatemeh, "Reliability of Information Systems Based on the Critical Success Factors—Formulation," *MIS Quarterly,* June 1987, pp. 187–203.

Zmud, Robert W., "Supporting Senior Executives Through Decision Support Technologies: A Review and Directions for Future Research," *Decision Support Systems: A Decade in Perspective* (ed.), E.R. McLean and H.G. Sol (North-Holland), 1986, pp. 87–101.

QUESTIONS

1. Differentiate between organizational-level and application-level information requirements. Which one does an EIS address? Why?
2. What are four strategies for determining information requirements? Which one(s) are most applicable to EIS? Why?
3. Discuss the four levels of critical success factors.
4. What are four methods to obtain information requirements for EIS? Are any of these applicable to other CBIS? How?

12

Selecting Information for an EIS: Experiences at Lockheed-Georgia

The MIDS system is recognized as a successful Executive Information System (EIS) used by the management of Lockheed Aeronautical Systems Company [2,3,4]. It has been in operation since 1978 and has remained effective throughout significant changes to the executive staff which it serves.

In the 11 years of its operations, the MIDS system has been examined by many organizations (government and private) seeking to emulate its success. The areas of most interest and concern to these investigators have been expressed in these questions:

1. How do you select and treat the executive information to include in MIDS?

2. How do you determine the most effective presentation of the information in MIDS?

3. What is necessary for good management of the MIDS system?

We will provide interesting issues concerning the first question. The other two questions are addressed only in the areas where they overlap with the first question.

George Houdeshel, "Selecting Information for an EIS: Experiences at Lockheed-Georgia," Proceedings of the Twenty-Fourth Annual Hawaii International Conference on System Sciences, 1990. Used with permission.

The methods used to determine informational contents of the MIDS system are examined in terms of initial requirements and sustaining requirements. The roles of hard information and soft information are addressed, as well as the interplay between them. The importance of comprehensive information coverage and the dynamics of information requirements were found to be vital aspects of the MIDS experience and these areas are also included. Each EIS must fit the executives it supports. All of the Lockheed MIDS system experiences will not be applicable to those faced with a specific application, but some of the long-term MIDS experiences should be beneficial to those responsible for EIS operations and especially for those in the EIS developmental stage.

THE MIDS SYSTEM

The Management Information and Decision Support (MIDS) system has been supporting senior executives at Lockheed Aeronautical Systems Company (LASC) since its formation in 1987 [3–7]. LASC was formed by combining the Lockheed-Georgia Company, the Lockheed-California Company and the Lockheed Aircraft Service Company into a single operating company. Prior to the formation of LASC, the MIDS system had supported Lockheed-Georgia Company executives since 1978.

MIDS was originally requested by Robert Ormsby, then President of Lockheed-Georgia. He set the objectives of the system as an online information system to provide concise, timely and complete information relevant to senior management's needs. His office was being supplied with voluminous quantities of data, but lacked organized, easy to locate information to support the executive decision-making process.

The system combines off-the-shelf hardware with in-house developed software. It began with a prototype for the president, spread to his staff, and evolved into the current system. MIDS is now available to thirty senior executives, 40 other executives, and 37 managers. It has a primary executive portion and several subsets for middle management. It serves executives in California, Georgia, and Washington, DC. The executive portion covers a wide range of subjects and yet remains concise enough to be contained in 750 display screens. MIDS is top-down oriented, with summary graphics followed by support graphics, then support tables and text as needed. MIDS has proven effective through changes in executive users, changes in organizational structure, and the fluctuations in the aerospace business. It has evolved through technological changes in the users' terminals and the host computer operating system. The users initially used Intelligent Systems Color Graphics terminals and progressed through several changes to the current IBM PS2 Model 50 personal computers.

THE TASK OF SELECTING EXECUTIVE INFORMATION

Determining what information an executive needs can be elusive even when a specific executive has been identified. An attempt to identify a set of generic executive information requirements for universal application would become a real enigma[8]. Information requirements are obviously related to the individual executive's position, but other factors have been identified as having an influence on the information requirements. These "other factors" are identified in rather vague terms, i.e., cultures, styles, politics, and soft information. Despite these obstacles, the installation and operation of an effective EIS containing vital executive information can be achieved.

In the selection of executive information for the MIDS system, there seemed to be two distinct phases. These two phases might be considered the *Initial Approach* (work with what information is immediately available) and the *Sustaining-Enhancing Phase* (develop a rapport with executive users that enables a continuous enhancement of information contents).

THE INITIAL APPROACH TO IDENTIFY
INFORMATION REQUIREMENTS

In the development of MIDS, we believe three factors greatly aided our initial approach to identifying pertinent executive information requirements and then locating the best source of that information. These factors were:

1. An executive sponsor for a pilot system focus (in our case it was the company president)
2. An operating sponsor with in-depth knowledge of the organization
3. A reasonably good flow of some pertinent executive information or the data sources for obtaining such.

The MIDS experience in the initial approach can be summarized as follows. With the sponsoring executive as support (Bob Ormsby), the EIS development had a specific target for required information. The top organization chart provided the staff and operational positions in a format to suggest their importance. The Critical Success Factors (CSF)[9] were identified for each of these positions and the current performance of these CSFs were developed into the initial MIDS screens.

Another approach used by the MIDS team required the assistance of the president's secretary. We asked her to identify three categories of reports currently being received by the president. The categories were:

1. Those put on the president's desk
2. Those filed and frequently retrieved at the president's request
3. Those filed and seldom retrieved.

This provided us with a screening of reports that the president and his secretary had already made. We then asked the president to identify what portions of those reports in categories (1) and (2) were of most interest. He often added why he was interested. These "whys" added to our understanding of the support requirements. For example, if he compared data from one report to data in another report, it immediately suggested a comparative graphic.

We also attempted to obtain answers to the following questions:

1. What portions of what reports are of interest?
2. How is it used?
3. Is other information related to it?
4. What are the correlations?
5. Would a different summary or format be better?
6. Is the level of detail proper?
7. Is the frequency proper?
8. What is the confidence placed in its accuracy?
9. Is it considered timely?
10. Is it complete?

These questions are more effective when asked in dialogue rather than in any form of survey.

It is important to work toward these answers in the manner that best fits the executive. The important point is that the executive think about his job when providing clues to the information requirements, rather than concentrating on the information itself. Examples of situations where information was of key importance and examples when insufficient or late information hampered his job are of great value to the EIS developer.

The luxury of being able to invade the executive's office for considerable periods of time is not available in most cases, so other methods of determining his or her information needs have to be found. The operating sponsor[10] can be of value here. The operating sponsor can be a member of the executive's staff or a member of a support function knowledgeable about the executive function.

Bob Pittman was a member of our financial staff department with the responsibility of providing executive presentations, speeches, and some high level reports. He was acutely aware of current executive issues, the preferred manner of presentation, and the CSFs for the industry and company.

When Bob became the MIDS development team leader, a great reservoir of past experience was available to influence the basic formation of executive information requirements. It is not necessary to know all the requirements to make the EIS effective. We took our initial input from the secretary, the answers to the report questions, and Bob Pittman's knowledge and developed about 30 key displays in full color. We had immediate success. This early success provided several advantages.

1. A fast response to the president's request with some real benefits from the system. (MIDS was on-line for the president six months after authorization to proceed.)

2. Experience with hardware, software, communications, and system management was gained while the system was being used. /phase

3. Information sources and channels were developed. phase

4. The president's staff members were stimulated to think of increased applications.

5. The role of cultures, styles, politics, and soft information could be better understood.

6. A trust relationship among information providers, information analysts, and executive users was developed. team work

The developers of the MIDS system never planned a two-phase development; it just evolved that way. A prototype phase for an executive, who was enthusiastic about the EIS concept, played a key role in the success of MIDS. The spread of MIDS to the other executives and the continuing system enhancements never allowed for a pause between phases.

THE SUSTAINING-ENHANCING PHASE

The timing of these phases is not precise. Some areas of MIDS were not started when other areas entered the sustaining-enhancing phase. The sustaining-enhancing phase is best described as the period following the initial on-line presentation of a given subject of information. For example, if five display screens with summary graphics and support tables were placed on-line to "cover" the subject of overhead, then "overhead" would enter the sustaining phase.

Status reports, however sophisticated, are a snapshot view of a portion of the company's operations and therefore represent only a segment of the information required by an executive to do his or her job. In our

MIDS experience, we found that to some executives status reports were central to their managerial style, to others they were important adjuncts, and to the remainder they were of little value.

The initial phase essentially took existing data, organized it, and added the value of color graphics and on-line accessibility. This was appreciated by the executives, but it was only the beginning of effective support. Each MIDS display screen had to be accurately and timely sustained while we developed a cooperative effort with the executive users to enhance the basic information. The enhancement was most often the addition of associated information, which provided more comprehensive coverage of given situations.

This phase required:

1. Persons capable of developing a rapport with the executives
2. An understanding of hard information relationships
3. The ability to assess the value of soft information
4. The ability to express the composite information (hard and soft) in an effective manner.

The enhancement of the initial information into decision-support information had to be tailored to the individual executive. Each user has his or her needs, styles, and available time to participate in this enhancement. Some are better able to define their needs than others. Therefore, it is important for the executive to know that the best system for him or her can be achieved only through the cooperative efforts of the executive and information system personnel. Experimentation is expected, encouraged, and generally necessary for maximum effectiveness. In the continuing development of MIDS, we often develop a specific information display to cover a specific subject area and make it available to an executive or a designated staff member for evaluation. When these displays are determined to be in their most effective form, they are made available to others and become an intrinsic part of the system.

The scope of executive information is often difficult to define. The terms "hard" versus "soft" and "basic" versus "associated" appear vague. The MIDS team did not find it necessary to clearly define these terms in nonoverlapping definitions, but Figure 12–1 may be helpful in understanding the relationships.

The hard/basic information has a direct bearing on the performance of Critical Success Factors for the individual executive. The soft/basic information has the potential to influence the performance to the CSFs and must be assessed. The hard/associated information, while not directly affecting the individual executive's area of responsibility, will impact the overall operational arena. This hard information is evaluated

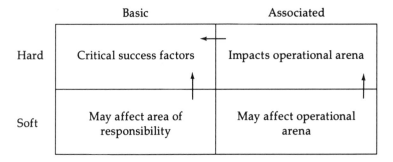

Figure 12-1. *Scope of Executive Information*

in terms of what impact will it have and when. Soft/associated information may influence the broad operational arena and that may produce a ripple effect that may reach the individual executive's area of responsibility or it may not. An illustration of how each of these terms may fit a hypothetical situation may be helpful.

If the Chief Financial Officer (CFO) has cash flow as a CSF, we can identify the types of information concerning cash flow. The monthly financial performance of actual cash flow to an established budget or goal is hard/basic information. Weekly or daily reports of cash receipts or disbursements are also hard/basic information. If a hazard is suspected to an anticipated large receipt, it is soft/basic information. It is soft because it is speculative and basic because it would affect a CSF of the CFO. This hazard could be identified in many ways and an understanding of the business might be required to identify it.

If a delivery of a major order is required to collect a large payment (cash flow) and the production management announces a delay in that delivery; the delivery schedule performance may be hard/basic information to the production vice-president, but the resultant effect on cash flow would be hard/associated information to the CFO. It is hard because it is a fact and associated because it impacts one of the critical success factor of the CFO.

If it is rumored that a major competitor is about to lose a major account to our company, this is soft/associated information. It is soft because it is a rumor and associated because the CFO does not have a prime responsibility to secure the new business. Should it happen, however, it would affect the operational arena of the CFO.

Much of vital executive information is very wide in scope, has many sources, and is time sensitive. To capture this comprehensive information in the EIS requires cultivated information sources and a developed rapport with executives and support personnel.

In developing the MIDS system, we found the *importance* of information is based on the users evaluation of the specific information. The purpose in considering the scope of the information provided is to recognize the comprehensive nature of executive information needs and to determine the extent of coverage that may be effective in an EIS. We sought to provide the most complete range of information possible and to let the executive evaluate its importance. Information received from external sources was added to the internal information.

HARD INFORMATION REQUIREMENTS

It is generally accepted that hard information is information that can be termed "facts" and resides as data/information somewhere accessible to the user. It can be internal or external to the operation. These facts can be collected, assimilated, analyzed, and presented as having some bearing on the executive's responsibilities.

Locating, collecting, filtering, and accurately presenting this hard information in a timely manner has its challenges. Financial information is perhaps the easiest. Standard accounting practices, rules for audits and governmental definitions of terms and methods have established a universal basis for identifying and presenting much of this essential hard information. However, even in this area of established rules, there is a continual redefining of the terms and methods. These changes require that very careful attention be paid to presentations of historical trends.

Other hard information, (i.e., marketing, production, quality, material) have generally more narrow rules. They may have units of measures established by precedence within industries, locations, or specific operations. Hard information concerning engineering, research, planning, and perhaps human resources have even fewer information standards.

Each of these areas has unique opportunities for effective use of hard information and generally each area has employed some method for reporting significant information. Effective treatment of hard information can be as simple as providing standards for terms and developing a common denominator for measurements (i.e., nonconformances per 1,000 hours worked for a quality measure) or correlating data to provide relationships (i.e., employee turnover to training hours required.)

Graphic treatment of hard information can be enhanced by trend graphics and exception reporting. Innovation in the treatment of this data (i.e., 3D graphics or icons) increases the risk of executive nonacceptance, but also offers unique opportunities to provide tools for better evaluations.

In MIDS, we often reduce typical Gantt schedule charts to chronological listings of major milestones and then record the actual performance using green for "ahead of schedule" conditions, yellow for "on schedule," and red for "late" items. Executives lose the time relations shown on

Gantt charts, but can quickly evaluate schedule performance and see the next major event due date.

No matter how clever the treatment of hard information, it rarely conveys the total picture. Often it prompts questions of why, how, when, and so on. If a favorable condition is presented, the questions might be:

- Is it the best it could be?
- What factors contributed?
- Can we apply whatever made it good to other situations?
- How long will the favorable position last?
- Who is responsible?

Unfavorable conditions might suggest some different questions. Some answers to these questions can be provided by inserting comments on the displays. Some questions lead to "soft information" answers and thereby open the door to another area of consideration for inclusion in the EIS.

SOFT INFORMATION CONSIDERATIONS

Soft information has been discussed by Henry Mintzberg: ". . . a great deal of manager's inputs are soft and speculative—impressions and feelings . . . hearsay, gossip, and so on" [11]. A universally accepted definition of soft information is not available, and some information seems to have degrees of "softness." A plan is soft in the sense that it represents actions to be taken within a set of parameters that may change, thus giving way to a contingency plan—if the changed conditions were anticipated. A plan is hard in the sense that it can be very formal and committed to paper. A schedule may be considered hard, but an "estimated completion date" may introduce an element of softness.

MIDS provides for soft information in several ways. Early in MIDS development we provided an on-line display to convey any item of information that a member of the president's staff wished to share with other MIDS users. This display is called a Daily Diary and its contents are generally on-line for one day. It serves as a news bulletin and often includes hearsay and impressions that a staff member wishes to share. A Daily Diary item might be: "A C-130 pilot from Peru told me that the recent South American Airlift Exercise went very well, except for communication equipment installed locally." or "A rumor from Egypt—the five-year military procurement plan will be revised to divert funds from ground transportation to airlift." Each item carries the name and telephone number of the contributor.

Opinions are often included on the individual displays under the comments area. A MIDS display dealing with a potential sale will often contain opinions relating to conditions which might impact the sale. This soft information is at least as important as the hard information having to do with product specifications and dollar values.

Soft information credibility is assigned by the viewer and is usually based on the viewer's assessment of the source and how well the information fits into other information known to the viewer. MIDS information always identifies the source(s) and relates the soft information to hard information when possible. Soft information can be contradictory to hard information or other soft information, but even so, it provides a fuller assessment to the presented subject.

HARD/SOFT INFORMATION COMBINED

An example of adding soft comments to hard information has been given, and that is a very effective way to combine the two. Sometimes the two can become interwoven to a much greater extent. A display containing the schedule for a given series of events will depict the official schedule and the actual performance measured by the schedule (all hard information). This display presents a schedule status and may be sufficient to convey the situation.

An elaboration of the situation might be as follows:

1. Assume the actual performance is behind schedule, an "estimated completion date" (ECD) would be added to provide management with an experienced forecast of completion (quasi soft information). This ECD can be used to determine the impact on other events.
2. A comment might be added to say that the ECD was contingent on performance in another event (additional hard info).
3. The comment might also include an opinion that the contingent event was likely to be performed on time (additional soft info).

The executive viewer would now know the schedule status (hard info), the expected completion (quasi soft info), a possible clause to further delays (additional hard info), but that it is not likely to happen (additional soft info).

A subsequent update might confirm that the contingent event was performed on time and the ECD was not *firmer*. The term "firmer" verifies that degrees of reliability are assigned to soft information.

The above is a simple example of combining hard and soft information to obtain a more complete assessment of a given subject. Often the necessary combinations are not directly related. An executive may use a measure of employee voluntary participation in company sponsored activities over time as an indicator of employee morale. Many bits of information would have to be assembled for a full assessment of employee morale.

The MIDS system has a tool to help the information analyst keep related information synchronized. When information is updated and a relationship to other information is known, a MIDS system file sends a message to the analyst. The message says, "Information on MIDS display(s) X, Y, and Z (displays are identified) may be affected by the changes you have just made." This tying together of known relationships is performed for both hard or soft information. Changes in the organizations' objectives, structure, and executive personnel are likely to have a major impact on the system contents, but subtle changes in operational procedures, regulatory requirements, and implemented policies also affect the operations of the executive, and therefore the requirements of his or her information system. The developed rapport with the executive users enables the MIDS system personnel to be aware of these changes and to make the necessary changes in the MIDS displays. The final objective of the MIDS system is to provide the scope and depth of information most supportive to the executives.

CONCLUSION

The Lockheed MIDS system is a successful Information System. The selection and treatment of information for the MIDS system was performed in two phases. The initial phase examined the existing flow of data for information of value to the executives and then used color graphics to add the values of trends and exception reporting.

The second phase of information selection and treatment is an ongoing sustaining and enhancing phase. This phase involves application of a knowledge about the business, the company and industry cultures and individual executive users requirements and styles. Knowledge and application of the business requires identification of the critical success factors, understanding the interrelationships of organizational entities and an awareness of the noncritical or supportive factors that support the executive users. The culture and style issues require the EIS to provide the executive users with a useful blend of direct and associated hard and soft information in a manner which is comfortable for the individual executive user.

In analyzing the success of MIDS, we are unable to specify the step-by-step procedure to select information for a generic EIS. We were initially successful by using the available information, determining its pertinence and improving its presentation with effective graphics. Our long-term information selection involved the effective blend of hard/soft and basic/associated information to match the culture of our organization and the individual styles of our executive users. The consideration of a two-phased approach to EIS information selection and an evaluation of soft information requirements to complete the executive support should be helpful to both the EIS initiate and the EIS operative seeking to improve their current system.

REFERENCES

1. Alexander, Michael. "Executive Information Systems Catch On," *Computerworld*, February 17, 1989, p. 31.

2. Kroeber, Donald W., & Watson, Hugh J. *Computer-Based Information Systems*, 2nd Ed., Macmillan, New York, 1987, pp. 568–570.

3. Hoffman, Susan S. "Lockheed Execs Fly MIDS," *Information Week*, September 7, 1987, p. 36.

4. Senn, James A. *Information Systems in Management*, Wadsworth, Pacific Heights, CA, 1987, pp. C56–57.

5. Houdeshel, George, and Watson, Hugh J. "The Management Information and Decision Support (MIDS) System at Lockheed-Georgia," *MIDS Quarterly* (10:5), March 1987.

6. Rockart, John F., & De Long, David W. *Executive Support Systems: The Emergence of Top Management Computer Use*, Dow Jones-Irwin, Homewood, IL, 1988.

7. Applegate, Lynda M. "Lockheed-Georgia Company: Executive Information Systems." Case study No. 9-187-135. Harvard Business School, Boston, MA, 1987.

8. Isenberg, D. J. "How Senior Managers Think," *Harvard Business Review*, November–December, 1984, pp. 81–90.

9. Rockart, John F., & De Long, David W. *Executive Support: The Emergence of Top Management Computer Use*, Dow Jones-Irwin, Homewood, IL, 1988, pp. 202–203.

10. Rockart, John F., & De Long, David W. *Executive Support: The Emergence of Top Management Computer Use*, Dow Jones-Irwin, Homewood, IL, 1988, p. 153.

11. Mintzberg, Henry, "Planning on the Left Side and Managing on the Right," *Harvard Business Review*, July–August, 1976, p. 54.

QUESTIONS

1. Describe the two phases of executive information selection at Lockheed-Georgia.

2. What three factors helped to initially identify pertinent executive information requirements?

3. What are advantages that may result from having an early success with an EIS?

4. Discuss the 2 by 2 matrix of the scope of executive information.

5. Define hard information, soft information, and the interrelationships between the two.

6. What are the differences, if any, between obtaining information requirements for an EIS and obtaining information requirements for other types of CBIS?

Key Question

13

Selecting EIS Software: The Western Mining Corporation Experience

Hugh J. Watson
Betty-Anne Hesse
Carolyn Copperwaite
Vaughan deVos

Executive information systems (EIS), or executive support systems (ESS) as they are sometimes called, are increasingly found in organizations. They provide senior executives with easy access to external and internal information relevant to their critical success factors. Many systems also provide support for electronic communications (e.g., e-mail), data analysis capabilities (e.g., decision support systems), and organizing tools (e.g., electronic calendars) [4].

An important issue in developing an EIS is selecting the software to use. Prior to the mid 1980s, there were few options. Systems designers could either custom build the software or patch together an assortment of available products. Some firms were successful with this approach. Lockheed-Georgia custom built their EIS software [2]. Phillips 66 used a combination of FOCUS (an IBM demonstration software package) and in-house developed software [1].

Since the mid-1980s, a wide variety of EIS software has become available. Table 13–1 provides information about some of these products. The software varies considerably in terms of cost and capabilities. At one extreme is a product like RediMaster that costs approximately $1,000 but

Used with permission from the authors.

Table 13–1. *Commercial EIS Software*

Product	Vendor	Description
CA–Stratagem	Computer Associates 711 Stewart Avenue Garden City, NY 11530-4787 (516) 227-3300	A set of products that can be integrated to create an EIS
Command Center	Pilot Executive Software 40 Broad Street Boston, MA (617) 350-7035	Full capability
Comander EIS	Comshare 3001 S. State Street Ann Arbor, MI 48108 (313) 994-4800	Full capability
EASEL	Interactive Images 600 West Cummings Park Woburn, MA 01801 (617) 938-8440	Supports EIS screen design
RediMaster	American Information Systems P.O. Box 367 Wellsboro, PA 16901 (717) 724-1588	Supports EIS screen design
Resolve	Metapraxis 900 3rd Avenue 36th Floor New York, NY 10022 (212) 935-4322	Full capability

only supports screen design. At the other extreme are products like Comshare's Commander EIS and Pilot's Command Center that typically cost in excess of $100,000 but provide a full range of capabilities. Table 13–2 lists many features of the full capability products.

A study recently completed at the University of Georgia provides insights about the software used to develop an EIS [5]. Fifty organizations with an EIS were surveyed and among the questions asked was whether custom built, a mixture of custom built and vendor software, or vendor software was used. The results were 24 percent of the firms were using custom built software, 52 percent a mixture, and 24 percent vendor software. The most popular software for the mixture of custom built and vendor was EASEL while the most popular vendor supplied software choices were Command Center and Commander EIS. When the data

Table 13-2. *Features of Full Capability EIS Software*

• Support for multiple user interfaces	• Application shells
• Online, context dependent help screens	• Data extraction from existing organizational databases
• Command files	• Graphical, tabular, and textual information on the same screen
• Multiple methods for locating information	• Integration of data from different sources
• Access to external databases (e.g., Dow Jones News Retrieval)	• Security for data, screens, and systems
• Interfaces to other software (e.g., Profs, Lotus 1-2-3)	• Support for rapid prototyping
• Integrated decision support (e.g., System W, IFPS)	• System usage monitoring
• Easy screen design and maintenance	• Support for hard copy output (e.g., paper, overhead transparencies, 35mm slides)
• Screen design templates	

were analyzed with age of the EIS as a consideration, newer systems tended to rely more on vendor software.

TWO APPROACHES

Even with the availability of full capability EIS software, some firms prefer to go with software already available in-house or to purchase software with limited capabilities. There are several reasons for this. An obvious one is cost—full capability EIS software is expensive. Another reason is time—get the initial version of the EIS up and running quickly while executive interest is still high. The time associated with justifying, selecting, purchasing, installing, and learning the limited software is less. A final reason is that there might not be a full commitment from management to the EIS. It may be that the system is viewed as a research and development project and that time and cost are to be minimized until there are strong indications that the project will be successful.

Systems that are successful tend to spread rapidly in terms of number of screens, users, and capabilities. Keeping up with the demands is one of the major challenges faced by the EIS development/support staff. Firms that have not elected to purchase full capability EIS software may find it especially difficult to keep up because of inherent limitations associated with the software used. Faced with this situation, firms once again have an important software selection decision. Should they try to kludge on additional capabilities or should they incur the time, cost, effort, and possible negative executive reactions associated with a conversion? Many firms choose to bring in full capability EIS software.

SELECTING FULL CAPABILITY EIS SOFTWARE

Given the cost and potential ramifications associated with the EIS software selection decision, a formal process should be used. An important first step is the formation of the evaluation team. Its composition should include representatives from all of the groups that will be affected by the EIS, including:

- The *executive sponsor* who makes the initial request for the system, makes the necessary resources available, stays on top of the system's development, handles potential resistance, and communicates strong and continuing interest in the system [4].
- The *operating sponsor* who manages the day-to-day development of the system. This person may be an executive but is most typically an information systems (I/S) manager [5].
- *Executives* who will be the users of the system.
- The *EIS development/support staff* who will develop and maintain the system. This group should contain business analysts and technical specialists.
- *Functional area personnel* who will provide data to the system.

The EIS software evaluation team provides the rich variety of perspectives that are needed. Each member participates in the team's activities in a way that is appropriate for their perspective; see Figure 13-1.

The EIS software evaluation team should use a multi-stage process that might include the following steps:

- End-user needs assessment
- Critical success factor identification
- Feature analysis and capability review
- Resource needs assessment
- Demonstration prototype development
- External user surveys.

This process is similar to one successfully used with DSS software [3].

End-user needs assessment is a systematic, organized, and structured procedure for identifying and evaluating features needed in the EIS software. It requires considerable input from future users of the EIS and lays the foundation for the feature analysis and capability review. The

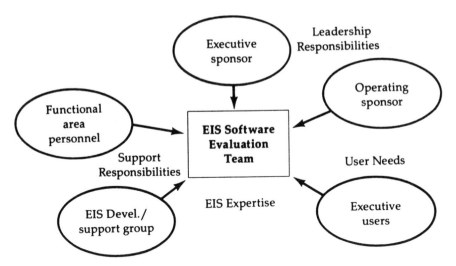

Figure 13-1.   *The EIS Software Evaluation Team*

assessment may reveal, for example, the need to provide information by functional area, product, and geographical location; the inclusion of e-mail capabilities; and the ability to access external databases.

Critical success factor identification establishes a minimum level of performance for key criteria and prioritizes the criteria used in selecting the EIS software. It reflects information gained in interviews with future users and technical people. For example, it may be deemed critical that the software requires no additional hardware, that it supports either a touchscreen or mouse mode of operation, and that its cost be below some maximum level.

Feature analysis and capability review involves the identification of specific features and capabilities important in evaluating the EIS software alternatives. The software alternatives are then evaluated using a checklist of features and capabilities. Possible features include ease of use, graphics capabilities, and methods for handling data.

The resource needs assessment explores the computer system resources required by the EIS software alternatives. It examines the computing platforms, operating systems, communications networks, and memory required by various products.

A prototype EIS should be developed by the vendors of the EIS products under consideration. The prototype should use real data and serve a current organizational need. Future EIS users should view the prototype.

An external survey should be made of the experiences of other organizations using the EIS products being considered. The survey should explore the product and the support provided by the vendor.

THE WESTERN MINING CORPORATION

Western Mining Corporation of Australia recently went through the process of selecting full capability EIS software. Their experiences, especially in the feature analysis and capability review step, should be of interest to other organizations.

At Western Mining Corporation, the EIS study was initiated by a senior executive. Two managers, one from MIS and one from Accounting, were appointed to oversee the study. Interviews were conducted with 20 representative executives across Australia to roughly determine their information requirements. This exercise revealed many insights and indicated a definite potential for EIS development. Most importantly, it allowed the organization to formulate its own perspective on EIS and to define what EIS could and should do for its executives. With steering committee approval, the software evaluation and selection process began.

The evaluation team consisted of two full-time MIS staff members and a part-time accountant. The decision was made to use a full capability EIS product and two products were selected as candidates. Only two products were considered because of what was available and supported in Australia at the time. Each product would also run on Western Mining's existing computing equipment. The evaluation team prepared a case based on a real business problem. The prototype EISs that were developed using the vendors' products were based on the case. A feature analysis and capability review checklist was created to compare the products. What began as a simple checklist became more comprehensive and detailed as the evaluation process proceeded. Appendix A provides the final checklist that was developed. It might be of use to other firms that are evaluating full capability EIS software.

Three weeks were devoted to the evaluation of each product. The initial week involved vendor demonstrations and some training. During the second week, the evaluation team experimented with various aspects of the software, using the evaluation checklist as a guide. Questions were prepared for the vendor who returned during the third week for assistance in developing the EIS prototype.

It became apparent that the case study was too simplistic to fully explore the potential of the software. Extra time available during the third week allowed the vendor to supplement the case study, demonstrating features of their choice. At the end of the third week, the evaluation checklist was reviewed with the vendor. The checklist was a valuable tool for comparison of the products.

Research into the implementation of EIS in the local and international arena was also undertaken to incorporate the experiences of other companies into the study. The net result enabled the project team to confidently recommend a product for detailed evaluation. Steering committee approval was attained to proceed to the next phase.

Over the next six weeks, two EIS applications were developed with vendor assistance. This experience not only served to confirm the software selection decision but also provided further in-house training. The applications developed during this period formed the basis for the initial version of the EIS at Western Mining Corporation.

CONCLUSION

The EIS software selection process used at Western Mining corresponds closely with the generic process presented earlier. It also shows, however, the iterative and evolutionary nature of the process. The case that provided the basis for the prototype EIS demonstrations was too simple to provide an adequate test of the various products' capabilities and had to be augmented. The feature analysis and capability review checklist evolved as more experience with the EIS products grew. After an initial decision on an EIS vendor's product was made, further testing was conducted in order to confirm the decision. A similar process might be effectively used by other organizations.

APPENDIX A: WESTERN MINING CORPORATION'S CHECKLIST FOR FEATURE ANALYSIS AND CAPABILITY REVIEW

1.0 Ease of Use
Development
Applications to be easy and quick to develop
New users to be easy and quick to add to the system
Suitability for quick prototyping
Display alternative output formats quickly
Learning
Learning time for developers
Learning time for users
Availability of appropriate documentation and tutorials
End User
Menu system
Customized menus for each user
Ability to bypass menus not required
Various modes of use (mouse, touchscreen)
Minimal number of keystrokes
Consistent use of functions

Maintenance

    Easy to add and modify data

    Ability to maintain integrity and timeliness of data (handling of frequent updates)

    Easy to add and modify screens, reports, and graphs

    Availability of standard templates

    Ability to copy existing screens, graphs, etc.

    Ability to monitor system usage

    Easy to add additional users

    Ability to incorporate changes to corporate structure

2.0 Reporting Capability

    Reports to be presented as both graphs and tables

    Ability to display graphs, tables, and text on single screen

    Ability to switch between tubular and graphic output

    Ability to color code exceptions on the current screen

    Ability to present a summary screen listing all exceptions throughout the system

    Support analysis of budgeted, actual, and forecast figures

    Effective presentation of time series data

    Ability to highlight variations

    Support interactive user defined variance criteria

    Retrieval of historical data as required

    Maintain historical data and discard after a user defined period

    Analysis of historical data and identification of trends

    Built-in restrictions to protect historical data

    Facility for personalized queries (i.e., ability for users to scan the data base according to interactively defined criteria)

    Explanatory notes to be attached to reports

3.0 Graphic Presentation

    Quality of graphics

    Speed of presentation

    Effective use of default color coding

    Ability to highlight areas of concern

    Availability of individual color schemes

    Ability to include explanatory notes for each graph

    Ability to produce a variety of graphs (pie, bar, 3D bar, line)

    Automatic generation of simple, default formats which can be customized

    Easy to produce executive defined graphs

    Automatic scaling

Graph limitations
Automatic legends

4.0   General Functionally
Drill down capability
Built-in statistical capabilities
Lookaside capability for interrupting a process to use another facility
Screen scrolling (horizontal and vertical)
Multiple tasks to be operating and displayed concurrently (e.g., windows, split screens)
Access to notepad facility
Integration with DSS
Import data from spreadsheets/word processing
Minimal screen repainting
Ability to display other languages

5.0   Data Handling
Version checking to ensure all users are accessing the same version of software, applications, and data
Interfaces with external databases and internal WMC systems
Efficient storage of time series data
Stored aggregates for rapid access
Built-in periodicity conversions
Efficient indexing and retrieval mechanism
Instantaneous distribution of new data among users
Ability to consolidate various sources and formats of data into an EIS database via manual input or electronic data transfer from other systems
Ability to sort screen data according to user defined criteria

6.0   Output Options
Laser printer, plotter, color printer, transparencies, dot matrix
Large screen presentations for meetings

7.0   Performance
Response times
PC-mainframe communications uploading and downloading data
Efficient resource usage
Capacity issues (i.e., number of users, volume of data)
Reliability of software
Recovery facility

8.0   Electronic Mail
Ability to run VAXMAIL
Ability to incorporate EIS reports and graphs into mail facility

9.0   Security
        Restricted system access
        Restricted function access
        Add/edit/delete restrictions for applications and data

10.0 Environments and Hardware
        Local access
        Across networks
        Multi-user access to the same data (only 3 users tested)
        Portability
        PC-mainframe links

11.0 Documentation
        Reference manual, introductory guide, tutorials
        Overall style of documentation
        Online, context sensitive help screens
        Meaningful error messages
        Appropriate cross-referencing and indexing
        Stand-alone chapters

12.0 Vendor Support
        Training courses for developers
        Technical support
        Local support
        Timeliness and smoothness of initial installation
        Availability of off-the-shelf applications
        Availability of source code
        Hot line support

REFERENCES

1. Applegate, Lynda, and Osborn, Charles S. "Phillips 66 Company Executive Information System," Harvard Business School Case 9-189-006, Cambridge, MA, 1988.

2. Houdeshel, George, and Watson, Hugh J. "The Management Information and Decision Support (MIDS) System at Lockheed-Georgia," *MIS Quarterly,* Volume 11, Number 1, March 1987, pp. 127–140.

3. Meador, C. Lawrence, and Mezger, Richard A. "Selecting and End User Programming Language for DSS Development," *MIS Quarterly,* Volume 8, Number 4, December 1984, pp. 267–281.

4. Rockart, John F., and DeLong, David W. *Executive Support Systems,* Dow Jones-Irwin, Homewood, IL, 1988.

5. Watson, Hugh J., Rainer, Kelly, and Koh, Chang. "Executive Information Systems: A Framework for Development and a Survey of Current Practices," working paper, University of Georgia, Athens, Georgia, 1989.

QUESTIONS

1. What are three reasons that some organizations choose to custom build their EIS or to customize a generic multipurpose software package?

2. What are three reasons that an organization might choose full capability, vendor supplied EIS software?

3. List the groups that should be represented on the EIS software evaluation team and the reasons each should be present.

4. Discuss the EIS software selection process.

5. What are the 12 major areas of Western Mining Corporation's feature analysis and capability review? Can these areas be applied to other computer based information systems as well?

14

What Users Want Today

Richard Laska
Alan Paller

One way to evaluate executive information systems is to ask the people who have already acquired systems and who create and use EIS applications what they like or dislike about the systems they have used, and what features they would like to see added to those systems. When the authors asked those questions, they were more surprised by what wasn't on the priority list than by what was on the list. Here, in decreasing order of popularity, is a wish list compiled from the responses of seasoned EIS users and developers:

1. SPEED

Experienced EIS directors say that new reports must appear in less than 2 seconds and new graphs in less than 6 seconds. Systems that take as little as 30 seconds per display are roundly ridiculed for their molasses-like quality.

One developer describes an early EIS she created for an electric utility company. "Our system answered hundreds of questions," she reports. "All the executives had to do was select an option from a menu. The system would take the request, tabulate the data, and display it on their screen. It took about 45 seconds for each display. That was too long. Our executives saw it as unresponsive. All work on the project was halted." On the other hand, if there's no other way to get critically needed information, the executives will probably be willing to wait.

Adapted by permission from "The EIS Book" by Alan Paller and Richard Laska, published by Dow Jones-Irwin, Homewood, IL.

2. GRAPHICS FLEXIBILITY

Executives want systems that allow them to choose the graphics format they like best. EISes that don't offer that flexibility can come under heavy fire.

One developer says she has worked for more than a year on an EIS but can't seem to produce graphics in a format that users want. "They don't like it," she says. "They want the bar charts to have numbers at the top and want dollar signs in front of the numbers. I use an EIS interface development language and have called the developer for help. They act as if I'm being picky. It's not picky when your users have a simple request and the software can't do it."

"Executives have been using graphics for a long time," notes Alan Greif, director of the executive information systems practice at Booz, Allen & Hamilton and perhaps the most experienced consultant in government EIS. "They're used to having a staff that can put whatever they want on a chart and modify it as they desire. They know what they like and what they don't like. Unless the EIS can give them what they want, it may as well give up."

In addition to design flexibility, seasoned EIS directors want a system to be able to deliver charts produced outside of the EIS. Some of the specific software packages mentioned were Harvard Graphics, CATellagraf, CADisspla, SAS/Graph, ICU, AS, Lotus 1-2-3 and Freelance Plus, SuperCalc 5, and Super Image. There is a strong feeling that existing charts can, and should, be part of the EIS delivery system.

3. OPEN EIS ARCHITECTURE

An EIS application developer should not be forced to reprogram existing reports into the EIS vendor's language. EIS software should be—must be—able to deliver reports and graphs produced by any popular program. Another dimension of such open architecture is access to other programs while the EIS is running. In other words, experienced EIS directors recognize that no EIS developer can create all the functions that might be needed, so a good EIS should embrace other programs and make them part of the EIS delivery system.

To find out how open a vendor's EIS is, bombard the vendor's representative with the following questions: Can the executive press a button inside the EIS to run dBase and return a report? To allow drilldown through that dBase report? To display graphs produced in Harvard Graphics and/or SAS/Graph? To send an SQL query to a server and present the answer? To search a very large Word Perfect text file?

This is a sophisticated demand, both on the part of the requester and as a requirement for the EIS developer. The developers who asked for this capability included nearly every EIS application builder in our survey who had worked on a system for more than six months. All had encountered one of two problems: Either they had been frustrated by limitations in the EIS software that they could not overcome (as with the developer who could not put numbers on bar graphs), or they had encountered a person in the organization who had developed the charts and tables the executive wanted and who asked: "Why rewrite the programs in some obscure EIS language nobody knows when I can use existing programs written in a language we all know?"

4. SUPPORT FOR OLD PCs

Many of the EIS developers in our survey emphasized the need to support old personal computers as well as new ones. In organizations that already have a substantial investment in personal computers, the ability of the EIS to support existing equipment keeps the cost of EIS workstations within prudent limits. Here the developers asked that the EIS allow existing PCs to serve as delivery systems. Even if the pictures do not look quite as elegant as on newer machines, companies want to give access to the system to as many managers and executive secretaries as practical, as well as to executives on the road. Where the firm already has a substantial investment in PC hardware, the developers want the EIS to support the old color graphics adapter and Hercules graphics adapters (common on most PCs sold in the past five years), as well as the graphics available on newer models.

More than 15 million PCs do not have enhanced graphics adapter (EGA or VGA) capabilities. Upgrading the monitors and internal graphics processors from CGA to EGA or VGA costs from $500 to $1,200 for each computer. That's too much for some organizations to swallow for a single application. If the EIS can deliver its information to CGA-equipped machines, it will save that much money and still make the information available to everyone who needs it.

5. MACINTOSH SUPPORT

Although Macintosh computers represent only about 10 percent of all business PCs, Macs are almost everywhere. At least a few Macintosh systems can be found in upwards of 85 percent of organizations now building EISes. Many EIS directors are demanding that their EIS software function equally well on Macintosh systems as on IBM or IBM-compatible PCs.

6. FAST APPLICATION DEVELOPMENT

Another capability experienced EIS developers look for is fast, automatic application development systems. Automated application development systems reduce EIS development and maintenance costs. Developers who cite this requirement are primarily users who want to develop multiple applications and/or have recently lost key staff members who were familiar with the appropriate EIS programming language. These developers abhor the helpless feeling they get from being dependent on writing and maintaining programs written in a proprietary language that few people know and that requires countless arcane statements to set up even the most basic display screen.

Here's the way one senior technology manager describes what he wants: "I have a whole array of reports and graphs. I would like to start by making those instantly available, in a logical way. Give me something that will let me tell the system what reports and graphs are available and what reports can be accessed from what other reports. Then let the system do the work of laying out and programming the screens."

That doesn't sound like much of a request, but you'd be astounded at how few EIS systems are capable of even such rudimentary capabilities.

7. SECURITY

Where systems are actually used, security becomes an increasingly important consideration. Security techniques range from encryption of data to thwart file thieves to sophisticated retinal pattern recognition systems to ensure that only the right people get to the sensitive data. The security problem remains largely unsolved at this writing, but it must be solved if executives are to trust their most sensitive information to the EIS.

8. DIAGRAMS, ICONS, AND GRAPHIC MENUS

Graphical user interfaces such as diagrams and icons are the most common face of an EIS. Sometimes they are useful; sometimes they are essential.

In EISes, icons are useful for building executive confidence that the system is truly easier to use than information systems of the past. Asking for information from an EIS can be simplified by using pictorial menus rather than textual ones. This is not to say that the system needs to use a picture of a letter with a stamp on it to represent electronic mail, or cartoon people to represent personnel. Icons and graphical pointing are necessary, however, to turn maps, diagrams, and charts into dynamic menus. Everyone agrees that executives are bombarded by too much information. The EIS menu should speed and simplify efforts to locate needed information.

The following is offered by an EIS builder for a chemical company: "We want our plant managers to have a system that shows real-time information on the status of each part of their operation. The best interface is a diagram of the process. Parts of the diagram should change color depending on current data. A problem area, for instance, should flash red. Then the system should allow the plant managers to point, using a mouse or their finger, at those items they want. The EIS should instantly display the data or graphs describing the performance of that component."

The chairman of a large software company has a quality-monitoring system that charts the organization's responsiveness to clients' requests for technical assistance. With hundreds of products to monitor, the menu that lets the executives use the system could have been cumbersome. To avoid the clutter, the EIS director simplified the interface by using graphs as menus. The first graph that appears when the executive asks for quality information shows a horizontal bar chart with the product groups ranked in order from most requests for help to fewest. By pointing to one of the bars, the executive gets another bar chart showing the products in that group. Pointing to one of those bars then brings up a line chart showing trends.

Most of these comments have a similar ring: The graphical menus must be dynamic. If the status changes, users want the color or length of the bar to change, and they want to be able to point to the problem area and get the information automatically.

9. MULTIPLE VIEWS OF DATA

After starting with an EIS that provides only fixed displays, many experienced EIS directors encounter a growing need to be able to cut the data any way the executives want it. Each executive looks at the organization from a unique vantage point. The EIS should allow straightforward reformatting of various views of the data to meet each executive's needs.

At one sales company, for example, the president wanted management displays at the divisional level, sorted by cost and by the variance of revenue from the budget. At the same firm, the chief financial officer wanted reports down to the department level, with performance indicators that showed ratios of travel and commissions to head counts. Finally, the financial control manager wanted detailed account-level displays to allow her to explain variances discovered by the other executives.

Perhaps surprisingly, one related capability that few EIS directors mention is executive-level ad hoc data analysis or gaming. Although this type of "what-if" analytical tool is viewed as an important requirement by EIS vendors and novice EIS directors, seasoned EIS managers learn differently. What the vast majority of executives really want is data focused through lenses crafted explicitly for them, to their specifications, with consistent format and content.

Some executives do want to look at data from many angles, but they want each view to have been developed and tested before they use it. They don't often use data manipulation tools such as spreadsheets regardless of how friendly such tools become. These executives worry that they might misuse the spreadsheet or database language, saunter into a meeting carrying the wrong numbers, and look downright foolish.

CONCLUSIONS

The requirements cited above were learned the hard way by experienced EIS directors. Unfortunately, most do not match the capabilities currently available in many popular, off-the-shelf EIS packages. Yet many of our respondents were among the EIS pioneers who acquired off-the-shelf EIS packages. How do the respondents explain this inconsistency?

Expediency is the most common answer. One federal manager acquired an EIS just a few months earlier. He explains that the rigors of federal contracting procedures made it necessary to purchase the package even after he had learned of its unacceptable weaknesses.

"I saw the EIS package being used at another agency," he says. "It looked good, so I showed it to our executives. They liked it. So I started the paperwork. It took nearly a year to get the paper through the contract shop. By the time the money became available, I had learned that the EIS I selected was not going to do the job I wanted. At that point, it was a matter of spend the money on the flawed system or lose it and get nothing at all. So I bought it."

The head of a new EIS search team at a consumer products company makes the point even more clearly. First, he explains why he was getting rid of the EIS he had purchased: "We are getting new EIS software because our old package is too slow and because its graphics are not good enough for executive presentations. Apparently the executive vice president saw a demonstration and was hooked. He knew the guy who ran the company that developed the EIS package, so he purchased it."

In both of these cases, a demonstration triggered the desire to buy. No one analyzed what capabilities were essential for the business problem that the EIS was to help solve. Both organizations soon regretted the purchase.

QUESTIONS

1. Why is a 30 second response time for an EIS considered to be unacceptable?
2. Why is graphics flexibility an important feature of an EIS?
3. Is an open EIS architecture a necessity? Explain your answer.
4. Why is the security of an EIS an important consideration?
5. Why are graphical user interfaces the most common user-system interface?

15

Product Spotlight on EIS

Eileen Carlson
Michael L. Sullivan-Trainor
Rudolph Pizzano

WHAT COLOR IS YOUR EIS?*

Defining an executive information system (EIS) calls to mind the old TV game show *What's My Line?*, where through a series of questions, panel members tried to determine the occupation of an anonymous contestant.

A lot of people are stumped by what an EIS actually is, and that is understandable. Until a year or so ago, it was easy to point at three vendors and say, "they sell an EIS."

Comshare, Inc., Pilot Executive Software and, more recently, Execucom Systems Corp. all offered software packages in the price range of $100,000 to $200,000, and all offered an easy-to-use interface, access to databases throughout and external to the organization, drill-down capacity, exception reporting and combinations of graphics and text to capsulize information for the busy executive.

During the last couple of years, however, more products have hit the market; while some of these claim full functionality, most are scaled-down versions of EIS or tools to help users build their own systems. With these alternative routes, the definition has become a little more hazy, with enhanced spreadsheets, EIS front ends, prototyping tools and even fourth-generation languages (4GL) vying to fit into the category.

People are looking beyond the "big three" and studying these alternatives. In fact, as many as 50 percent of all EISs currently in place and one-third of those planned at IBM mainframe installations will be

* This section was written by Eileen Carlson.

generated from application development tools, according to Clare Gillan, senior analyst for application solution software at International Data Corp. in Framingham, Mass.

As users select the functionality they need for the price they want to pay, no two companies can claim to have the same EIS.

To confuse the issue further, decision support and executive support system (DSS, ESS) characteristics are creeping into commercial and homegrown EIS systems, stirring debate as to how much of a role they need to play and to whom these systems are most valuable.

The paths that users can take to achieve some degree of EIS functionality are numerous, including the following:

- Build an EIS using in-house tools such as a spreadsheet, 4GL, applications generator, programming language and their favorite graphics software.

- Put a front end customized for executive access onto a DSS, be it an off-the-shelf or in-house package.

- Use a vendor EIS package to display a handful of reports to a small group of executives.

- Build robust applications with a vendor EIS package for a large number of executives and managers.

However, for each path taken, functionality differs widely. Consider the following three approaches, in ascending order of sophistication:

At Motorola Corp.'s corporate headquarters, 45 executives—from the chairman of the board to the assistant general manager—use personal computers to view economic forecasts, quality measurements and financial information as well as access the Dow Jones News/Retrieval service and the mainframe electronic mail system.

The in-house-built system is based around a graphical interface, which took about one year to develop. This interface serves as the

Function	Application	Percent Cited
Finance	Budgeting/Forecasting	64%
Human resources	Head-count reporting	36%
Marketing	Sales forecasting Sales/Share reporting	56%
Manufacturing	Inventory management	20%
Sales	Sales reporting	45%

Source: Pizzano & Co.

Figure 15-1. *Where Does the Money Go?*

delivery vehicle for information sprinkled throughout headquarters in various databases.

At this point, the system is manually updated. Motorola chose to create the interface first and save the feeder system for the next phase. ①

Inland Steel Co., a steel manufacturer in East Chicago, Indiana, also took a build-your-own approach, primarily because it was working within a one-month time frame and wanted tools that they were comfortable with. The company put a front end onto its Lotus Development Corp. 1-2-3 spreadsheet, integrated the spreadsheet with Ashton-Tate Corp.'s Dbase files and used some add-in products to write custom applications. ②

The finished system accesses financial, marketing and human resources databases and brings this summary data into the file server. Forty people—from the vice-president of manufacturing down to the section managers—currently use the system, which provides a drill-down function and ad-hoc queries.

While Inland had intended to finesse the system with an off-the-shelf EIS after presenting it to executives, the users were so happy with the results that it no longer seemed necessary. These executives are somewhat technically oriented and don't mind typing in a few extra commands, as opposed to icons.

The fact is that drill-down on the Inland system differs from what an off-the-shelf package would offer. Drill-down in the strict sense means that by clicking on or touching an item on the screen, users access more detailed information, whether it's in graphical or textual form. On the Inland system, users hit "page-down" and merely see more preset screen detail, not information relating to any particular item. Additionally, the Lotus graphics are not as high-quality as a vendor package.

Stone Container Corp., on the other hand, began with a custom-built system and replaced it with Pilot's Command Center after the first attempt "didn't work out too well," according to Donna Dreczko, project manager of EIS.

Dreczko attributes the failure to the system's use of function keys and the fact that there were no icons or graphics; users selected menu items with a text-based interface.

The new system clearly displays applications in five colored boxes that executives touch for more detailed information.

The system was implemented in two months and runs five applications, including accounts-receivable, orders, shipments, production and backlog. Users range from the chief executive officer to the senior vice-presidents from each functional area.

When considering what off-the-shelf packages have to offer, it becomes clear what an EIS *can* do. Comshare's Commander offers two primary applications—Briefing Book and Execuview. With Briefing Book, information is down-loaded from the mainframe to a PC. With standard reports, drill-down, color-coding, trend analysis and commentary features, the product presents the user with his own customized EIS.

Execuview's Executive Edge handles ad hoc reporting, where the executive views the data from the mainframe, file server, or PC. The product was designed to work with System W or One-Up, Comshare's DSS products.

Execucom, on the other hand, works with preformatted templates, which a company writes applications to fit.

Pilot's Command Center offers drill-down, trend analysis, exception reporting and ad hoc query. It also offers a number of code generators, including Advantage, Dimension, and Multipath.

ROADS TAKEN

A large percentage of companies, however, willingly give up some of the functionality of the vendor packages, believing they can do so for a fraction of the software cost. In addition, they see no reason to pay so much for software that requires a huge degree of customization—usually one to six months' worth before an application is up and running.

One homegrown approach is to use a very powerful 4GL product to provide EIS capabilities.

One such product comes from Information Builders, Inc., which just released Focus EIS. Focus EIS sells for $995 per copy and requires either PC Focus, which lists for $1,295 per copy, or the mainframe version, which costs $180,000.

Focus EIS uses drill-down, trend analysis and exception reporting to improve data access and reporting capabilities for systems built in Focus or PC Focus. Its open architecture allows access to data across many platforms.

Information Builders claims you can bypass the mainframe Focus database and go right to the source systems; however, the ideal method is to pull data from the different sources, bring the data into the Focus database and then present it to executives with Focus EIS.

In addition, Focus EIS is ideal for companies that already have a sophisticated Focus database.

PROTOTYPE, THEN IMPLEMENT

Another approach is to first prototype and then implement a production system. Two products commonly used for this purpose are American Information Systems, Inc.'s Redimaster and Interactive Image's Easel.

At Central and South West Services, a Dallas-based holding company for four electric companies and a gas pipeline company, "The prototype approach was a lot more attractive to our management than making an up-front commitment and going with any of the particular EIS products," says Dick Groff, manager of planning.

Central and South West chose Easel, a general-purpose screen design and prototyping tool. The product creates screens from mainframe databases to present on a PC, complete with color-coding, graphical trends and drill-down capabilities.

It took the IS department about eight weeks to create a demo for the eventual EIS. It included three modules, showing operational information, status reports and organizational charts. From there, six months were spent preparing a more in-depth prototype and standardizing on the use of the three applications.

The project is now on hold until strategic plans are finalized. Nevertheless, it is still less expensive to have a prototype fail than a full-blown EIS.

One drawback to sticking with an EIS created in this manner is that once you enter production mode, maintenance becomes costly and difficult. Each screen that is displayed to the end user has several PC files associated with it, each of which needs to be maintained. If the executives decide they'd like a change in screen format, it is a big job, since hundreds of screens may be at stake.

Another way to start small is to take a departmental, distributed approach with a LAN-based system.

"The architecture of the future will be an intelligent workstation providing the human interface and personal productivity functions," says Richard Crandall, president of Comshare. "These will have engines behind the scenes performing the bigger analytical and data management work," he says.

Abbott Laboratories went with Comshare for just this distributed approach. "We could offer executive information systems without them becoming incredibly costly because the preponderance of the work is handled on the PC while the executive is using it," says Nancy C. Boyd, a consultant in the firm's corporate MIS department.

Another downscaled approach to PC-based EISs is offered by Channel Computing Inc.'s PC-based Forest & Trees.

Users of the system define critical success factors or vital signs and set up their applications accordingly. While the $495 product is not a bad step toward eventual EIS functionality, there are a few drawbacks. For one, it is necessary to hard-wire the data to the application as well as program every part of the screen that will be activiated. Channel Computing claims that executives can do their own screen modification, but the number of steps involved in this process makes that claim doubtful.

As users choose between large- or small-scale systems, they also are faced with another issue: the degree to which ESS and DSS characteristics should creep into their EIS.

Executive support systems are umbrella systems that enable the executive to communicate with others via E-mail, review people's schedules to set meetings, make travel arrangements and perform other administrative and support functions.

The EIS is the core piece of the ESS that provides the financial, marketing, operational, personnel and competitive information.

The more comfortable the executive is with using a computer, the more ESS functions he'll want in the EIS. For example, on some systems, E-mail is embedded within the EIS application so that the executive doesn't have to go to a separate screen to mail a message about a particular report.

A DSS, on the other hand, is usually targeted at managers and analysts. Whereas an EIS is a presentation vehicle of summary information, a DSS is an analytical tool. EISs do perform some analytical functions, such as sorting, basic mathematics, selection and limited what-if, but DSSs add more sophistication to the picture, performing strategic planning, budgeting and forecasting, consolidated reporting, what-if analysis, goal-setting and optimization on larger volumes of data.

Does 'E' Stand for 'Everybody'?
Kevin D. Green

The "E" in EIS doesn't just have to mean "executive." Once targeted at the top brass, executive information systems are now marketed to—and used at—other levels of the organization. EIS can mean "everybody's information system" to some and even "enterprise intelligence system" to others.

The question is, how far down in an organization can an EIS be effectively used? And, at what point might decision support technology or other information systems better serve needs?

In the traditional view, EISs give top executives a means of tracking critical success factors. With the new approach, "everybody is sharing information and networking from the same ubiquitous database," says Michael Watson, senior manager at Price Waterhouse's Applied Technology Center, which uses the term "enterprise information network." The enterprise view includes all of the people within the organization from the senior-level executives down to the people responsible for the operational work.

Another advocate of this theory is Pilot Executive Software. "EIS is not about executives. It's about a technology that solves a class of information problems," says David Friend, the company's founder and chairman.

"It's about hypertext data navigation, access to multiple data sources, graphical data displays to aid interpretation, multiple ad hoc views of data and so forth. It's just as applicable at the middle-management level as at the top."

Friend even recommends EIS at the operational level. For instance, a plant manager would look at detailed summaries of plant activity to determine the level of efficiency.

Further down in the organization, however, people's information requirements do change, usually growing too specific for an EIS to handle. Friend concurs that decision support system capabilities need to be used at these lower levels.

In Pilot's product, the issue is tackled by assigning different users of the system different access levels to the database. Chief executive officers may access the top three levels of the database, for example, including salary information. Mid-level management and employees on the operational level would view more applicable levels of the database.

Others take a modified view, believing that EIS was designed for more than the top executives, but it's not for everyone.

"Directing the EIS to the top two levels of management is too narrow," says Richard Crandall, president of Comshare. "An EIS must also be designed to include the people who analyze, process, package and deliver information to decision makers. On the other hand," he continues, "EIS is not relevant right down to the bottom of the organization. There you will start to compete with other products, such as Microsoft and Lotus, that have different functionality than an EIS."

Far Reach

People who have used EISs see practical reasons for the filtering-down process. Inland Steel Co. intended from the very beginning for its home-grown EIS to reach beyond top executives, says Kevin D. Green, EIS project manager. "If you had the executives looking at the business using one approach, and the rest of the company is looking at the business using a different approach, it would create problems," he says.

At Inland, 40 people—ranging from the chief operating officer to section managers—use the system, and it is currently being made accessible to analysts. Inland follows Pilot's approach, in which employees at different levels of the organization have access to different parts of the database.

EIS purists argue that the democratization of EISs trivializes the technology and undermines the leadership role of top executives. "The purpose of an EIS is to send signals to the organization as to what is important, to indicate movement toward a new direction and to help executives monitor the progress towards that direction," says Wayne C. Burkan, president of Alternative Visions, Inc.

"The organization will succeed or fail based on the leadership of the executives," he adds.

EIS OF USE

An EIS is also more user-friendly than a DSS. Most vendor packages include a touch screen, mouse or remote control to activate the system.

With a DSS vendor package, the user either types in commands or uses function keys to activate the system.

EIS purists hold that executives want only capsulized information and no analytical capabilities. "An executive will take a large report and scan for items that are interesting to him," says Wayne C. Burkan, president of Alternative Visions,Inc., an EIS consulting organization in Farmington Hills, Mich.

"An analyst is far more methodical in gathering and analyzing information," he says.

Those who see DSS merging with EIS also expect that lower levels in the organization will use EIS.

The top three vendors have a close affiliation with DSS: Comshare and Execucom started out as DSS vendors and later added EIS products, and Pilot started as an EIS vendor and just last year added a DSS component to its product line.

A fourth vendor that is traditionally strong in DSS, Information Resources, Inc., is beta-testing its EIS product. While companies have used its DSS, Express, to build EISs, the firm has added an EIS tool kit to its PC Express with the intention of easing and speeding the EIS application building process. This kit is scheduled to be released next month and will cost $50,000 along with an additional per-user fee.

In all four cases, the DSS can be added for $150,000 to $200,000. Used in combination with the EIS, these systems work well to consolidate and massage the raw data on internal systems.

Despite these advantages, stacking an EIS on DSS or vice versa does not produce the integration one might desire. For example, to perform more sophisticated DSS applications on data presented in the EIS, flat-file transfers or other preformatting steps are necessary to present the information in a user-friendly format. It would be nice to say that you get what you pay for with EISs. In some senses, this is true; $495 won't buy the functionality of a $50,000 package.

However, high price alone cannot guarantee a successful system. There are many implementation concerns that will influence your eventual failure or success [CW, June 25].

The good news is that as the EIS definition changes and blurs, there are that many more types of EIS packages on the market, and companies can choose between luxury and economy models.

COMMAⴖD CEⴖTER SLIPS PAST COMMAⴖDER *(BARELY)***

Coke or Pepsi, Burger King or McDonald's, Ford or GM—which do you prefer? If you find those choices hard, then you begin to understand the

---

** This section was written by Michael L. Sullivan-Trainor.

difficulty information systems professionals face in choosing between executive information systems (EIS) rivals Comshare, Inc. and Pilot Executive Software.

While Comshare's Commander owns an imposing 55 percent of the installed base, as opposed to Pilot Command Center's 34 percent, the two are nearly equal in the types and qualities of features they offer, according to *Computerworld's* Buyers' Scorecard survey of 50 users of each product.

Introduced in the early 1980s, Pilot's EIS products lost an early lead in share to Comshare, which introduced Commander in 1985. These were followed in October 1988 by Execucom Systems Corp.'s Executive Edge, which has 5.7 percent of the installed base (See Executive Edge ratings and methodology).

Varying Views
Eileen Carlson

There are as many ways to view data through an EIS as there are ways to view the organization. The most common applications include the following:

- **Financial.** The executive may monitor profitability, analyze expenses or look at the breakdown of revenue—whether by region, corporate division, department or product.
- **Marketing.** The system may display market share, demographic makeup of the customer base and product popularity in various geographic regions.
- **Operational.** The executive may view productivity variation across a number of plants, how the actual production rate compares with the plan and how a strike would affect productivity.
- **Human resources.** May include executive succession planning, number of employees that fit into certain categories according to their skills and experience, actual head count vs. planned head count and background information on individual employees.
- **Competitive.** May include news stories regarding the competitors' financial performance and product mix.
- **External factors.** Execs may want on-line access to interest rates, government regulations, indicators of the general economy and industry trends.

Any of these applications can also be viewed simultaneously; for instance, executives can look at head count vs. financial performance or internal vs. external factors.

The closeness of Pilot's and Comshare's packages is reflected in a whisker-thin difference in the overall ratings. Command Center edged ahead with 58.1 points to Commander's 57.9. The point totals are derived from multiplying the ratings each user group gave his own product by the importance factors all users assigned to the 17 criteria.

Despite the closeness in overall scores, the two packages do have different approaches in key areas. For example, Command Center is a host-based product, with data downloaded to personal computers on request. Commander, on the other hand, uses host-based data but requires all screens to be downloaded to the PC.

Another feature that wins user points for Command Center is an automatic program generator that supports screen design and maintenance. The product received its highest rating—8.8 out of a possible 10—in the area of screen design, which is one of the most key considerations for users. Screen design was rated 8.7 in importance by all users on a one to 10 scale. Command Center also topped other application development categories.

Commander scored higher, however, in data access and integration categories. The package comes with specific links to different types of internal databases. This feature was reflected in a rating of 7.5 for data extraction from existing databases. In addition, Comshare was the first to forge relationships with other vendors that offer external database services. Users recognized these ties with a 7.5 rating for access to external databases.

The strength of Commander's System W decision support system was reflected in a score of 7.7 for well-integrated decision support.

Methodology

Products rated in *Computerworld's* Executive Information Systems Buyers' Scorecard were chosen based on the following criteria:

Products selected for review by users had to be full-capability EIS, which means they had to be designed for use by top-level management and offer the following functions: drill down; exception reporting; data extraction from existing databases; access to external databases; support for multiple-user interfaces; on-line context-dependent Help screens; command files; multiple methods for locating information; integrated decision support; screen design templates; application shells; graphics, tables and data on the same screen; hard copy output; and integration with office software.

The products also had to be one of the share leaders in both installed base and revenue. For example, Comshare leads the pack with 55 percent of the installations, followed by Pilot and Thorn EMI, which both sell Command Center and have a combined share of 34 percent. The firm with the third-largest base of users, Execucom, has 5.7 percent of the market.

Execs say, it's nice, but . . .
Alan Radding

Top executives may not know every technical detail of how their executive information system (EIS) works, but once they use one, they're pretty sure what they want to do with it.

While a number of executives contacted by *Computerworld* said they were generally pleased with their systems, most could see room for improvement. Displeasure arose mostly when the EIS promised more than it delivered.

The improvements most wished for varied widely, depending on the executive's usual work habits.

"What I want from an EIS most executives probably don't need," says John Betak, assistant vice-president of asset development at Conrail in Philadelphia, who puts great value on analytical capabilities. On his wish list is specialized software to help analyze the data provided by the EIS.

Matters of taste

The need for analysis tools ranges from the basic to the very sophisticated. Thom Faria, vice-president of agency operations at The New England, a financial services company, for instance, says he would be satisfied with basic modeling capabilities such as what-if scenarios on his EIS from Comshare, Inc.

Sophisticated graphing is in demand at Connecticut Mutual Life Insurance Co. in Hartford, Conn. "Sometimes I'm working with numbers that are in the millions of dollars and numbers that are below half-a-million dollars at the same time," says Richard McGeary, chief financial officer for information systems at the firm. "I need to have logarithmic graphing so I can show orders of magnitude."

Predictive capabilities are gold to some, but they're worthless to others.

"We built our system on the concept of what's happening, not what-if," says Robert Wallace, recently retired president of Phillips 66 in Bartlesville, Okla., a pioneer in EIS. Of more importance is up-to-the-minute accuracy of data.

Other executives just can't get enough information. Conrail's Betak, an experienced computer user who is accustomed to accessing many Conrail databases, says he would like to meld all of these databases into the EIS.

Wallace would like to have more types of data in the EIS, such as information on laws and regulations from legislature and trade associations. To handle this load, he says, the EIS needs to be faster, at least operating "in a speed frame consistent with our mental process."

At Comdisco, Inc., an equipment leasing firm in Rosemont, Ill., James Stanton, vice-president of administration, has access to a massive amount of information through his EIS—the equivalent of 175,000 reports internally plus external data sources. He wouldn't refuse if he were offered more: "If we had better capability to drill down for more detail and if it were easier to get data from outside sources, I'd support that," he says.

The need for detail is echoed by Steve Bonville, second vice-president of individual disability marketing at Unum Life Insurance Co. in Portland, Maine. "I have charts and graphs, but I can't get at the raw numbers," he says. A new version of his Pilot Executive Software EIS promises to remedy that situation.

Other executives seek the comforts of home. "We can't use the EIS from a laptop, but that's something I would very much want," The New England's Faria says. The problem, suggests Connecticut Mutual's McGeary, is the sheer volume of information that would have to be transmitted.

Others chafe at predefined reports and long for unstructured output capabilities, "I wish I could dump [the information from the EIS] on a floppy and move to the desktop publisher or just transfer it to the publisher," Betak says.

Promises to keep

Real dissatisfaction with an EIS arises when it doesn't live up to its billing. At Metropolitan Life Insurance Co. in New York, the problem is not with the EIS but with the incomplete or out-of-date information it delivers.

"They gave me a PC and told me I would have access to a lot of information with a mouse," says Ted Athanassiades, executive vice-president at the firm. "Unfortunately, they aren't keeping up the databases, so it is useless to me."

The screen gives him a colorful display of the information he can select with the click of a mouse, but when he requests that information, he is disappointed. "If I try to access, say, human resources, they give me a report that's dated December 1989. It's useless to me," Atanassiades says.

The company is planning to connect the EIS to the central databases so files can be accessed immediately.

Those who are pleased with their current systems see almost limitless potential for enhancements, including expert systems capabilities. "I would love to have the system become intelligent to who you are and what you like to see through your touch stroke," McGeary says. "I'd also love to be able to say 'sales' and see sales information open up."

Others, such as Comdisco's Stanton, think the current technology could use a few improvements. Stanton's particular peeve is touch-screen design. "At times the lines are too close together for thick fingers," he says.

Because of the large market share difference and a consequent difference in the number of users available to be surveyed, the user ratings for Execucom's Executive Edge are presented separately from those of Commander and Command Center. While Commander and Command Center are installed in more than 200 sites per product, Executive Edge is installed in only about 50 sites. While respondent populations of 50 per product were used for the Commander and Command Center ratings, a population of 20 respondents was used for Executive Edge. In addition, less than one-third of the Commander and Command Center respondents were supplied by the vendors, while more than 80 percent of the Executive Edge respondents were supplied by the vendor.

The ratings were based on telephone surveys conducted by First Market Research in Austin, Texas. Result tabulation was performed by IDG Research Services in Framingham, Mass.

The total scores, which are weighted according to the criteria that all the respondents find most important, are computed by multiplying the mean scores all users assigned to the importance of each criteria by the mean scores each user group gave to its own product.

For example, the criteria—ease of screen design and maintenance—received a mean importance rating of 8.7 on a scale of one to 10. Command Center users gave their product a rating of 8.8 for performance in this criteria. To develop a total score, these two factors are multiplied for a total of 76.56. This total is then added to the other totals of criteria importance ratings and performance ratings. This sum is divided by the total number of ratings for a total score for all 17 criteria.

Table 15–1. *Pilot's Command Center vs. Comshare's Commander*

Product	Best Relative Features	Worst Relative Features
Pilot's Command Center SCORE **58.1**	Integrating data from different sources Ease of screen design and maintenance Quality of service and technical support Ease of customization Interfaces to other software, such as Profs & Lotus 1-2-3	Presenting graphics, text, and tables on the same screen Data extraction from existing databases Support for rapid prototyping Support for multiple interfaces Security for data, screens and systems
Comshare's Commander SCORE **57.9**	Presenting graphics, text and tables on the same screen Data extraction from existing databases Support for rapid prototyping Support for multiple interfaces Security for data, screens and systems	Integrating data from different sources Ease of screen design and maintenance Quality of service and technical support Ease of customization Interfaces to other software, such as Profs & Lotus 1-2-3

Total scores reflect all criteria and their user-assigned importance. Response base: 50 users per product.

Table 15-2. *User Ratings*

User Importance Rating	Data Access	Command Center	Commander	User Importance Rating	Application Development	Command Center	Commander	User Importance Rating	User Features	Command Center	Commander
8.7	Integrating data from different sources	7.9	7.8	8.7	Ease of screen design and maintenance	8.8	7.5	8.9	Well-presented graphics, text, tables on screen	8.5	8.6
8.4	Efficient data extraction from existing databases	6.4	7.5	8.4	Ease of customization	7.9	7.5	8.5	Quality of service and technical support	7.4	7.3
8.0	Efficient access to external databases	6.3	7.5	8.3	Support for rapid prototyping	8.1	8.1	7.9	Effective interfaces to software such as Profs & Lotus 1-2-3	7.5	7.0
7.5	Multilevel, ad hoc query capability	7.2	7.3	8.0	Effective support for multiple user interfaces	7.4	7.4	7.2	Pricing of installation & maintenance	6.7	5.7
7.1	Well-integrated decision support system	6.2	7.7	7.8	Good security for data, screens and systems	6.8	7.6	7.2	Easy to create hard copy output	7.2	6.4
				7.4	Varied application shells	7.7	7.0	6.5	Useful online Help screens	6.3	6.1

Each product shows its strengths in user ratings of EIS capabilities. Commander wins by a considerable margin in three of the five data access categories and takes a fourth by a hair. Command Center has a slight edge in integration, price, and user features and excels in several ratings related to ease of use.

Table 15–3. *A Closer Look*

How many executives use these products?		How much do the executives use these products each day?	
Number of Executives	Number of Respondents	Time	Number of Respondents
1:		15 minutes or less:	20
2–10:	11	16–30 minutes:	18
11–20:	12	31 minutes to an hour:	7
21–60:	15	More than an hour:	1
61 or more:	11		
1:	1	15 minutes or less:	12
2–10:	15	16–30 minutes:	16
11–20:	13	31 minutes to an hour:	9
21–60:	14	More than an hour:	6
61 or more:	7		

How long has the package been in use?		How much did it cost to get the EIS up and running?	
Number of Years	Number of Respondents	Cost	Number of Respondents
0–1 year:	21	Less than $10,000:	1
		$11,000 to $100,000:	4
2–3 years:	22	$100,001 to $300,000:	17
		$300,001 to $500,000:	8
4–5 years:	7	$500,001 to $1 million:	6
		More than $1 million:	2
0–1 year:	32	Less than $10,000:	1
		$11,000 to $100,000:	3
2–3 years:	18	$100,001 to $300,000:	13
		$300,001 to $500,000:	9
4–5 years:		$500,001 to $1 million:	9
		More than $1 million:	3

The top numbers are for Command Center and the bottom are for Commander.

Table 15-4.   *EIS Packages*

Vendor	Product	Hardware Platform	Operating System	Disk Space Necessary to Load Program (Bytes)	Graphics Capabilities	Imports Graphics from External Sources	Office Automation Tools Interfaced With
Ashton-Tate Corp. (213) 329-8000	Framework III	IBM PC AT, XT, PS/2 and compatibles	DOS, OS/2	3M	Bar, line, pie, scatter, stacked bar, XY	No	Communications, databases, E-mail, spreadsheets, word processing
Channel Computing, Inc. (800) 289-0053	Forest & Trees	IBM PC AT, XT, PS/2 and compatibles	DOS 3.1 and higher	750K	Bar, line, pie, XY	No	Databases, spreadsheets
Cogent Information Systems, Inc. (201) 795-4003	EIS/Corporate Performance Analysis	Any minicomputers that support operating systems listed at right	Unix, Unidata, Universe, Prime Information, Pick	28M	Bar, line, pie, XY, others from external graphics packages	Yes	Databases, E-mail, spreadsheets, word processing
Comshare, Inc. (800) 922-7979	Commander EIS	DEC VAX 3000, 6000 AND 8000 series, IBM PC and compatibles, IBM 9370 series, PS/2, Apple Macintosh	VM, MVS, VMS, DOS, OS/2, Apple Macintosh OS	10M for PC, 40M-100M for host	3-D, bar, line, pie	Yes	Communications, databases, E-mail, spreadsheets, word processing
Decision Technologies, Inc. (203) 327-4000	Probus EIS	Apple Macintosh	Apple Macintosh OS	500K	Bar, line, pie	Yes	Communications, databases, E-mail, spreadsheets, word processing
Dialogue, Inc. (212) 425-2665	Access Executive	IBM 370 series DEC VAX, Unix machines, IBM PC	CMS, TSO, VMS, Unix, DOS	8M	3-D, bar, line, pie, text, XY	No	Communications, databases, spreadsheets, word processing

All products perform exception reporting. All have drill-down capabilities except those from Ashton-Tate Corp., Meta Media, Inc. and new Generation software, Inc.

The companies included in this chart responded to a recent survey conducted by *Computerworld*. When a vendor is unable to provide specific information about its product, the abbreviation NP (not provided) is used. When a question does not apply to a vendor's product, the abbreviation NA (not applicable) is used. Further product information is available from the vendors.

Table 15-4. *(Continued)*

Report Generation (Static or Ad Hoc)	Update Procedure (Automatic or Manual)	Automated Application Development	Networks Supported	Windowing Facility Supported	Eternal On-Line Services Accessed	User Interfaces Available	Other Features	Price
Both	Automatic	Yes	3Com, AT&T Stargroup, Banyan, IBM PC LAN, Novell Netware	Proprietary	Dow Jones News/Retrieval, Compuserve, Ashton-Tate BBS, others on request	Keyboard, mouse	Outlining capability	$695
Both	Automatic	Yes	Any PC-based, Token-Ring	None	None	Keyboard, mouse	None	$495
Ad hoc	Either	No	Primenet	None	Dow Jones News/Retrieval, Mead Data Central, Reuters, UPI, AP	Keyboard	Built in on request	$35,000+
Both	Automatic	Yes	3Com, Banyan, Decnet, SNA, Novell Netware, Token-Ring	OS/2, Apple Macintosh Multifinder, proprietary	Dow Jones News/Retrieval, Infoglobe	Mouse, touch screen, keyboard optional with DOS machines	CD-ROM support, imaging capabilities, large screen display, on-line tickler file, voice annotation	$48,000
Static	Automatic	Yes	3Com, Appletalk, Novell Netware, other AFP-compatible networks	Apple Macintosh Multifinder	Dow Jones News/Retrieval	Keyboard, mouse	CD-ROM support, imaging capabilities, large screen display, video, voice annotation	$45,000 for site license
Both	Automatic	Yes	DEC PCSA, Novell Netware	None	No direct support, but interfaces written on request	Keyboard, mouse	None	$1,000–$200,000

Table 15–4. *(Continued)*

Vendor	Product	Hardware Platform	Operating System	Disk Space Necessary to Load Program (Bytes)	Graphics Capabilities	Imports Graphics from External Sources	Office Automation Tools Interfaced With
Dun & Bradstreet Software (404)239-2000	Smartview	IBM 370 series, IBM PC, PS/2 and compatibles	MVS, DOS 3.1 and higher, OS/2	6M for PC, 300 cylinders for host	3-D, bar, line, pie, XY	No	Communications, databases, E-mail, spreadsheets, word processing
Execucom Systems Corp. (800) 531-5038	Executive Edge	Any machines that support operating systems listed at right	MVS, VM, AIX, SCO-Unix, VMS, Micro VMS, Ultrix, RISC Ultrix, MPE-XL, HP-UX, Dynix, DOS 3.3 and higher Apple Macintosh OS	360K-720K for workstation, 20M for host	Area, bar, high-low-close, line, pie, variance, XY	Yes	Communications, databases E-mail, spreadsheets, word processing
Ferox Microsystems, Inc. (703) 684-1660	Encore EIS Toolkit	IBM PC AT and compatibles	DOS	20M	Bar, line, pie	Yes	Communications, databases, E-mail, spreadsheets, word processing
Global Software, Inc. (800)326-3444	Global EIS	IBM PS/2 and compatibles	DOS 3.0 and 4.0 OS/2	3M	3-D, bar, high-low-close, line, pie, scatter, xy	No	Communications, spreadsheets, other built in on request
IBM Contact local office	Executive Decisions	IBM 370 series, PS/2	VM, MVS, OS/2 Extended Edition	2M	3-D, bar, line, pie, XY, others from external graphics packages	Yes	Databases, E-mail, spreadsheets, word processing; communications optional
IMRS (203) 323-6500	IMRS On Track	Compaq 286, 386 and compatibles, IBM PC AT, PS/2 and compatibles	DOS	1M–2M	Bar, line, pie, XY	Yes	Communications, databases, E-mail, spreadsheets, word processing, Micro Control and Fastar financial packages
Information Resources, Inc. (617) 890-1100	Express/EIS	Any machines that support operating systems listed at right	MVS, VM, VMS, MPE/XY Primos DOS	2M	3-D, area, clustered and stacked bar, line, pie, XY	Yes	Communications, database, E-mail, spreadsheets, word processing

Table 15-4. *(Continued)*

Report Generation (Static or Ad Hoc)	Update Procedure (Automatic or Manual)	Automated Application Development	Networks Supported	Windowing Facility Supported	Eternal On-Line Services Accessed	User Interfaces Available	Other Features	Price
Both	Either	Yes	Novell Netware, IBM PC LAN	Microsoft Windows 3.0	None	Keyboard, mouse, track ball, touch screen	Large screen display, on-line calendar	$50,000
Both	Either	Yes	Any PC-based network	Microsoft Windows, proprietary	Dow Jones News/Retrieval, others on request	Keyboard, mouse, remote control	On-line calendar, scheduling template, CASE-style application generator with object-oriented capabilities, icon library	$50,000–$300,000
Ad hoc	Both	No	Novell, Imaginet, Token-Ring	None	None	Keyboard, mouse	None	$3,000
Ad hoc	Either	No	3Com, IBM PC LAN, Novell Netware, others on request	OS/2 Presentation Manager	Dow Jones News/Retrieval, Compuserve, others on request	Keyboard, mouse, touch screen	Large screen display	$75,000–$100,000. annual lease available
Both	Automatic	No	Any supported by OS/2 Extended Edition Communications Manager	OS/2 Extended Edition Presentation Manager	Dow Jones News/Retrieval, others via service workstation	Keyboard, mouse, touch screen	Automatic telephone dialing, imaging capabilities, large screen display, on-line calendar and address book, stock trends graphing capability, voice annotation	$7,500–$68,400 (host component), $500 per workstation, $100 for optional communications feature
Static	Automatic	No	3Com, Ethernet, IBM PC LAN, Netbios, Novell Netware	Microsoft Windows	No direct support but can access any on request	Mouse, touch screen	Large screen display, on-line calendar	$35,000–$50,000, includes five end-user licenses
Both	Either	Yes	3Com, bisynch, asynch, Banyan, Ethernet, Novell Netware, Token-Ring, SNA, SDLC	Proprietary	Dow Jones News/Retrieval, Compuserve	Keyboard, mouse, remote control, touch screen	CD-ROM support	$50,000+

Table 15-4. (Continued)

Vendor	Product	Hardware Platform	Operating System	Disk Space Necessary to Load Program (Bytes)	Graphics Capabilities	Imports Graphics from External Sources	Office Automation Tools Interfaced With
Interactive Images, Inc. (617) 938-8440	Manager's Portfolio	IBM PC, PS/2 and compatibles	DOS, OS/2	2M+	3-D, bar, line, pie, XY	Yes	Communications, databases, E-mail, spreadsheets
Interactive Software Services, Inc. (800)288-8550	AMIS (Advanced Management Information System)	IBM AS/400, System/38	OS/400, CPF	35M	Bar, line XY	No	Any externally defined file
Manageware, Inc. (203) 359-9397	Compete	IBM PC, AT, PS/2 and compatibles	DOS, OS/2	1M	Dependent on external graphics package	No	Databases, spreadsheets, word processing, ASCII files
Meta Media, Inc. (404) 892-7921	Executive Information System	IBM PC and compatibles with Video Show hardware/software unit	DOS 3.3 and higher	1M	Line	Yes	Communications, databases, E-mail, spreadsheets, word processing
Metaphor Computer Systems, IBM (800)255-5803	IBM Data Interpretation System	IBM PS/2, 386-, I486-based PCs	DOS, OS/2	200K, plus that required for dedicated file server	Bar, curve, line, pie, XY	No	Databases, E-mail, spreadsheets, word processing
New Generation Software, Inc. (916) 920-2200	I.Q.	IBM AS/400, System/38	OS/400, CPF	18M	Bar, line, pie, XY	No	Spreadsheets, word processing
Pilot Executive Software (617) 350-7035	Command Center EIS	IBM 370 series, DEC VAX, HP 9000, IBM PC XT and compatibles, Apple Macintosh	VM, MVS, VMS, Unix, DOS, Apple Macintosh OS	400K for PC, 20M–30M for host	3-D, bar, line, pie, scatter, symbol, XY	No	Communications, databases, E-mail, spreadsheets, word processing

Table 15–4. *(Continued)*

Report Generation (Static or Ad Hoc)	Update Procedure (Automatic or Manual)	Automated Application Development	Networks Supported	Windowing Facility Supported	Eternal On-Line Services Accessed	User Interfaces Available	Other Features	Price
Both	Manual	Yes	Any PC network	OS/2 Presentation Manager	Dow Jones News/Retrieval	Keyboard, mouse, touch screen	Imaging capabilities, large screen display, on-line calendar	$7,500+
Ad hoc	Automatic	No	None	None	None	Keyboard	Large screen display, multidimensional database	$25,000–$75,000
Both	Either	Yes	Any that can run under Microsoft Windows	Microsoft Windows 3.0	None	Keyboard, mouse	None	$4,995
Static	Automatic	No	Any that are PC-based, Netbios-compatible	None	Signal, Reuters	Digi Pad, keyboard, mouse	Imaging capabilities, large screen display	$50,000 licensing fee
Both	Manual	Yes	Ethernet, Token-Ring	Proprietary	Dow Jones News/Retrieval	Keyboard, mouse	None	$40,000 plus $4,000 per work-station
Ad hoc	Automatic	No	None	None	None	Keyboard	None	$1,750–$13,500
Both	Automatic	Yes	Any supporting HLLAPI, EHLLAPI, EEHLLAPI, Ethernet protocols	Apple Macintosh Multifinder, proprietary	Comtex, Dow Jones' Dow Vision, News Net, Reuters, others	Keyboard, mouse, touch screen	4GL, CD-ROM support, large screen display; imaging capabilities and voice annotation on Apple Macintosh	$45,000–$150,000

Table 15-4. *(Continued)*

Vendor	Product	Hardware Platform	Operating System	Disk Space Necessary to Load Program (Bytes)	Graphics Capabilities	Imports Graphics from External Sources	Office Automation Tools Interfaced With
SAS Institute, Inc. (919)677-8000	The SAS System	IBM 370, 4300, 9370, 3000 series, PC AT, PS/2, DEC VAX, Data General and Prime minicomputers, Sun and HP workstations	MVS, CMS, VSE, VMS, DOS, ADS/VS, Primos, HP-UX, Sun OS	10M+	3-D, bar, line, pie, XY	No	Communications, databases, spreadsheets, word processing
Software 2000 (506)778-2000	Vision 2000	IBM PC and compatibles, AS/400	DOS 3.1 and higher, OS/400	750K	Bar, line, pie	No	Databases, spreadsheets

Table 15–4. *(Continued)*

Report Generation (Static or Ad Hoc)	Update Procedure (Automatic or Manual)	Automated Application Development	Networks Supported	Windowing Facility Supported	Eternal On-Line Services Accessed	User Interfaces Available	Other Features	Price
Both	Either	Yes	Novell Netware, Ethernet, Decnet	OS/2, DEC, X, proprietary	None	Keyboard, mouse	Large screen display, on-line calendar	$595 for PC component, up to $19,000 for host component
Ad hoc	Automatic	No	Any PC network	None	None	Keyboard, mouse	None	$15,000, plus $2,500 per five users

As of 1989

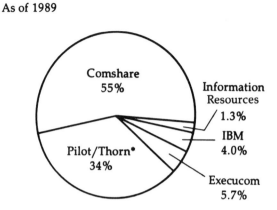

Source: International Data Corp.
*Thorn sells Pilot's Command Center

Figure 15-2. *Vendor Shares of Worldwide Host-Based EIS Installations*

PRODUCTS THAT ALREADY UNDERSTAND THE LINGO*

Executive information systems (EIS) now come in special-purpose flavors.

Several software developers have recently released packages that cater to particular industries, such as financial services or medical institutions, or to specific business departments, such as human resources and information systems.

In some instances, these packages are really just applications software with a twist—an EIS front end that provides a graphical user interface, drill-down capabilities and exception reporting. In others, they began as specific applications and grew into full-blown EISs that can be used independently of the original software. In both cases, these packages have something to recommend them.

For one thing, tailored EISs can reduce customization time because they are geared to the vocabulary and practices of a particular area and written to gather and present data accordingly. While a hospital administrator tracks "DRGs," a television network programming director may monitor "overnights," and the leveraged buyout specialist who owns both firms watches the yield curve.

These departmental and vertical EISs can also save money. Buying an EIS front end for a departmental application costs approximately $50,000 per application—well under the price range of a general-purpose EIS, which typically costs from $100,000 to $200,000.

* This section was written by Rudolph Pizzano.

A departmental EIS is only cost-effective for one or two applications, however. For three or more departments, it is more economical to purchase a general-purpose EIS and customize the interface to each departmental system.

For vertical-market EISs, prices range from less than $50,000 to $150,000.

To develop EIS capabilities in their systems, applications software vendors either license technology from traditional EIS vendors or go it alone.

All three of the top EIS vendors—Comshare, Pilot Executive Software and Execucom Systems Corp.—are currently licensing their technology to software firms.

Pilot has formed a relationship with HBO & Co., a software developer for hospitals in Atlanta. HBO's system keeps track of financial data, which administrators must report to insurance companies or government agencies. It also tracks patient care information, such as drugs administered, hours of physical therapy and surgical procedures. With Pilot's EIS front end, administrators can more easily access both types of data.

Medicus Systems Corp. in Evanston, Ill., another healthcare software developer, formed a similar alliance with Comshare, which also offers an EIS tailored for the retail industry.

For its part, Execucom has licensed its front end to Telos Corp., a telecommunications company.

Several software firms have developed EIS capabilities internally, including Legent Corp., Multitrak, Software 2000, Inc. and Information Resources, Inc. (IRI).

Whereas Legent's and Multitrak's EIS offerings are designed to work with their applications software, Software 2000 and IRI are pitting general-purpose systems against offerings from the top three EIS vendors.

Legent, based in Vienna, Va., and Boston-based Multitrak both offer project management software for IS. These systems track the progress on projects as well as capacity planning.

After finding that its clients spent a lot of time pulling together information generated from their system to prepare management presentations, Legent decided to add the EIS function.

Multitrak's original project management software was IBM mainframe-based; when it came out with a personal computer version, it decided to add an EIS front end. Legent and Multitrak each price their systems at less than $50,000.

Software 2000 in Hyannis, Mass., is a vendor of human resources and accounting software that licensed an EIS front end from Forest & Trees, Inc. in Portsmouth, N.H. With this technology, Software 2000 has developed a general-purpose EIS that can work with many other applications packages than its own. Now in beta testing, the product is intended to compete directly against Pilot, Comshare and Execucom with a price point of less than $50,000.

Similarly, IRI in Waltham, Mass., is positioning its Express/EIS against the "big three," although its original data retrieval software was intended for consumer packaging firms. Express/EIS, now in beta testing, is priced at $50,000, plus $2,500 per workstation.

With the popularity of graphical interfaces, exception reporting and drill-down capabilities, this trend of adding these EIS capabilities into systems will most likely continue.

QUESTIONS

1. Discuss the four paths that organizations can follow in implementing an EIS. Include advantages, disadvantages, costs, and relative effectiveness.

2. Briefly discuss how Carlson compares and contrasts DSS and EIS.

3. Should the "E" in EIS stand for "executive," "everybody," or some combination of the two? Discuss your answer.

16

Avoiding Hidden EIS Pitfalls A Case Study: What You See Isn't Always What You Get

Hugh J. Watson

How many things can you find wrong with this true-to-life scenario?

Bill Perry, vice president of information systems at Genericorp, had advocated the development of an executive information system (EIS) to support the information needs of the firm's senior executives. From trade writings, conferences and conversations with other information systems managers, Perry had heard of EIS successes at firms such as Xerox Corp., Phillips Petroleum and Lockheed-Georgia. Perry believed that besides helping top management, an EIS would also improve the image of the IS department. For too many years, company executives had approved multimillion-dollar budgets without much IS support. An EIS would change that situation, however.

Perry arranged for one of the EIS vendors to present a demonstration to the chief executive officer and other senior executives. The demonstration was very well received. With a touch of the screen, charts and reports quickly appeared in a rich variety of formats and colors. The executives were impressed and, after a brief meeting, authorized the development of an EIS. The project was allotted a budget of $250,000.

The next step was to put together a team of people to develop the EIS. Sam Johnson, who had worked at Genericorp for 20 years in a variety of areas, was recruited to head the project. Johnson was a good choice because of his knowledge of the business, executives and politics of the organization. Perry also assigned two of his best systems analysts to the project.

After reviewing the software and hardware alternatives, the EIS team chose what they thought would be a good approach. A major EIS vendor's software would be used. The product was designed around the co-processing concept, in which the personal computer performs graphics functions and the mainframe handles data storage. The executives would have IBM Personal System/2 Model 50 machines connected to an IBM 4381 by a Token-Ring network. Most of the hardware was already in place.

Getting the initial set of executive users to specify their information requirements proved to be a problem. The EIS staff found it difficult to arrange time with the executives because of the latters' travel and job requirements. Even when they did meet, the executives were often vague and uncertain about their information needs. Consequently, the executives' staff and secretaries became important sources for determining what should go into the EIS.

Three months later, the initial version of the system was rolled out to five users. The 50 screens provided key financial reports that were previously available only in paper form. The system also provided information on key performance indicators that had been identified in Genericorp's strategic planning processes. The screens were efficiently updated by automatic downloading of data from existing databases.

The executives' initial reaction to the system was generally positive. One executive said, "I've never been able to get my hands on this information this quickly before." Several of the executives seemed proud to finally be able to use a computer. Only one older executive seemed to have little interest in the EIS.

Having delivered the system, the focus turned to maintenance. Johnson was assigned to another project. The systems analysts were given responsibilities for developing a new, important transaction processing application. Two maintenance programmers were assigned the task of handling the evolution and spread of the system to more users, with additional screens and new capabilities.

Little happened with the system during the next few months. It took the maintenance programmers a while to learn how to use the EIS software. Even after they knew how to develop screens, the programmers discovered that this activity always seemed less critical than working on other applications. Besides that, the executives seldom requested additional screens. To some extent, the maintenance programmers viewed the EIS as an "executive toy."

Nine months after the introduction of the EIS, little evolution had occurred. There were no new users, and usage-tracking software revealed that three of the five executives were not using the system at all. Few new screens had been added, and there were no new system capabilities.

At about this time, Genericorp began to encounter financial troubles. To maintain a healthy bottom line, any nonessential expenditures were eliminated. At a key meeting, the executive who had never taken to using the EIS proposed that it be terminated. "We've put a lot of time and money into this system, and I don't see that we have gotten much out of it," he said. "If we are honest with ourselves, all we are getting is the same information that we used to get before—except now it is on a screen with fancy graphs and colors. We can save money by trashing the system and not lose much." After discussion, the executives agreed that the system had turned out to be a disappointment that should be scuttled.

When Perry learned of the decision, he was crushed. The EIS had seemed so promising, and things seemed to have been going so well. What had gone wrong? He'd gotten executive support, assembled a good staff, selected appropriate hardware and software and quickly delivered an initial version of the system. These were frequently mentioned keys to success. Maybe the executives just weren't ready to use computers. One thing Perry did know, however, was that the EIS experience smeared his reputation, as well as that of his department.

While the scenario and company are fictional, the situation is very much like the EIS experiences of many firms. An EIS is developed with high expectations, but it often ends in failure.

WHAT WENT WRONG?

The Genericorp scenario has many problems in it. The longer you look, the more faults you find. Some problems are not fully appreciated even by experienced EIS developers. Taking a look at the following problems can help you steer your organization away from an EIS failure.

Problem One: Lack of Executive Support

Conventional wisdom says that an EIS requires an executive sponsor. This person supports the project, makes the necessary resources available and handles the political problems that occur.

In the early days of EIS (from the late 1970s to the mid-1980s) senior executives tended to drive EIS development. They had a specific information need and thus a strong interest in EIS. More recently, IS managers, sensing a chance for increased visibility and recognition, began initiating interest in EIS. Although they may get executive support, that support is weaker, and as Genericorp learned, there is a difference between support and commitment. Come economic hard times, the system may be abandoned.

There is another reason that an EIS should have a broad base of executive support. More than one EIS has failed after the executive sponsor left the company. The highly touted EIS at Northwest Industries died after Ben Heineman left. When the EIS has multiple supporters, it can better withstand the loss of an executive sponsor. Having a broad base of support requires the creation of a system that meets the needs of many users.

Problem Two: Undefined System Objectives

There can be a variety of motivations for creating an EIS. A firm's executives may need information that is more comprehensive, relevant or timely. An EIS can be used to improve communication within an organization. It may be used to change executives' mental models: for example, how executives view the firm. It might be employed to analyze specific organizational problems.

Many firms fail to clearly define the objectives for their EIS. One outcome is that the system may lack needed features and capabilities. An otherwise excellent EIS that does not serve its intended purposes is likely to fail. At Genericorp, system objectives were never clearly defined, thus contributing to the failure.

Early in the development of an EIS, it's important to assemble key executives and clearly define why the EIS is being developed. A clear purpose suggests the capabilities and features that should be included in the system. Some organizations have used an EIS executive steering committee with good success to not only define system objectives but also provide on-going planning and control for the project.

Problem Three: Poorly Defined Information Requirements

Most organizations know that an EIS should supply relevant information that will aid success. Less obvious are some subtleties and potential problems that need to be understood and addressed when designing an EIS.

There are four basic types of critical success factors: industry, organizational, work group and individual. In mining, for example, key factors include world demand and price for tin, copper and other metals. These factors remain relevant over long periods of time. Organizational factors differ by company. These might include the market share for tin or the cost per ton for extracting copper. Such factors are relatively stable over time. Work unit factors apply to the division, group, department or other organizational unit. Examples might include the number of accidents per month or the number of tons of tin produced per day. Such factors are stable only as long as the responsibilities of the work unit remain the same. They are also unique to the work unit. Finally, individual factors are things that the executive must do well in order to be successful. These factors tend to change relatively quickly as job responsibilities and concerns change and are unique to the particular executive.

Information about industry and organizational success factors tend to be available to all EIS users. (One exception might be sensitive competitive information that only a few executives can access.) Work unit and individual critical success factor-related information is usually of interest to only a few or perhaps even a single executive.

Most organizations take one of two approaches when designing the initial version of their EIS. The first approach is to *focus on the executive sponsor's information needs.* This approach is logical because it reinforces the interest and commitment of this key person. The type of information provided is likely to vary considerably. It will include industry, organizational, work unit and individual critical success factor-related information. A problem with this approach is that it does not build a broad base of support. Thus, it is critical to expand the information provided by the EIS so that it meets the information needs of more users.

The second and most common approach is to focus on *providing key financial and strategic information.* This was the approach used at Genericorp. Once again, this seems to be a logical approach because it provides information that senior management needs to run the business.

This approach runs the risk, however, of what may be called "the six-month phenomenon." For the first six months, everything seems to be going well, but then executive use of the system starts to decline. As was the case at Genericorp, the system may even be discontinued. The problem is often that the information provided does not grow in depth or breadth. This type of system may not allow executives to drill down to the level of detail needed. It may provide information about only a few of the areas that are important to users. Very little, if any, information is provided about work unit or individual critical success factors. After a while, executives perceive that the EIS is satisfying only a small percentage of their information needs and that it is unlikely that the situation will change. Enthusiasm and interest in the EIS decrease, use of it declines and the system is terminated.

Even when the EIS support staff realizes the importance of providing individual success factors-related information, there are problems when users are unwilling to commit the time to discuss their information needs. While executive support personnel can provide important insights about what information is required, regular interaction with the executives makes it not only possible to respond to information needs but also to anticipate them.

A portfolio of methods should be used to identify information requirements. Some of the methods involve direct interaction between executive users of the system and the EIS support staff. It is seldom possible to get as much executive time as wanted. Consequently, analysts must use indirect methods, such as discussing executives' information needs with support personnel.

All these methods merit consideration. Those used will depend on factors such as how accessible the executives are, the relationship between the analysts and the executives, whether the information requirements are for the initial or ongoing version of the system, the level of the success factors-related information that is needed and the software used.

It is important to recognize that multiple methods are needed, because no single method is likely to serve all purposes.

Problem Four: Inadequate Support Staff

A good EIS support staff is critical. Genericorp got off to a good start by naming Johnson to direct the project. He knew the company, the executives and the politics. He was well regarded and had the requisite business, technical, managerial and interpersonal skills. His staff was also first-rate.

The staffing problems began when people started to think that the EIS could be placed in a maintenance mode, like most other applications. An EIS needs to spread to additional users, accommodate new and changing information needs and evolve to provide additional capabilities. These requirements demand a permanent staff that promotes the EIS, interacts often and effectively with executives, understands and anticipates information needs, has a vision of what the EIS can be and is ready and able to overcome problems when they are encountered.

Even though EIS support staffs can be assembled in a variety of ways, three organizational roles must be filled. *Technical supporters* must perform tasks such as testing and installing hardware, handling communications needs and writing data extraction routines. Such people typically come from IS, whether they are permanently assigned to the EIS support staff or have a dotted-line relationship to it.

Another role is filled by *business information analysts.* These people perform tasks such as identifying information needs and designing displays. They must work closely with the executives and may even have been the staff that supported the executives before the EIS was created.

The final role is the *data provider.* These people obtain data and enter it into the EIS. This role is often performed by functional area personnel, including secretaries.

In our case, Genericorp created a permanent EIS support staff that was unable to perform the business information analyst role. Their organizational location, training, experience, other job responsibilities and attitudes made them terrible choices for providing long-term EIS support.

Problem Five: Poorly Planned Evolution

The initial version of an EIS can take many different forms, depending on the motivation for creating it. The EIS at Genericorp provided financial and strategic information. The initial version may provide information about an important problem. It may focus on communications support. There are many legitimate starting points, depending on the company's needs.

Regardless of the starting point, there should be a plan—or at least a planning process—for the evolution of the EIS. Genericorp had neither. Ideally, an EIS planning committee includes the operating sponsor, executive users, EIS support staff manager and IS personnel. Their purpose is to give direction to the EIS.

To maintain executive interest in the EIS, evolution must occur quickly. Changes and enhancements must be made almost daily. The EIS at Genericorp was in trouble when months passed while the new support staff learned to use the software. Even then, little change was forthcoming.

An important part of the evolution of an EIS is to ensure that it helps address significant needs or problems. The information and capabilities provided should make a real difference in the performance of the organization. Efforts should be made to assess tangible benefits from the EIS. Without this, the EIS is at risk from economic hard times (as was the case at Genericorp), turnover of the executive sponsor and political resistance.

When an EIS is successful, it almost always expands to other users. The spread can be lateral to different areas of the firm or downward to lower organizational personnel. Other people want to have access to information on which important decisions and actions are based. Priorities for the spread of the EIS should be governed by the areas of greatest need.

Ultimately, the EIS may serve everyone in the organization. Having relevant information that is easily accessed is appealing to more than just the senior executives of a firm.

EPILOGUE: IS IT WORTH DOING?

For most organizations, an EIS is a high-risk application. It serves users who have poor computer skills and are skeptical about whether computers can help improve their job performance. Organizations often have little experience in developing applications of this kind. An EIS often involves learning, selecting, implementing and using new technology. Additional data sources typical have to be used. Potential political problems abound.

So a logical question is, is it worth the trouble? For many organizations, the answer seems to be yes. Providing information that is more comprehensive, consistent across the organization, relevant and timely has value.

It lets organizations communicate better, especially when units are separated by time and distance. The perspective and information presented by the EIS focuses attention on those areas that are judged to be important. An EIS can improve the productivity of individuals and groups, thus enhancing the productivity of the organization. An EIS can reduce costs by facilitating the reduction of systems (for example, systems for developing executive-quality presentation materials), staff personnel and management personnel.

IS managers who successfully develop an EIS also benefit. They are afforded the opportunity to work with leading-edge technologies. An EIS provides more visibility with top management than almost any other kind of application. A successful EIS typically results in greater management satisfaction with IS. In some firms, the system has helped IS management join the select group of senior executives who determine the strategic direction for the firm. It could happen to you.

QUESTIONS

1. Discuss the EIS failure at Genericorp. What are the reasons for the failure? What are solutions to correct the failure?
2. Discuss the five problems that can lead to EIS failure. Can these five problems lead to failure of other computer-based information systems? If so, how?

17

EIS Experiences at Marine Midland Bank, N.A.

Linda Volonino
Stephen Robinson

In 1987, Marine Midland Bank, N.A. implemented an executive information system (EIS). Initially, enthusiasm for the EIS was high because top officers were impressed by its capabilities, especially the graphics illustrating trends, its quick delivery of relevant information, and the ability to make departmental comparisons. During the first year, users were pleased with its easy and rapid access to current information and, in part, by the gimmickry. As the novelty wore off and response times increased, signs of system faltering became evident. There were reductions in system usage and several requests for paper copies of screens rather than the screens themselves. Usage reductions were symptomatic of fundamental problems stemming from an incomplete understanding of how information was used to support executive activities, insufficient integration into management processes, loss of the executive sponsor, and hardware problems. The EIS experiences of Marine Midland are not rare. They exemplify many of the challenges that EIS designers confront during the early stages of development or appear after implementation. Lessons learned from the Marine Midland Bank can help others conduct an EIS-readiness assessment and formulate a development plan to reduce risks associated with this type of application.

Previously published in *Journal of Information Technology Management,* Volume 2, Number 2, 1991. Used with permission.

MARINE'S EIS: COMPASS

Senior-level managers at Marine Midland Bank are supported by a sophisticated mainframe-based EIS called *Compass*. *Compass* is administratively set to support 100 users from the CEO to divisional vice presidents. As Table 17–1 illustrates, *Compass* represents a progression from an early rudimentary sneaker-brigade phase that began in 1985. During that phase, executive-level support was provided via PCs to approximately 25 users with data managed by corporate financial planning and analysis personnel. The sneaker brigade periodically loaded updated spreadsheets into PCs from floppy disks. After two years, Marine dropped this low-technology PC-upload system in favor of a high-technology mainframe-based system.

DEVELOPMENT PROCESS

The consideration of a mainframe-based EIS began when the CFO, Howard Phansteil, learned about Pilot Command Center EIS Software which ran on the same VM machine as their decision support system (DSS). Having the DSS already in place was important from a development viewpoint because it provided the infrastructure needed to supply information quickly and in the proper format to the EIS. The DSS serves as the central repository of summarized and aggregated data so that the EIS does not need to pull raw data from physically distributed operational systems.

Table 17–1. *Compass History*

1984	Requirements research: Asking the users what they needed.
1985	The sneaker brigade PC-based EIS is implemented.
January 1987	More requirements research: Asking the users what they wanted.
May 1987	Pilot Command Center installed. The prototype is completed, approved, and accepted enthusiastically by 10 officers.
Early 1988	Growth as Compass is rolled out to other top managers and applications are added.
Mid-1988	Executive sponsor exits Marine Midland Bank (MMB). System performance declines and some data integrity questions arise. Initial signs of system faltering become evident.
1989	Usage declines. Interviews are conducted with users to identify problems and reasons for system faltering.
1990	MMB restructured. Nonessential applications within the bank are targeted for deletion.

The CFO, Howard Phansteil, who became the senior executive sponsor, urged the development of an EIS to serve as the foundation for automated executive offices of the future using Command Center. His objective was to provide a tool to Marine's top three levels of management that would further filter data, transform it into information supportive of critical decision making, and present it in easily interpretable formats. In January 1987, a team of six developers was formed led by Charles Hubbard, vice president of management and financial information systems (MFIS), and Robert Pofsky, director of MFIS. From the outset, Charles Hubbard planned to build accountability into the system by addressing not only technical concerns such as user-friendliness and database access, but also managerial concerns such as determining information requirements of specific executives and quality and integrity issues.

Determining Information Requirements

Conducting executive interviews to determine information needs was very difficult. First there was the difficulty of getting the intended users to focus on a technology that was unfamiliar to them, with the notable exception of those who managed the technology-sensitive businesses. The uninitiated group tended to voice their frustrations with the content and currency of available data to the point where the delivery vehicle seemed irrelevant to them. The second difficulty, which was exacerbated by the first, was securing sufficient executive time for the specification of information needs. Faced with this situation, initial information requirements for *Compass* were obtained from intermediaries who reported directly to the executives. It was later realized that this approach led to too many assumptions about how information from *Compass* would be used by executives.

Addressing Quality and Integrity Issues

Issues of quality (i.e., accuracy, availability, timeliness, and completeness), security, data integrity, and credibility were addressed during the systems design. *Compass'* database resides on a single mainframe to avoid confusion. It draws its data from the corporate database and four functional areas: accounting, finance, human resource, and retail. *Compass* displays the names, addresses, telephone numbers, and dates of all sources of information on each screen so that users do not attribute data values to those who support the system. Preformated displays are stored hierarchically on PCs to facilitate drill down. The credibility of *Compass'* database is ensured by gathering information from other systems automatically to eliminate errors resulting from re-entering data. *Compass* does not create information that is not already resident in the bank's financial databases. This approach prevents the production of data that might conflict with those databases or that is unavailable to other systems. Due to the nature of much of the data and applications thought to be needed by the targeted user group of executives, it was built primarily to have weekly updates, although some types of information were to be refreshed on a monthly basis. The infrequent update schedule occurred because executives, when asked about their information needs, responded "what we have is pretty good, so do that." Eventually, this proved to be a critical mistake.

Architecture

Executives gain access to a database of applications and standard reports via a window-based graphical interface running on the PCs. Applications reside on Marine's network of IBM 3090, 308X, and 3033 mainframes linked via coaxial cable to the XTs, ATs, or PS/2 Model 50s and 60s that are located in executives' offices. Current *Compass* applications and their functions are listed in Table 17–2.

In May 1987, a prototype consisting of six applications was demonstrated for the Chairman John Petty, President Geoffrey Thompson, and eight other top officers who made up the bank's operating committee. The prototype was well received and appreciated by the 10 executives. Subsequently, they helped refine and enrich the screen reports and formats of the prototype. Information requirements were tailored and tested through prototyping and executive hands-on sessions.

Initially, *Compass* was considered a success as judged by frequency of use by the original users and requests for access by others. Even though *Compass* was intended for use by senior level executives only, demand for access led to it being extended to the controllers and administrative assistants who serve as providers and filters of information. In this way, *Compass* also began supporting those who support the executives. To manage dissemination, the system was rolled-out to others three at a time. To facilitate use of the system, users received personal training sessions and reference cards explaining the applications and navigation paths. However, as *Compass* spread beyond the top officers, response time degraded.

In mid-1988, warning signs that the EIS was no longer sustaining the initial level of executive excitement were evident. Usage rates, which were constantly monitored, dropped to the point where *Compass'* economic justification came into question by all concerned. Robert Pofsky and Stephen Robinson, who became director of *Compass* in 1988, conducted personal interviews with the users to determine what had gone wrong. During the interviews, users were asked what they liked and

Table 17-2. *EIS Applications at Marine Midland Bank*

Application	Function
Profitability analysis	Provides profitability measures for each department and comparisons of departments' performances relative to each other. Also supports business investment decisions. Reports are based on a single template that can be used to present different types of data and views of similar data. Approximately 1,500 different views are available for drill down or to access specific data for an executive's particular division.
Financial analysis	Provides eight different reports for pre-close balance sheet analysis, criticized assets, statement of condition, and reserve position to support funding decisions and post-closing adjustments.
Economic analysis	Provides a weekly interest-rate spread report together with a monthly interest-rate forecast to support marketing and funding decisions.
Consumer trend	Tracks consumer credit trends, consumer credit delinquencies, and product demand across demographic variables to support marketing programs.
Human resources	Tracks staff counts, personnel expenses, recruitment, training, turnover rates, staffing trends, salary analysis, fringe benefits as a component of total compensation, and other related statistics.
Calendar	Group calendar and personal calendar for scheduling decisions.
Outside news services	*American Banker* to support environmental and competitive awareness.

disliked, what information and applications they used and did not use, and most importantly, why. In the next section, guidelines for EIS design based on the lessons learned from their design process and interviews with the executive users are discussed.

GUIDELINES FOR EIS DESIGN

We recommend several guidelines—some of them provocative—to avoid situations that lead to system failure and to improve the potential for EIS success. As a framework for the guidelines, we present them as core issues to be resolved in the course of an EIS project.

Existence of an Information Delivery Problem

The firm contemplating the adoption of an EIS, or any new technology, should ask itself the question: Is there a real business problem the technology is designed to address? If designers cannot find and focus on an executive information problem, the technology is acquired for its own sake—a "solution to a nonexistent problem," in effect. If an EIS is introduced because the technology is fashionable, without real thought to the practical application in the existing managerial environment, it is doomed to fail.

Technological Maturity of the Organization

The technological maturity of an organization and its executives needs to be considered prior to adoption because the *degree of technology comfort* influences EIS receptiveness. Low-technology organizations like banks tend to have a management culture that is less sensitive to technology and its capabilities. Their senior management are inclined to be conservative and not encourage innovative use of IS. This type of corporate culture is less likely to embrace a progressive tool like EIS. It may be wiser, perhaps necessary, to wait until technologies are widely used and accepted in the industry prior to introducing them into such firms.

Understand the Management Process

Senior level management processes must be understood prior to design because they are not processes that can be molded around a new technology. For lower-level job functions, it is possible to enact significant alterations in activities and decision-making processes. But for executive-level functions, there is precious little latitude in the degree of change that will be tolerated. Failure to tailor the EIS to fit corner offices will result in EIS that disturbs rather than supports the dominant coalitions in an organization. Changes can be expected after EIS implementation, but if the initial version does not fit and facilitate the way executives work, they are in the position to summarily reject the EIS. This reaction leaves the designers with little or no recourse.

Incentives for Use

Given the characteristics of users, it is necessary not only to fashion the new tool around senior management's processes, but also to provide "carrots" to encourage changes in those processes. A top priority should be to get the executives hooked on the EIS by basing it on existing internal information and communication structures within the organization. Afterwards, attempts can be made to foster improvements in those structures. An approach to increasing acceptance is to ensure that the EIS is perceived as a trapping of power and prestige, especially for executives who are unfamiliar with PCs. For many senior managers, the keyboard is a hurdle and a mouse is not a solution. Executives may consider PC use belittling unless the symbolism surrounding the EIS reflects a befitting amount of status and the interface is executive-friendly. Status symbolism elevates PC usage from the realm of clerical activity to executive support.

Information Customization

Continuing efforts to further customize and refine information delivery are needed because initial information requirements differ from sustaining information requirements. Houdeshel [4] has observed that selecting executive information occurs in two phases. During the *Initial Phase,* work focuses primarily on the information that is immediately available. Frequently this focus occurs because those who are involved in EIS implementation think initially in terms of information and reports that are currently being used [2]. A consequence of this approach is an EIS whose primary value is its ability to supply users with quick access to new views of existing information. Information contents are enhanced during the *Sustaining-Enhancing Phase* with the addition of more comprehensive and customized coverage. By this time, designers have developed rapport with executive users, thus increasing their ability to customize and provide extended information coverage. Progression to the second phase of information requirements is critical because expediency as an impetus for usage is not compelling enough.

Executive Sponsorship

The executive sponsor should be someone highly visible to provide the "look what I have that you don't have" type of motivation. When an EIS is used conspicuously by such a user, it entices other executives to employ the system and initiates the cascade downward. This is essential to get and keep key people on the system. Knowing that colleagues or superiors are using an EIS to access information acts as a powerful motivator. When an EIS is used by top officers of the organization to brief themselves on a regular basis, its usage is encouraged. Executive involvement also is needed to ensure financial support for maintenance. An EIS becomes destabilized when there is a loss of executive sponsorship.

Currency of Data

Developers need to adjust their thinking to consider the new practicality and advantage that an EIS can provide to decision makers. The electronic delivery mechanism has a clear advantage over paper with regard to speed and efficiency of distribution. This is best leveraged when applied to information that is refreshed frequently. External news services, for example, are updated continuously.

Development Mentality

Developers need to be aware of the temptation to design systems, applications, screens, and so on, that they *think* will be most useful to others. Often developers develop systems that *they* want. Too frequently systems are implemented with fancy features of which the developers are proud, but for which users have little use [5]. Even worse, systems may lack some really useful features that the users need. "What is missing is the reality test—a thorough understanding of how users actually do or will perform their jobs and of the environmental conditions of the user organization" [5]. This predicament arises when executives are unwilling to participate actively in the initial EIS design phase.

Response Time

Executives are intolerant of slow response. Response times from instantaneous to 5 seconds are acceptable, but longer response times cannot support *just-in-time thinking* (i.e., being able to access information while still thinking about it). As EIS spread with the addition of new users, data sources, applications, and services, response times can increase exponentially. The hardware and technology must be able to support increased demands without impairing the system.

Exclusivity of Information

An EIS should never be used to deliver only information that is available entirely through other media. Providing something that is not available otherwise, such as hypertext, graphical displays, or data with textual annotations, is necessary to ensure that executives remain EIS users rather than return to previous information sources. Exclusivity of information can be the stimulus that fosters acceptance of the new technology, maintains the allure of the EIS, and ultimately makes executives EIS-dependent. If all information is otherwise provided, it can lead to "is this all there is" types of reactions.

Quick Turnaround

Once the decision to develop an EIS is made, a prototype should be developed and refined through quick iterations. Because information requirements change, executive information problems intensify, and users do not want to wait 12 months to see the completed system solution, it is important to provide quick turnaround of new applications or functions.

The Importance of Paper and the Feedback Process

Prior to the elimination of any conventional source of information, the potential impacts of that change have to be identified and analyzed. In most organizations, paper still constitutes an essential part of the feedback loop. People are accustomed to writing notes and comments on paper copies for their later use and, more importantly, for circulating that information to others to elicit their comments. This part of the feedback process cannot be ignored when designing a new delivery system. Screens are most suitable for graphical analysis and less so for textual and tabular presentation formats because people tend to prefer viewing and receiving tabular reports on paper.

Screen Design

Screens need to be designed to display a useful message. Screens that are too busy or have too many colors detract from their usefulness. Graphical screen design is an art form whose importance often is underestimated. In addition, designers should be conscious of the way information is presented to prevent information bias, particularly with graphics.

While following these guidelines do not guarantee EIS success, ignoring these issues can lead to system failure. In the next section, the primary factors contributing to the weaknesses of *Compass* and the proposed redesign efforts to rectify them are discussed.

COMPASS WEAKNESSES AND REVITALIZATION STRATEGY

There are several fundamental factors contributing to dampened enthusiasm and low usage rates. Foremost was the loss of the senior executive sponsor. *Compass* is not integrated thoroughly into the management process. It provides information retrieval capabilities, but does not function as a communication tool. Electronic-mail continues to run in a totally separate software environment. E-mail had existed first and there was strong resistance to change. Attempts were made to integrate *Compass* with e-mail, but it did not come out seamless and the fact that it is not remains an impediment to acceptance. Response times became inconsistent because *Compass* lacked dedicated hardware. The update schedule became unacceptable as the executives' level of expectations increased. Unreliability of certain data, which was a problem prior to the EIS, continued to be a problem because of the infrequent updates. Finally, weakness in the design, which were a result of trying to provide users with extensive flexibility in how they viewed data, made several applications too complicated for executives to use.

Addressing these impediments requires that changes be made to the EIS. Toward this end, the following changes were planned:

- Find a new sponsor who is willing to use his or her business as a pilot for testing new applications and changes to management process.
- Integrate *Compass* into the management process by targeting it as a primary communication tool.
- Eliminate information and entire applications, if necessary, to increase speed of the EIS.
- Eliminate alternative access methods to provide some degree of information exclusivity.
- Provide access to more external sources of information.
- Provide fast, easy conversion from screen to paper.
- Integrate *Compass* into e-mail to exploit the synergies that occur when the two are used together. In this way, *Compass* becomes a primary vehicle for management communication.

Enacting these changes necessitates improvements in the infrastructure surrounding the EIS, including a bigger or dedicated processor, changes to the telecommunications network configuration, as well as improvements to the MIS applications that feed the EIS and their interfaces. As the price tag for these improvements grew into the hundreds of thousands, the question had to be asked: Can the expenditure be justified for such a limited user base in a world of severely limited IS budgetary resources? Even though the EIS itself was relatively inexpensive to run, its environment was becoming prohibitively expensive because of competing demands for organizational resources.

CONCLUSION

The high visibility of EIS technology and the ever increasing expectations of the audience heighten the risks associated with systems design. Traditionally, executives have been insulated from the information systems development process. With the advent of EIS, IS departments must respond to challenging business imperatives coming directly from the executive suite. Implementors must understand what makes servicing this class of end users unique. One paramount consideration must be that the requirements of this user set are as fluid as the environment in which they work, and not subject to reengineering on the part of the implementor to fit a preconceived process model. As a result, even successful EIS applications become eternal prototypes, that never free themselves of the burden of refinement and re-validation.

An EIS that serves only to provide electronic delivery of data to the executive will most likely fail to satisfy the expectations that have become associated with the technology. Given the level of exposure involved, the price of such a failure is high. The reaction is often one of pessimism and skepticism [3]. Most executives associated with an unsuccessful EIS rarely consider reviving it in their lifetime [1].

Maintenance of the link between the functionality of the application and the mission of the organization is the function of both implementor and the executive sponsor. It is this link that sustains the life of the application, and allows the impact of the technology to grow. In the case of MMB, the link was never adequately established, and, in the absence of an executive sponsor to address the issue, the EIS never found its role in the management process. Ultimately, its contribution to the organization's mission amounted to an additional item on the list of budget reductions. The irony here is that, in other organizations in crisis, an EIS has proven to be a vital tool for helping executives cope with the challenges of adverse business conditions.

REFERENCES

1. Burkan, W. C. "Making EIS Work," *Proceedings of the Eighth International Conference on Decision Support Systems,* E. Sue Weber (Ed.), Providence, RI, The Institute of Management Science, June 1988, pp. 121–136.

2. Burkan, W. C. "Wringing Every Last Dollar from Your DSS/EIS Investment," *Proceedings of the Ninth International Conference on Decision Support Systems,* George Widmeyer (Ed.), Providence, RI, The Institute of Management Science, June 1989, pp. 5–10.

3. Clippinger, J. "Mind Over Mountain," *CIO,* January 1990, pp. 60–62.

4. Houdeshel, G. "Selecting Information for an EIS: Experiences at Lockheed-Georgia," *Proceedings of the Twenty-Third Annual Hawaii International Conference on System Sciences,* Jay F. Nunamaker (Ed.), 3, January 1990, pp. 178–185.

5. Stone, C. "Warm-Blooded Technology," *CIO,* Jan. 1990, pp. 74–78.

QUESTIONS

1. Much is being said and written about the need to redesign jobs to take advantage of the use of information technology. Is this a realistic objective

in terms of expecting senior executives to change their work processes to take full advantage of an EIS? Discuss.

2. A possible incentive to encourage EIS use among senior executives is to make it a trapping of power and prestige by restricting who has access to it. Is there a downside to this approach? Discuss.

3. Evaluate the plan to revitalize *Compass*. Are there any other plans that you would recommend?

18

Identifying the Attributes of Successful Executive Support System Implementation

David W. DeLong
John F. Rockart

The use of computers by top management, known as Executive Support Systems (ESS), is a steadily growing phenomenon, one that can have major impacts on the nature of executive work and the way organizations function. Like any new application of information technology, however, ESS is fraught with pitfalls. Technological, organizational, psychological and educational issues all contribute variables that make the implementation of Executive Support Systems difficult.

Much has changed in the four years since Rockart and Treacy first identified the executive computing phenomenon (Rockart/Treacy, 1982). At the time they found only a handful of top managers making use of the technology. But, in late 1984, a survey of 45 randomly-selected Fortune 500 companies revealed that two-thirds of them had at least one executive, and usually several, with a computer terminal on his or her desk (DeLong and Rockart, 1984). Slowly but steadily the concept of top management computer use is gaining credibility.

One of the major barriers to the spread of ESS has been our lack of understanding of how to implement these systems. Unlike more mature

David DeLong and John Rockart, "Identifying the Attributes of Successful Executive Support System Implementation," Transactions of the Sixth International Conference on Decision Support Systems, 1986. Used with permission.

I/S applications, such as transaction processing and Decision Support Systems, we have lacked sufficient experience to develop an appropriate methodology for implementing ESS. Implementation of executive systems presents problems not experienced in systems designed for middle management. The fragmented nature of executive work, the high degree of environmental uncertainty at this level of the organization, and the political ramifications of giving top management more and better information make implementing ESS a special challenge.

The purpose of this paper is to propose an outline of critical ESS implementation issues, based on a preliminary analysis of field studies done at the Sloan School's Center for Information Systems Research over the last year and a half. Our framework is based on an in depth study of almost 30 companies which have tried to install ESS. The research involved extensive field interviews with both ESS developers and users in firms representing a broad cross-section of industries. To illustrate many of the critical points in the outline we will use a case study of one computer company's attempt at implementing an Executive Support System.

One of the problems with implementing Executive Support Systems is the difficulty in defining the concept. There is still great confusion about what really constitutes such a system. What one firm might consider an Executive Support System, another will discount as "just a personal computer" or "just electronic mail." But, unless the boundaries and purpose of an ESS are carefully conceived, it is hard to implement an effective system.

Levinson (1984) defined ESS as "terminal-based computer systems designed to aid senior executives in the management of the firm." We have defined it a little more specifically (DeLong and Rockart, 1984) as "the routine use of a computer terminal by either the CEO or a member of the senior management team reporting directly to him (or her). The use may be for any management function, and these systems can be implemented at the corporate and/or divisional level."

FACTORS IN ESS IMPLEMENTATION

There is a substantial body of literature on Information Systems implementation (Markus, 1979). Unfortunately, there is no clear agreement in this literature as to the factors that are most significant in making the implementation process successful or as to the best process to follow. As we have looked at dozens of attempts at implementing ESS, there seem to be eight critical factors in assuring top management acceptance and use of a system. They are:

1. *A Committed and Informed Executive Sponsor.* There must be an executive who has both a realistic understanding of the capabilities (and

limitations) of ESS, and who really wants the system so badly that he or she is willing to put considerable time and energy into seeing that a system gets developed.

2. *An Operating Sponsor.* Because the executive sponsor usually lacks sufficient time to devote to the project, it appears very worthwhile to have an "operating sponsor" designated to manage the details of implementation from the user's side. This person is usually a trusted subordinate or an executive assistant who is well acquainted with the sponsor's work style and way of thinking.

3. *Clear Link to Business Objective(s).* The ESS must solve a business problem or meet a need that is addressed most effectively with I/S technology. There should be a clear benefit to using the technology. It must provide something that would not otherwise be available, such as graphical displays, data with textual annotations, etc. Simply getting access to the "same old data" through a terminal may not be as good as the existing paper-based system, unless there is some value added to the data.

4. *Appropriate I/S Resources.* The quality of the ESS project manager on the I/S side is most critical. This person should have not only technical knowledge, but also business knowledge and the ability to communicate effectively with senior management.

5. *Appropriate Technology.* The choice of hardware and software used has a major bearing on the acceptance or rejection of a system. One of the early barriers to executive support has been the lack of hardware and software that could meet the demands of highly-variable executive work styles and environments. Things are getting better, however, as more and more products are being designed specifically for the ESS market.

6. *Management of Data Problems.* The physical and technical ability to provide access to reliable data can be a major issue in ESS development. Aggregating, accessing and managing production data bases in a corporation with multiple divisions can be the biggest physical roadblock to ESS implementation.

7. *Management of Organizational Resistance.* Political resistance to ESS is one of the most common causes of implementation failure. An ESS alters information flows and this always has the potential to significantly shift power relationships in a company. Anticipating and managing the political ramifications of an ESS will remain a potential problem throughout the life of the system.

8. *Management of Spread and System Evolution.* An installation that is successful and used regularly by the executive sponsor will almost inevitably produce demand by peers or subordinates for access to

a similar system. Managing this process of "spread" means identifying the specific job function, technical orientation, work style, and specific information support needs of each potential user, and taking that into account when expanding the system.

It is worth pointing out that these eight factors in ESS implementation are essentially prescriptive, based on a sample of about 30 cases. Most, or all, of the eight elements appear to be present during the implementation of the systems we have studied, which have been deemed most successful by both the executive users and the developers. While we cannot prove that the factors listed above will lead to system acceptance, we do have substantial evidence that failure to consider these issues certainly increases the chances of system failure.

To illustrate these eight factors more effectively, we present a case of one computer company's attempt at implementing an Executive Support System. The case is helpful because it clearly illustrates each of the factors we have discussed above. The case has been significantly disguised.

STOWE COMPUTER CORPORATION

In the early 1980s, Stowe Computer Corporation (SCC) experienced serious financial difficulties. The firm lost $75 million in 1981 and was on the verge of bankruptcy. Survival was the fundamental issue for the company when Roger Weathers was brought in as the new president and CEO that year. Weathers' word quickly became law and decision making was very centralized in the early days of his tenure at SCC. During this period, about 8,000 people, or one-third of SCC's workforce were laid off, and the president worked on an entirely new product strategy in an effort to reverse the company's sagging performance.

SCC was a technology-driven company whose major hardware business was selling mainframes to data processing departments. The concept of end user computing was still relatively unknown in 1981, and the emerging personal computer segment of the market was not regarded as strategically important by the SCC culture.

Corporate Information Systems (CIS) was the firm's very traditional, centralized DP department. The head of CIS, Warren Zink, had no secretary and operated his department with a primary objective of keeping costs down. This strategy was traditional in CIS, and resulted in the department running the oldest mainframes and operating systems available. It often used equipment that had been returned by SCC customers for newer models. Several executives characterized SCC's internal information systems as "archaic."

Two other executives joined SCC at the same time Weathers became CEO. Phillip Dutton was named executive vice president for sales and marketing, and Richard Brohammer became chief financial officer.

One of Weathers' top priorities after he arrived was to change SCC's technology-focused culture and its product strategy, and he saw Executive Support Systems as a key part of this plan. Weathers wanted to improve productivity at the executive level, while providing a laboratory and a showplace for new product development.

In addition to these objectives, the CEO felt personally frustrated by the lack of management information that was available to him to run the company. At his previous company Weathers had a terminal on his desk with direct access to the corporate mainframe. Not only did he now feel he did not have enough information, but the CEO also believed the corporate controller was providing the existing information too slowly.

To address these problems Weathers asked one of SCC's mainframe-oriented product development groups if they could help. They proposed a 50-person project to tackle the problem of executive support. Weathers looked for another more practical alternative and found it in a small internal consulting group managed by Bill Hatfield. Hatfield, who had extensive experience as an internal auditor and as a systems developer in CIS, reported directly to CFO Richard Brohammer.

The CEO asked Hatfield and his group of senior consultants to develop an Executive Support System. Hatfield agreed and, in April 1982, he began a study of the information currently being used by SCC's senior management. When CIS Manager Warren Zink heard about the project, he urged Weathers and Brohammer to shift Hatfield's reporting relationship to CIS. Top management, however, decided that Hatfield should continue to report to the CFO.

In July 1982, Hatfield's group produced a report recommending the development of an ESS prototype with the ultimate objective of providing SCC's 500 + core managers with user-friendly access to essential performance information. Top management had put two constraints on any system Hatfield would develop. First, it had to be capable of being made secure against any unauthorized access. Second, only SCC products were to be used because of the strategic nature of the system.

Hatfield's report recognized that ESS implementation would require support staff with broad exposure to business as well as technical competence in both the hardware and software used. It estimated full implementation of the system would take 15–20 months and argued that implementation should be done by a small group which would report directly to a senior executive.

The report presented two options for implementation. The first was to identify critical performance factors based on the company's strategic objectives and to identify management information needed to support them. Hatfield explained that the problem with this option was that Weathers had only recently set out a new strategy for the company, and the consultant felt he couldn't get top management support for entering a process of again redefining what the company was about. Hatfield said he didn't consider the option "politically feasible."

The second option was to identify current planning activities and integrate the plans and actual data currently used in those activities into the ESS prototype. Hatfield's report acknowledged that the drawback of this approach was that it relied on the existing plan and actual data to design the new system, even if they were not what should be included. Despite this drawback, Hatfield's group chose this approach when the CEO approved development of the prototype. "We were looking for relatively quick results, and this was the pragmatic approach," he said.

In December 1982, Hatfield's group returned with a prototype ESS that used SCC's Lynx terminal, one of their most successful products. After a demonstration of the Lynx ESS, Weathers and CFO Richard Brohammer told Hatfield to produce the prototype and install it in the offices of the corporation's 14 senior managers. Using the Lynx terminal, the system would be networked to a mainframe at the firm's data center 20 miles from corporate headquarters.

Lynx Design and Installation

In March 1983, Malcolm Livingston was named the new manager of CIS, replacing Zink, who left the company. Livingston was chosen over Hatfield who had made a bid for the job.

Soon afterwards, in a move that Weathers did not consider significant, CFO Richard Brohammer shifted Hatfield's reporting relationship to Livingston. The CFO said he did not have enough time to manage Hatfield properly. Hatfield had a very uneasy relationship with his new boss, whom he thought ran CIS "like a batch computing bureau." Hatfield said:

> Shifting my reporting relationship to Livingston affected the visibility of my group. Livingston pretty much gave me free reign, but I lost some of the direction I had been getting from Weathers and Brohammer. I think some of the inspirational direction from Weathers started to decline because he assumed Livingston was providing it. But he wasn't.

Through the spring of 1983, Hatfield's group spent time trying to overcome technical problems with the mainframe operating system the Lynx terminals would be using. Among the problems the development group faced was a lack of applications-oriented software suitable for executives and a very unfriendly operating system, which was difficult to log into. As technical problems continued to plague the project and as the design process progressed, it became clear to Hatfield that his group was going to spend more time on technical rather than business issues.

"As a result," he said, "we didn't approach the project from a full understanding of how the system would be used. Rather our purpose was just to help share more information among the executives."

But even the task of providing information proved more difficult than expected. Hatfield had a very difficult time getting the corporate controller to release information for the system. "We represented a challenge to the corporate staffs, and the controller was upset at the idea of the CFO coming to us for information," Hatfield said.

The controller's primary argument for not releasing information for the Lynx system was security. His concerns, however, were not unjustified. SCC had gone through a very embarrassing experience several years previous when some of the company's confidential financial information inexplicably had appeared in a local newspaper. That experience made the finance department extremely cautious about releasing data to anyone.

By the summer of 1983, Lynx terminals had been installed on the desks of 13 senior executives. (The vice president of personnel refused to allow one in his office, contending he had no use for it.) Hatfield and his three consultants showed each executive the capabilities on the system and then asked them how they would like to use it. The system had a menu with five applications directly available, including corporate performance summaries and modeling. Technical problems, however, continued to make the software difficult to learn and use. For example, different packages required different "log off" procedures and data was outdated. As a result, the Lynx system was all but ignored by executives shortly after it was introduced, even though Hatfield's group continued to try to encourage its use for some time. Marketing EVP Phillip Dutton described his reaction to SCC's first ESS:

> Initially, it was going to be a product that we could network together and put up a financial data base, so I could get into it and look at instantaneous trends, results, etc. But the LAN didn't work very well and it kept breaking down, so the system wasn't up a lot. Also, because it was a special project, the system was always late getting the data loaded onto it, so the data was always out of date. After finding the system out of date or broken a few times, then I just began referring back to the printed reports.

> It was also a terrible job to get through the security system. Security was a major issue because the controller was fanatical about it. He made damn sure that the system went through the nth level of security. But, in the end, it would take the normal ad hoc user ten minutes to get through the security section.

In the end, there was a lot of interest but no direct use by the executives themselves, conceded Hatfield. To get at a particular "what if," the executives would actually get a staff member to operate the terminal for them.

Reorganization

In May 1983, Weathers began a major reorganization within SCC. The product development and marketing people were integrated into 15 product centers each with a product line or industry focus, such as mainframes, insurance industry, or the federal government. The product centers defined markets and developed the products/services to be brought to those markets and sold by the geographically organized sales units.

The Management Support Product Center (MSPC) was created to develop and market products related to DSS/ESS, knowledge engineering, and business graphics. MSPC was headed by Walter Edison.

Early Development of PC-based ESS

For some time, Weathers had been pressing MSPC management to get an ESS product into the marketplace, and simultaneously, he and Brohammer, the CFO, were still looking for something to support SCC executives. CIS remained responsible for implementing any internal ESS, but they had to rely on the product centers to do the actual hardware and software development for their systems, which would also ultimately be sold as products in the external marketplace.

Meanwhile, product developers in MSPC felt unusual pressure to deliver something through CIS because Weathers had made it clear he wanted a system on his desk "tomorrow." It was decided that the capabilities of the new ESS would be based on external market research done previously by MSPC. No interviews were done inside SCC. Arthur Frost, who was in charge of ESS product development for MSPC, explained:

> The key lesson from the research was the need for relevance to the executive's job. Provided you gave them what they needed, a surprising number of executives were prepared to deal with complex interfaces. We also concluded that executives wanted access to many capabilities at once, and the ability to switch tasks and information sources quickly. This meant we had to put a lot of intelligence on their desks. Also, we were up against a very short time scale because Weathers had given us a deadline, which meant we couldn't design something new. We had to use existing equipment.

Hatfield's Lynx system was not ready to market and lacked the local processing capabilities MSPC wanted, so Frost began looking outside to see what high quality graphics terminal could be brought into SCC. The decision was made to use an intelligent color monitor built by a Japanese company, which could be linked to SCC's own recently-developed personal computer (PC). The PC offered more local processing power than the Lynx for individual applications, and using the Japanese-built monitor would give SCC the chance to market its first color graphics terminal.

Frost conceded that, from the start of the PC development project, things didn't move as fast as expected. But, because of the continuing pressure from Weathers, MSPC introduced a prototype of the ESS product to top management in October 1983. The developers had adapted some of the software technology from the Lynx system and created a generalized menu system that could be personalized for individual users. Walter Edison, head of the Management Support Product Center, introduced the PC system prototype of what MSPC planned to market as DSS for executives. The system included a graphics package, called "Giraffix," which was designed to create graphics on the PC once data was downloaded from the mainframe.

Decision Support Group "Deskilled"

Since Hatfield's team of consultants had been reassigned to CIS, they had become known as the Decision Support Group (DSG). Their primary responsibility continued to be encouraging and supporting top management computer use. By August 1983, Hatfield had begun to take on broader responsibilities within CIS, so he brought in Jill McMahon to manage the Decision Support Group. McMahon, whose primary strengths were in technical areas, was told the DSG's target population was the top 20 executives. Virtually no progress was made, however, in developing Lynx use among executives between July and October, in part because of communication problems that existed in trying to operate the ESS on a remote mainframe in the corporate data center. The system seemed to be "gathering dust" on most executive's desks.

In November, DSG was set up with access to half of a new mainframe at corporate headquarters in anticipation of its hardware needs for supporting top management in the future. But other things were happening to DSG that reduced its ability to support SCC executives. "Weathers wanted to deskill DSG activities so the group could be run by only four junior people," said Hatfield.

He explained that until McMahon took over the DSG in August there had been three senior consultants involved in the ESS activities who were used to dealing with top management. While three senior people could support more executives, Hatfield said that McMahon, with her staffing now restricted to junior people, could not cope with supporting more than a couple of top managers. By late 1983, DSG was staffed with two analysts and two programmers.

"We had junior people trying to provide support to Weathers. They just couldn't do it," said Hatfield. "In retrospect, I leaned too far on technical expertise."

PC System Development

Weathers was upset when the MSPC had not delivered its new PC-based executive support system by early 1984. As a result, CFO Richard Brohammer met in early February with CIS Manager Malcolm Livingston, Hatfield and McMahon to discuss the problem and make sure everything possible was being done to get the product out. At the meeting, Brohammer expressed doubts that Walter Edison's product center was going to be able to develop the PC-based ESS software on schedule, despite pressure from Weathers.

Thus some decisions were made. Brohammer told the CIS people that he wanted a new ESS terminal implemented for the top three people in SCC (Weathers, Brohammer and Dutton), and the CFO would decide what would be on the system. Brohammer then looked at what they could deliver in short order. He reviewed the original Lynx menu and said he wanted corporate performance summaries, inter-company comparisons, the five year planning model, and some product line profitability statements in the PC-based system.

Marketing EVP Phillip Dutton offered this perspective on Brohammer's decision to get involved in the ESS development:

> Primarily, I think, he wanted to get a system that would work and deliver things that he needed and not have all these different folks involved. He was primarily concentrating on the financial reporting parts of the system that he needed.

> At that stage we'd had a lot of non-progress, so Brohammer picked up the baton to get some system out so we could get at our own data and also use it to show customers what innovative people we were.

Hatfield explained the design problems that remained for CIS and the product centers:

> Despite Brohammer's plans and the summer installation deadline, as of February, the PC was not yet actually available, and the graphics, LAN, and applications software was still in development. None had been field tested or released as products. Thus, we were working to a time scale which effectively said, 'We expect to get software at X point and, meanwhile, the graphics are being developed and we hope the two will work together.'

After the meeting with Brohammer made it clear the PC project was top priority, a series of weekly meetings were set up between DSG people in CIS and those in the product centers involved with PC/ESS development. The weekly meetings went on until July but, despite the pressure from top management, the project slipped almost a month behind schedule because the software was still not available, said Hatfield.

Arthur Frost, ESS project manager for MSPC, offered this perspective on the process:

> Not only did lots of technical problems arise in the meetings with CIS, but personality clashes among those involved added to the tension. We were shouting at each other alot.

> The people from CIS were looking after senior management and their views of what the system should do were often at variance with our views. At the weekly meetings it became clear that SCC's top executives were very different individuals with different requirements and needs attempting to be satisfied with a single product. Weathers was happy with a keyboard, easily understood it, and could do complex things on the system. Brohammer expected that when the system was switched on it would automatically show yesterday's sales results. Other executives were more normal and as casual users needed something that was simple and clearly labelled.

In July 1984, a meeting was held to demonstrate the progress made on the PC-based ESS. Among those attending were Livingston, Hatfield, Brohammer, Edison, and a consultant who had been brought in to help keep the ESS project on track. Weathers showed up at the meeting unexpectedly.

McMahon demonstrated how the PC could do modeling on the mainframe and produce graphics on the PC. Weathers watched the demo and told Edison, whose group had developed the software, that the PC was too slow in generating graphics.

The consultant had a similar reaction. "It was painfully slow and too awkward to use. Too many keystrokes were needed. If I had work to do, I couldn't work at that speed," he said.

Despite his criticism of the PC's slowness, Weathers was encouraging. "OK, you've got something there. Now what are you going to do with it?" he asked. "I want to spread this around to the executive staff, and we should be using it in the product centers to improve their access to management information." Weathers then turned to Livingston and asked, "How many are you proposing to install this year?"

The CIS manager hesitated for a moment and then responded, "We've got a budget for 40."

Thus it was agreed that CIS would install 40 PCs—20 in the corporate offices and 20 among executives in the product centers—as soon as possible. This became known as the "40 PC project."

Dutton, sales and marketing EVP, offered this view of the decision to implement 40 PCs for executives: "Weathers made an emotional decision that we had to get PCs on people's desks. It was one of those gut feels. Get people more involved in what sits on their desks, then worry about what they're going to use it for."

Shortly after the "40 PC project" was initiated a major change hit SCC. The company merged with Electronics International Group (EIG), a large multi-national corporation. This led to a top management shakeup. Weathers became chairman of the SCC subsidiary and a senior executive in EIG. In September 1984, EVP Phillip Dutton became president of SCC. Shortly afterwards, Brohammer left the company and a new CFO was named.

PC Installation

PCs were installed in the offices (and some homes) of SCC's executives during the fall of 1984. Use of the technology by top management varied significantly, and depended a great deal on each manager's particular function and work style.

Weathers commented on his own experience and needs for computer support as SCC's chairman:

> So far they have been unable to provide me with support where I need it, such as at home. CIS came out with a bunch of junk which was so awful I sent it back. It was a PC with a modem, but it covered the whole desk.
>
> What I need primarily is facsimile, electronic mail, voice mail, and all the instant messaging capabilities; also, competitive assessment analysis, industry news, and, lastly, financial information about our own activities. I think that's the difference between senior people who tend to look at an industry from a strategic overview and line managers who are deeply engrossed in their own financial activities.

When CIS installed Dutton's PC, the new president found the experience not unlike the one he had with the Lynx system earlier.

> Guys came up and I had about two 45 minute training sessions. That was adequate to get going, but getting past the security checks was still a problem, although it was easier than with the Lynx. More important, the data was not useful enough for me to really want to spend a lot of time getting into the system. It was still often a month out of date.
>
> We were putting more management effort into that so-called Decision Support System than we were on trying to figure out how we could get our data faster, regardless of what format it was in. We were busy looking at the graphics and how to get it up onto screens, and how the LAN system worked, when, in fact, all the data we were looking at was three weeks out of date.

So, our priorities were in the wrong place. What we should have been doing is spending all of our management effort making sure that we could do the consolidations in two days, and then figure out how to use it.

The primary function of the vice president for technology planning is to make decisions about R&D investments. He commented on his experience with the PC-based ESS:

My hackles were up even before the system arrived. There was no way I was going to have a system someone told me I must have. I publicly made a point of how hard it was to turn on and to get the system up, and the response time was pretty awful. Also there were some real problems with the command structure. The screen would say press button X to do something when really you were supposed to press button Y.

Early on I made a nuisance of myself saying I don't want a package. Instead, I said I wanted an R&D project monitoring system, but CIS couldn't make the system flexible in that way. They tried to create a single package everyone would use, but they forgot that we all wanted to do something different. The fact that getting new capabilities took six months was too long.

Besides, the bulk of my job is communication, not analysis. My real need is for communications support between me and my staff. Very little information for decision making in my job is financially based. Most of the information I use is highly subjective, and at least 50 percent of it is external. So, basically, my systems needs are for electronic mail, the ability to build customized systems, and for visibility into some of our existing operational systems.

The vice president of SCC's Office Systems Division is responsible for five product centers, including the PC product center. He said he spends half his time managing the product centers and the other half on corporate business not directly concerned with the division. He described his experience as follows:

I have a double interest in the PC. It is one of my products and I want to use it for corporate I/S. My PC is at home, though, because I'm never in the office. When I said I wanted it at home that created a problem. I have an encrypting modem which is expensive and difficult to set up, but that's because the controller wouldn't allow data out of the mainframe without encrypting it.

The main thing I use it for is typing longer documents, such as a talk or a strategy paper. I print it at home and get it rekeyed at the office because I can't squirt it into electronic mail. I've got electronic mail, but it's extremely unfriendly.

I also use the PC to go into the corporate data bases to look at company and unit results. But I do this out of a sense of duty. I find the system clumsy to get into. You need three different passwords. But the real problem is there is nothing new in the data base. Corporate finance doesn't want to put anything in the data base until it has been presented at the monthly forecast meeting. As a result, they don't put data in until it's too old to be useful, so I never learn anything new from the system. Access to paper reports is faster.

I spend 70 percent of my time in reviews and meetings, and I'm in my office less than 10 percent of the time. When I do come in it is for a stack of tightly processed discussions. My time is tightly programmed. I do about 18 hours of reading a week, but almost always out of the office. For most of the stuff I read I attach a note with the action to be taken. Electronic mail wouldn't work for this.

Logistics is critical. Anything I can do to save time will give me more time for planning. Otherwise, I'm rushing from one pile of paper to another and from meeting to meeting.

CIS continued to install ESS applications on the PCs sitting on the desks of SCC's top managers through December 1984. On January 8, 1985, almost three years after Weathers had first asked Hatfield to implement an ESS, President Phillip Dutton sent a memo to CIS manager Malcolm Livingston and MSPC manager Walter Edison. These were the two people currently responsible for SCC's Executive Support Systems. Dutton wrote:

I have a Decision Support System hooked up in my office which I can assure you I never use . . . If I weren't such an optimist, I would despair. Please let me know when I can have something which is useful to me in my office.

STOWE COMPUTER CORP. AND LESSONS IN ESS IMPLEMENTATION

Let us look at Stowe Computer Corporation's experience in light of the eight factors in ESS implementation outlined earlier. How does the Stowe case illustrate the issues identified?

1. A Committed and Informed Executive Sponsor

In our research, rarely did we find an ESS being used by executives that had been initiated solely by the information systems department. Executive users must want and ask for the system themselves. There are three characteristics the executive sponsor must have. First, he or she must be committed to putting time and energy into the ESS project. Second, the sponsor's expectations of what is possible for the system must be in line with the physical limitations of the technology and data access.

Finally, the sponsor should have a realistic understanding of the implementation process itself and what the organization must go through to develop an effective ESS. The executive must: (1) understand the human and financial resources needed for the project; (2) recognize the need for an operational sponsor; (3) anticipate the organizational impacts of the system; and (4) anticipate and deal with political resistance to the system's perceived impacts.

SCC's executive support project clearly had a sponsor in CEO Roger Weathers. Weathers wanted the system and was willing to spend time seeing that it was developed. But it was also important for the executive sponsor to have a realistic expectation of both the ultimate capabilities of the system and the organizational issues surrounding the implementation process. Weathers seemed to lack both of these, although, in his defense, a desire to have the firm learn about the implementation process was one of the reasons he encouraged the ESS projects in the first place. Nevertheless, the predictable shortcomings of an ESS developed in this setting created frustration and disillusionment for the chief executive.

2. An Operating Sponsor

The task of managing ESS development is frequently, but not always, delegated to a trusted subordinate who becomes the "operating sponsor" (Levinson, 1984). This sponsor ideally is a person who can communicate easily with both the executive user and the ESS designers. He or she serves as a go-between helping to match business needs with technological capabilities. Quite often, where the CEO is the executive, or initiating, sponsor, the task of operating sponsor often falls to the CFO or the controller.

In the SCC case, the CFO assumed the role of operating sponsor at times, particularly with the PC project. Before that, however, he had delegated away the operating sponsor's role when he shifted Bill Hatfield's reporting relationship to the CIS manager. When that happened, the input Hatfield received from top management was diminished because he was reporting to the CIS manager, not the CFO, and his project came to be viewed as "just another DP function."

In general, the SCC case is an example of a lack of clarity about sponsor's roles and shows the confusion that can arise when the role of operating sponsor is not made explicit and is filled only intermittently.

3. Clear Link to Business Objective(s)

The irony of ESS is that often executives *demand* systems on what seems like such short notice that defining the business objective of a system is probably the most frequently ignored activity in the implementation process. It is assumed the executive is too impatient to go through such analysis, the ESS developers are too afraid to ask for such input, or the developers don't consider it important to identify a link between specific business needs and the technology. As a result, the systems usually do not take full advantage of the unique benefits the technology could provide, such as faster access to data or more effective communications.

Weathers identified a need for the system on several levels: (1) to increase his own access to information; (2) to improve executive productivity; and (3) to develop an ESS product for the marketplace. Not only are these multiple objectives in conflict with each other, but they are also too vague to be useful in linking the technology to internal business problems. In this case, Weathers seemed most concerned about getting an ESS product to the marketplace, while SCC's CFO Richard Brohammer was pushing CIS for a system that would meet the needs of his finance function. Thus, the ESS developers were getting mixed signals from the initiating sponsor, Weathers, and Brohammer, who at times acted as the operating sponsor.

In the case of the Lynx ESS, Hatfield actually decided the system's capabilities because he found it so difficult to get executive input. He conceded that his group didn't actually know what the system would be used for. Their only objective was to help executives share information better. Unfortunately, this was not an important business objective for top management. For the PC-based ESS project, the CFO dictated the applications. In this case, the only business objectives the CFO had in mind were those of his finance function, to the dismay of other executives.

A result of the failure to explicitly link the technology to business objectives in both situations was that neither system met the needs of the executives who were given terminals. Weathers, for example, made it clear that his needs were primarily in the communications area, as did the vice president of Technology Planning. Yet, the electronic mail package on the PC system was universally criticized by the executives as terribly unfriendly and totally unusable.

4. Appropriate I/S Resources

Weathers chose Bill Hatfield's small team of experienced consultants to implement an ESS over the monolithic, mainframe-oriented product development group that wanted to make it a 50-person project. In many ways, Hatfield was the ideal person to fill the critical role as ESS project manager on the I/S side. Not only had he been a systems developer in CIS, but he also had extensive business experience managing the firm's internal audit group. He was a good communicator and was viewed as very professional by SCC executives. One drawback was that he never had a good relationship with the head of CIS.

Hatfield's decision to bring in someone to replace him in running the Decision Support Group who had a technical rather than a business orientation was an unfortunate move. Hatfield's ability to understand business executives and to communicate with them was lost. This shift to a more technical orientation happened as Weathers was reportedly trying to "deskill" DSG. Reducing the quality of the support staff from senior consultants with a business orientation to more technically-oriented junior analysts unable to relate to top management was a costly mistake.

It is also worth noting that Hatfield's group existed outside the mainstream operations of CIS, reporting instead directly to the CFO. Our research has shown this to be not an unusual pattern. Often, a traditional I/S department just doesn't have the flexible, fast moving, sophisticated mindset needed to support executive users. ESS development teams are often composed of people like Hatfield who come from the finance department and who also have I/S experience. Being outside, or on the fringe of the I/S department, however, can make it very difficult for ESS developers to get access to I/S resources because of political infighting.

5. Appropriate Technology

Although the ESS developers had to use SCC's own products, it is not unusual for companies to have their ESS hardware choices predetermined because one vendor dominates the firm already. This explains, in part, the overwhelming predominance of IBM PCs that were found on executives' desks in our 1984 study of 45 Fortune 500 companies (DeLong/Rockart).

The major technology decisions are usually in the software area, and the common problems with existing software are evident in the SCC case:

- They can't be integrated easily.
- They don't allow multi-tasking.
- Response time is too slow (sometimes a hardware problem).
- Complex command structures make them hard to learn and remember.
- Extensive menus make the software easier to learn, but difficult to use quickly once they are mastered.

Often the capabilities of existing software—rather than user needs—determine the applications built into an ESS. What is presented to the user is, too often, crammed into what the software can deliver. Attempts to tailor a system to specific user needs often create a dilemma for developers. They are caught between users who want systems today and the realities of slow moving software development projects.

Response time is another common technology problem that must be anticipated. Our research shows that executives simply will not use systems when response time is more than a couple of seconds. The paradox is that when a system is initially successful and response time is good, more users inevitably want to get on the system. As a result, response time, unless it is well managed, can deteriorate and badly undermine the value of the system.

Compatibility with existing systems is yet another issue, and like the problems above, it too surfaced in the SCC case. Note that the SCC executives couldn't communicate with their secretaries' terminals. This is a frequent problem and one that needs consideration before technology choices are made because the executive-secretary link is critical.

6. Management of Data Problems

Anticipating data management problems was clearly not done in the SCC case, and it becomes evident in the comments of Dutton and the vice president of the Office Systems Division. Dutton pointed out that the fundamental problem was not the ESS design, but the fact that it took the company three weeks to close its books. He believed management effort would have been better spent trying to improve the firm's consolidation system, instead of trying to develop an ESS.

The office systems division vp raised another data management problem. Corporate finance wouldn't release data for the ESS until it had been presented at the monthly review meeting. This meant the data was effectively out of date by the time it got on the system. This raised an important question. At SCC, who owned the financial data—corporate finance or the company?

ESS implementation frequently raises questions of data ownership. To be of value, an ESS must provide data faster than traditional paper-based systems, but that means changing existing information flows and, thus, the distribution of power.

7. Management of Organizational Resistance

Executive Support Systems, to be effective, must change information flows, improving the timeliness, the type, and the quality of the information users receive. Shifting information flows inevitably means threatening the distribution of power in an organization. This potential power shift will almost always be met by political resistance. There are several examples of political resistance in the SCC case.

CIS management didn't like Hatfield's ESS development team operating outside of their department, and they continually lobbied the CFO to shift that reporting relationship. Finally, Brohammer agreed, and when Hatfield's group was reassigned to CIS, they lost a significant amount of the prestige they had in reporting directly to the CFO.

Hatfield found it very difficult to get the corporate controller to release financial data for use in the ESS. The controller's justification was security concerns, but he also recognized that Hatfield's system threatened to replace him as top management's primary source of financial information. Hatfield recognized that his group's system was a threat to the corporate staffs. And he said that, even if the technical problems with Lynx had all been solved, the staff groups would never have allowed his group to gain significant power. The ESS was too threatening to them. But this potential power struggle never surfaced because of the technical failures of the system.

Data security was a particularly sensitive issue at SCC because of problems the company had experienced previously. It is sometimes hard, however, to separate when security concerns are the real reason a manager resists providing information, and when they are just a smokescreen for political resistance, most specifically in response to the fear of losing power. Security is a much talked about issue during the implementation process, and is often used as a reason for not providing executive access to certain information through ESS. In practice, however, when executives at SCC were given the option of protecting their data by requiring passwords for access, they rarely used these optional security measures. "Security turned out to be mostly an emotional issue," said one product center manager.

Finally, one of the best examples of resistance came from the technology planning vp who outwardly rejected the PC-based ESS because he felt it had been imposed on him by someone else (the CFO).

8. Manage Spread and System Evolution

When an ESS is used by the executive sponsor, often the user's subordinates and some of his or her peers will also ask to be put on the system immediately. This is particularly true when the system contains information that reflects on the subordinates' performance. An effective system is also likely to result in a rapid increase in demand for new capabilities, as executives begin to understand how the technology can be applied to their work.

Both of these factors—spread and evolution—must be managed carefully. One important step is to identify explicitly who will be using the system and take into account their technical orientations, work styles, and job functions.

Brohammer's decision to design the PC-based ESS is a dramatic example of how a system can be implicitly designed for one executive when it is really intended to be used by a range of top managers. The response of the technology planning vp to the PC system best illustrates this problem. Not only was he defensive about being told to use a system designed by and for somebody else, but the PC didn't even begin to address his needs for communication support and an R&D project monitoring system.

When trying to identify who the users of an ESS actually will be, an important consideration is whether installation and use of terminals is voluntary or mandatory. Some chief executives, like Weathers, will just insist that all of their vice presidents have terminals on their desks. Given the inherent technical, data, application, and support shortcomings of the pioneering ESS's today, this is an unworkable managerial demand, except in the most bureaucratic of organizations. Executives with a bias against computer support quickly find multiple reasons to doubt the system's effectiveness and will soon ignore it. Use of the system must be voluntary.

The ESS development process at SCC identified different work styles and technical orientations that were never acknowledged in the system design itself. For example, both the technology planning vp and the vp of the office systems division spent very little time in their offices and did a great deal of administrative work at home. It is unrealistic to expect an executive who is rarely in his or her office to make significant use of an ESS, unless he or she has a terminal at home. In the SCC case, there was a clear correlation between amount of time spent in the office and the use of the ESS. All those executives who made significant use of computers at the office, spent more than 50 percent of their time there.

Another work style question concerns how an individual likes to absorb information. Some executives prefer looking at numbers, while others much prefer graphic presentations. Ironically, SCC's developers were convinced by their external market research that graphics were what executives wanted. But, at SCC, many top managers said they actually considered graphics unimportant, and they preferred getting information in numerical formats.

Technical orientation is a factor that also should be explicitly identified. Members of the design team assumed Weathers was very comfortable with a terminal and was willing to work with complex command structures. Brohammer, on the other hand, only wanted to hit one or two keys to get last month's sales report. Understanding these different technical orientations is essential when managing the spread of an ESS.

CONCLUSION

This paper has been an attempt to outline the critical ESS implementation issues identified in our field studies. Research in this area is difficult because there are a large number of potential variables and only a small number of success stories in ESS implementation. But, as the case of SCC indicates, there is much to be learned from some of the failures. And, we believe, it is useful to expose our current conclusions about ESS implementation to encourage further discussion.

REFERENCES

1. DeLong, David W., and Rockart, John F. "A Survey of Current Trends in the Use of Executive Support Systems," CISR Working Paper #121, Center for Information Systems Research, Sloan School of Management, (Cambridge, MA:) November 1984.

2. Levinson, Eliot "The Implementation of Executive Support Systems," CISR Working Paper #119, Center for Information Systems Research, Sloan School of Management, (Cambridge, MA: MIT) October 1984.

3. Markus, M. Lynne "Understanding Information Use in Organizations: A Theoretical Explanation," unpublished dissertation, Case Western Reserve University, August 1979.

4. Rockart, John F., and Treacy, Michael E. "The CEO Goes On-Line," *Harvard Business Review*, January-February 1982.

QUESTIONS

1. What are the eight factors critical to successful ESS implementation?
2. Discuss each of the eight factors in the context of Stowe Computer Corporation.

19

How Rockwell Launched Its EIS

David A. Armstrong

Having spent sizable sums of money to automate the grass roots operations of their companies, executives are now beginning to look for ways to bring automation to Mahogany Row. A good way to do so is through an executive information system (EIS). Such a movement is under way at the El Segundo, Calif.-based North American Aircraft (NAA) Division of Rockwell International Corp.

One of Rockwell's foremost reasons for adopting an EIS is to better respond to the changing climate in which it does business. As the prime contractor of the B-1B Air Force bomber, NAA is one of the major aerospace companies being affected by the downturn in defense spending. The division has seen this business dwindle as the B-1B production program comes to a close. Consequently, NAA is making major changes in its work force structure, its cost management and even in its physical facilities. The demands for relevant executive information to help manage these changes have prompted the move to EIS.

The division's executive council members, for example, found themselves spending several hours each month in a cost performance presentation. As described by Art Goudreault, vice president of material and one of the early proponents of EIS, the council would typically wade through pages of detailed cost and budget reports for each organization in the division. A question would surface occasionally, and a council member would be charged with coming up with a solution. Yet for every page that required action, there were many pages in the briefing that did not.

Previously published in *Datamation*, March 1, 1990. © 1990 by Cahners/Ziff Publishing Associates, L.P. Used with permission.

Goudreault wanted to know if there was some way to spend less time looking for problems and more time solving them. He approached Nick Corritori, director of the information systems department, and asked for help.

At about this time, a decision was made to move the executives from offices located in a centralized building to facilities located closer to their departments. The division president, John Pierro, then faced the problem of how to communicate with VPs who were no longer down the hall. Pierro's solution was to direct IS to equip each executive's office with a personal computer connected to a network with electronic mail capabilities.

The office automation and telecommunications groups began developing a plan to automate the executive suites. Their efforts resulted in an executive network based on a Digital Equipment Corp. MicroVAX 3100 hub and a Digital PC LAN 3100 server. The MicroVAX 3100 runs the electronic mail and calendaring systems. The 3100 server handles network communications among the 14 executive and secretarial workstations. A Systems Network Architecture gateway connects the PCs to IBM mainframe applications such as the Information Management System (IMS) database management system.

The workstations consist of IBM-compatible 386 PCs running MS-DOS, VGA color monitors, ink jet color printers for the executives and laser printers for the secretaries. Other services planned include electronic fax, scanners and connection to external news services such as Dow Jones News/Retrieval. With plans for the network in place, a question naturally followed: What else should we do with these machines besides write letters? The answer: EIS.

GOALS OF EIS

Pierro and Goudreault were joined by Howard Chambers, vice president and program manager of the B-1B program, as the primary sponsors of the EIS. They intuitively sensed the value of the EIS and its impact on the division. Pierro saw EIS as a tool to provide him and his VPs with information that would lead to better and faster decision making. It could also be used as a feedback monitor to gauge how effectively decisions were being implemented.

To accomplish these objectives, Pierro established several guidelines for those of us in IS to follow in developing the system.

Derived Information

The computer is great at storing mountains of data. But where in those mountains are the granules on which the executives should focus? Pierro coined the term "derived information" to describe mechanisms that tell not only what is wrong but why. The concept of derived information became the philosophical backbone of the EIS.

Anticipating Questions

The EIS must be more than an expensive page turner for static reports. It must have features that make it useful as an investigative tool. Executives, however, cannot always anticipate what they will need to know about a subject before they see it. And executive users cannot wait for IS to process a programming request just to create a simple report or sort a file.

Accordingly, we anticipated three requirements right away: a database, drill-down functions and what-if capabilities. Storing the data for the EIS in a relational database to a sufficient depth of detail is essential to anticipating unexpressed requirements for data. Drill-down refers to the ability to navigate through a hierarchy of increasingly finer levels of detail in the database. As the name implies, what-if describes tools for trend analysis and answering ad hoc queries.

Soft Data

Simply seeing numbers and graphs is not enough. To make effective decisions, executives need explanations and analysis information. For example, there may be pertinent background information on a manufacturing problem that is not portrayed by graphs or charts. The EIS must have a way to tie soft data to the hard facts.

Standards and Procedures

The EIS database should become the single source of information for executives so that they no longer receive conflicting reports based on different sets of data. When properly implemented, the EIS enforces a standard view of information where, for example, each executive sees the same departmental head-count charts with data taken directly from operational systems.

The information portrayed by the EIS must be of a high quality or it is of no use. So, the data must be accurate, timely, comprehensive and useful. Mechanisms must be built into the system to ensure these attributes.

Responsiveness

Many IS projects take too long to develop. Business problems are often short-lived moving targets. EIS development must be fast enough to deliver an application while it is still useful. Unlike traditional IS projects,

Rockwell's EIS Implementation Time Line

April 1989—Electronic cost performance briefing system is proposed.

May 1989—Executive e-mail network proposed. IS develops first EIS PC prototype. IS drafts network design. Division president approves network and EIS projects, sets budget and deadline.

June 1989—IS evaluates EIS software vendors and network component vendors.

July 1989—Command Center selected for EIS development. Digital selected as network vendor.

August 1989—Command Center installed and tested. Executive steering committee appointed to define EIS application subjects and formats.

September 1989—Executive network hardware arrives. Development team forms, and Command Center training for programmers begins. Executive steering committee writes first draft of EIS requirements specification. Developers begin first EIS prototypes. Executives move to new offices. Workstations and network installed. Secretarial training begins.

October 1989—Network and workstations operational. Six prototype applications available for executive review. Executive training begins.

December 1989—Five applications completed with live data. Executive steering committee refines EIS requirements. President appoints EIS program coordinator and accepts no more paper mail from VPs. Development of five new applications begins.

January 1990—EIS developers refine development methodology. Application development schedule established. Three more applications completed with live data. Executive conference room outfitted for EIS briefings.

where development is measured in man-months, EIS applications have to be built in a few weeks or even days.

Benefits

The bottom line on EIS is truly the fiscal bottom line. To simply make data more accessible is not the goal. Data are already accessible in a plethora of reports. Nor is the goal to enable executives to read reports faster. The system must produce dollar benefits that are reflected in financial statements.

Ultimately, there were two fundamental goals for our EIS: make the system simple enough so the executives *can* use their machines, and convert the cost performance reports from paper to electronic display so that executives *have* to use their machines.

Before EIS, only two of the 14 executives at NAA had office computers. These two used them mostly for limited inquiry transactions and to request reports. Persuading more of the executives to accept the PCs was a challenge that required some salesmanship. The conversion for some has been, and continues to be, a slow process.

In April 1989, we began to prototype our EIS by experimenting with technology already available in the department, such as PC graphics, mouse drivers and pop-up menus. Using these tools, we developed a crude prototype of the written cost performance briefing on a PC. When we showed it to the executives, we learned two important lessons. First, they wanted more graphics and fewer numbers. And second, what they had in mind was access to far more information than what was in the cost performance reports.

THE RIGHT PROTOTYPE

We found a sophisticated prototype package, called RediMaster, by American Information Systems Inc. of Wellsboro, PA. This program allowed us to do away with pop-up menus and introduce a more flexible graphical user interface. One of the important features of the interface is "hot buttons." A hot button is an area of the screen that accepts input from a mouse. Using RediMaster, we created another version of the cost performance briefing and learned that we were getting closer to what the executives wanted in terms of presentation and ease of use.

At this point, creating a strictly PC-based EIS posed some developmental and logistical challenges. How could we distribute growing mountains of data to the workstations and make sure they were always current? How could we protect the data once they get to the PC? To be acceptable, the EIS had to conform not only to executive needs but to sound IS standards.

ADDRESSING IS NEEDS

From what we learned from the prototypes and discussions with executives, we established a set of requirements for choosing an appropriate EIS technology from an IS point of view. These requirements addressed the needs for security, capacity for growth, data integrity, connectivity and low maintenance.

Security of information is important to any business. To an aerospace manufacturing and government contractor, it is critical. Our EIS technology had to provide for protecting executive information.

To be viable over the long term, any EIS must also be able to grow. In the beginning, we figured our EIS database would be small. However, we realized that it potentially could grow to hundreds of megabytes in order to support the drill-down and ad hoc features. There is no simple way to predict growth unless the number, type and size of applications can be predicted. Because of the potential for explosive growth, the technology must be able to support any conceivable growth pattern without significantly increasing the operations and maintenance burdens of the IS staff.

A key to having accurate information in the system is data integrity. This includes mechanisms for ensuring that data cannot be accidentally or intentionally tampered with or that data cannot be lost.

Connectivity refers to users' ability to access all of the functions and data they need at their workstations, regardless of where they may reside. The total executive network at NAA was designed to include a local area network and gateways to the corporate IBM wide area

---

Catering to Executive Needs

What makes an executive information system (EIS) suitable for executive use? After implementing an EIS at Rockwell International Corp., the development team found that four criteria must be met.

First, the displays must be graphic. Graphs and charts are the executives' principal methods for turning data into information. Identifying features and functions on screen with icons and colors makes the screens easier to understand.

Second, the technology should minimize use of the keyboard. As much as possible, executives should not be forced to use the keyboard to make things happen on the screen. Because most of the executives at Rockwell's NAA division have limited keyboard skills, all EIS information is accessible either through use of the mouse or a touch screen. Both input devices can be used to choose from menu items or activate hot buttons.

Third, the system has to be self-explanatory. Executives have little time for training. They have even less time and patience for thumbing through notes and reading manuals. If executives cannot just look at the screen and know what to do, it has failed the "intuitive" test.

Fourth, the system must be fast. Although studies show that subsecond response time is optimal, such quick response times may not be feasible when displaying graphic results of complex queries. But common sense says that busy executives will not wait 30 seconds for a response. For the EIS at Rockwell, we used the MTTA measure—Mean Time To Anger. We let the executives' reaction to the system tell us if we are achieving acceptable response time. So far, their reactions have been positive.

network and external communications resources. We knew the EIS would have to dovetail into this emerging environment.

Perhaps the strongest concern that faced IS management was the fear of having to supply a cast of thousands to support the EIS without a budget increase and without any relaxation in our service to other customers. The EIS technology had to be such that maintenance would be kept to a manageable level. In addition, it had to promote EIS application design that could be relatively immune to on-going changes in the environment.

Armed with these requirements, we began the search for the right EIS software. Like almost all requests to buy something, this one had strings attached. There were two primary constraints that affected our ultimate decision. First, we did not have a blank check. And, second, we had a schedule to follow. We wanted the EIS technology in place with some visible results by the time the executives had their office computers.

SOFTWARE SELECTION

Shopping for vendors was the first order of business. For the most part, the vendors found us once word got out that we were looking at EISs. The three main players in the EIS marketplace and their products are Boston-based Pilot Executive Software with Command Center and Advantage/G; Comshare Inc. in Ann Arbor, Mich., with Commander; and Austin, Texas-based Execucom Systems Corp. with Executive Edge. Other entries include the newly announced OfficeVision from IBM, DECDecisions from Digital, and EISEL by Interactive Images Inc. of Woburn, Mass.

Having identified potential products, we began comparing and testing them. During product demonstrations, we tried to evaluate the products from the perspectives of both executives and programmers. We paid close attention to what kind of graphic displays were produced and how the user interfaces operated. Then we viewed technical demonstrations of the products. The focus here was on the development tools and how the data for the system were organized and stored.

Part of the evaluation phase involved talking to users. We first talked to another aerospace company that had built its own EIS. We then saw a working version of Execucom's EIS system implemented by a local utility company. We interviewed and heard presentations by IS personnel in banking industry and manufacturing using Pilot's Command Center. Finally, we met various vendors and users by attending the EIS '89 national seminar.

The product we finally chose was Pilot's Command Center, supplemented by the Advantage/G application generator. The primary deciding factors in Pilot's favor were its mainframe-based architecture, IBM compatibility, data driven approach and powerful development tools.

Command Center consists of a mainframe engine for handling database maintenance and queries coupled with a PC front-end module for displaying graphics. Being mainframe-based offered advantages in data security, unlimited capacity for database growth and EIS access by virtually any division user with the PC front-end software. This final point is important because we believe that interest in the system will filter down through the executive ranks.

Our satisfaction should not imply that there are no disadvantages to a mainframe package. We have found response time to be generally slower on a mainframe than on a dedicated PC. Having a mainframe database also means sacrificing some flexibility in that the EIS does not easily accept files from outside sources. In addition, it won't capture and display graphic images generated by other systems, unlike certain PC-based systems. However, we felt the integrity, security and accessibility of a mainframe system outweighed the drawback of inflexibility.

The saga of EIS at North American Aircraft so far has been a happy one. We completed the evaluation at the end of June 1989. We brought Command Center in on a trial basis in August and tested it. We recommended acquisition and put a development team together to start training programmers in the Command Center language. The executives moved to their new offices, the PCs were installed and we demonstrated several prototype EIS applications by November 1.

We are now in the middle of full-scale development of EIS applications. In a subsequent article, we will explore the evolution of the development team and the organizational infrastructure surrounding the EIS. We will also describe the methodology we use to define and create the applications. And we will share some of the important results of this effort and some of the lessons learned.

QUESTIONS

1. Discuss the goals that North American Aviation established for its EIS.
2. What did the company mean when it " . . . looked at EIS software with IS needs in mind?" What IS needs are included here?
3. Discuss the firm's vendor evaluation process.

20

The People Factor in EIS Success

David A. Armstrong

In May 1989, the North American Aircraft (NAA) division of Rockwell International Corp. embarked on an ambitious project to develop a full-scale executive information system (EIS). In the March 1 issue of DATA-MATION, we outlined the initial requirements for our EIS and described some of the software tools we chose to implement them. This second part of the story looks beyond software and systems and reveals what we discovered to be even more important in EIS success—people.

We began our EIS journey last spring by talking to other EIS users, visiting trade shows and experimenting with implementation software. By November of last year, we went on line with the first part of the system, an office automation network linking 14 top division executives located in six sites spanning two states, including NAA's headquarters in El Segundo, Calif. That's when John Pierro, division president, and his vice presidents began communicating at their networked personal computers using electronic mail and calendaring software.

During the first half of this story, we evaluated EIS software that could help us deliver business reports and graphics to the executives' PCs. Last summer, we selected and installed an EIS implementation package called Command Center from Boston-based Pilot Executive Software, along with the company's Advantage/G application generator. Although this software makes it possible to deliver some prototype applications to the executives, we quickly discovered that EIS success is not guaranteed by technology alone. It takes commitment, teamwork and leadership to make EIS work on a daily basis.

Previously published in *Datamation*, April 1, 1990 © 1990 by Cahners/Ziff Publishing Associates, L.P. Used with permission.

With the onset of application development, what began as a rather informal team evolved into a more formal structure. This was a slow, trial-and-error process. No one was sure exactly what an EIS team should look like. However, with time and experience, we began to identify some key roles and players in the EIS infrastructure.

For the most part, the structure of our EIS project is not very different from other IS development projects. It consists of analysts, programmers and sponsors/users. However, the way these roles relate and interact becomes markedly different for EIS. A multifunctional team gradually emerged at NAA and became the backbone of EIS development.

Unlike most IS projects, which are sponsored by operational managers, our primary EIS sponsor was division president John Pierro. His vision provided the guidelines and inspiration for the system. He even got personally involved in the placement of the hardware in the executive offices.

As the primary sponsor, Pierro also shaped the philosophies behind the applications that would be developed. He wanted an intuitive system that required minimal training for the executives. It had to be mouse driven, with meaningful icons and menus. It also had to display what Pierro calls "derived information," meaning graphic displays that not only highlight problems but identify the source of those problems.

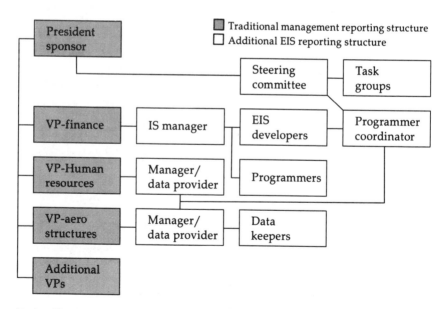

Rockwell's EIS project is a team effort that's coordinated by individuals both within and outside the company's traditional management structure.

Figure 20-1.   *Rockwell's EIS Executive Framework*

Perhaps Pierro's most significant contribution to EIS in the long run continues to be his role as a user of the system. He uses it, and he demands that his vice presidents do the same.

Loosely related to the sponsor is what we call the system champion. In its embryonic stages, EIS can be a thoroughly absorbing subject. A division president cannot afford the time needed to shepherd the details of a fledgling EIS. It is important, then, to appoint a high-level executive to take the system under his or her wing.

At NAA, the EIS champion was Howard Chambers, vice president and manager of the B-1B bomber program. His primary task is to promote the system among his colleagues by keeping the fires of interest stoked during the relatively quiet periods of evaluation, investigation and analysis. Chambers does this by championing frequent briefings, project status reports and prototype demonstration sessions, among other things.

Because information is the basis of corporate power, EIS challenges traditional lines of communication. It makes information more readily available and, in some cases, changes the source of information. For these reasons, the champion has to be sensitive to these cultural changes and know how to manage them. He must be particularly active in soliciting cooperation between members of the EIS structure, especially where cultural changes appear most threatening.

Managing the EIS Data Dilemma

Any EIS implementation is bound to raise new questions over the handling of corporate information. There are a number of important data issues that all EIS developers have to address, including the following:

Technical Problems. Data can reside on a number of media in a variety of formats. They can exist in mainframe databases or files, in personal computer spreadsheets, in word processors, in handheld calculators or in a person's brain. Obviously some of these media lend themselves better than others to electronic transfer to the EIS database.

Unfortunately, there is no simple solution to formatting data for EIS. The developer may have to learn some new languages and may have to negotiate with data providers, data keepers and IS personnel.

Direct Access vs. Repository. The question here is whether the EIS will tap directly into the operational databases of the enterprise or whether it will access only its own special database that is fed by the operational systems. The direct access method is most appealing to the executives but is most threatening to the political structure of the organization.

Executives typically like the idea of looking directly into the production databases because they get to see the raw data in the most timely fashion. They see information as it really exists, not as some staff person has scrubbed and fashioned it for them.

There are serious disadvantages to this approach, however. The raw data in production may not be organized for the most efficient retrieval for EIS. The EIS applications may be overly cumbersome and unresponsive when executives try to handle data not properly prepared. Even more important, the people responsible for the data will feel exposed. Knowing their executives can see every last detail of their operational data makes them uneasy. They fear that the executive will micro-manage them, and they cannot anticipate where the questions might originate.

Manipulation. If the decision is to base EIS on a repository, rather than on source files, the next question is, Can the data providers manipulate the data before they get into the repository? Giving them this option has two advantages. First, it allows the data providers to eliminate data errors in EIS that will save executives confusion and time. Second, the data providers maintain control over their information, and EIS will not seem like a monster that will take away their jobs. The disadvantage is that data manipulation takes time, which makes the EIS information less timely and somehow less real to the executives.

Refresh Rate. The refresh rate determines how often the information at the executive workstations is updated. The options for refreshing range from every time the executive accesses an application to a regularly scheduled cycle. To get the most up-to-the-minute refresh, the application must be on line to the operational database, with all the advantages and disadvantages already described. For the most part, weekly or monthly updates generally suffice.

Standards of Quality. The EIS is only as good as the information it delivers. Standards have to be set for the quality of information portrayed. Quality is measured by its accuracy, completeness and timeliness. Mechanisms should be built into the system to measure and communicate quality of data.

Ownership. An adjunct to data quality is data ownership. Ownership makes the data providers accountable. Every record in the EIS database should have a name and phone number attached to it. As the executives view their screens, they should always see the name of the data provider. In this way, they know exactly whom to call if they have a question.

STEERING COMMITTEE

To create the road map for his EIS concept, Pierro appointed a steering committee and directed its members to form task groups. The groups would define the subjects and formats that would be included in the first generation of our EIS. Chambers heads the steering committee, which includes Art Goudreault, vice president of material; Jim Richey, vice president of finance; and Paul Mason, division coordinator of automation projects.

Beneath the steering committee, two task groups were formed to mirror NAA's two concurrent structures. One committee consists of the traditional enterprise function, including engineering, finance, material and human resources. The other is oriented to specific business programs, such as B-1B production, aerostructures modifications and advanced systems and technology development. The interests and needs of these two structures diverge on some subjects and overlap on others. The two task groups are made up of directors and managers representing these two unique structures.

The task groups' original directions from the steering committee were relatively simple: identify four or five key business questions in their respective areas that EIS should address. Then outline the formats in which the information should be presented.

Implementing these instructions was not so elementary. Many hours went into investigating and analyzing existing reports and briefing charts. Brainstorming was often needed to determine new and better ways of presenting information. In many cases, four or five key points were not enough to give a clear picture of a function or business area. The task groups' efforts resulted in a 130-page book of sample reports and charts that formed the basic requirements document for EIS development.

A major challenge in implementing our EIS continues to be the identification of the data providers. A data provider is typically a middle-level departmental manager who creates, collects, maintains, analyzes or publishes information. He or she may or may not be a consumer of the information. While this appears to be clear cut, in fact it is a complicated arrangement. The reason: all the information for an application rarely is maintained by one department. Several departments may contribute pieces to make up the whole picture. We currently have identified 15 primary data providers at NAA, along with another six supporting providers.

DATA PROVIDERS

Data providers play significant roles in both the development and operation of EIS applications. During development, they define source data for an application. Although the executives may indicate what information they want to see, the data providers have to determine where that information comes from, to what levels of detail it will appear and how often it will be updated.

Once an application goes into production use, the data providers assume responsibility for the care and feeding of the information displayed. They review the accuracy of the data, and they often package the source data and stage them for import into the EIS database. Without the cooperation of the data providers, the EIS system cannot be effective.

DATA KEEPERS

Although the data providers are ultimately responsible for the information that gets into the EIS, they rarely are the individuals who actually maintain the data files and write the programs to capture and store the data. These people are called data keepers.

The job of data keepers is to manage and maintain source data and systems. Two roles are represented here: program keepers and file keepers. Program keepers write and maintain programs and systems for capturing, processing and distributing data. This is traditionally the job of IS professionals. However, with the advent of end user computing, PCs and fourth-generation languages, many user departments are creating their own systems and establishing departmental program keepers.

File keepers use the program or system to update the file and create the output reports. An analyst in the financial planning department is one example of a file keeper at NAA. This person is responsible for updating the capital-planning data maintained in our IMS-based production system. These data, in turn, are used to feed our EIS.

Occasionally, we find the program keeper and file keeper to be one and the same person. For instance, our Appropriation Request Status application is based on a spreadsheet report created and maintained by a staffer in the financial-planning department. Coordination is easy, communication is straightforward and development has progressed rapidly. We put this application together in less than two days. Still, most program keepers at NAA are members of the IS department staff.

On the other end of the spectrum are situations where data providers rely on file keepers in other departments, who in turn rely on program keepers in IS. In NAA's Indirect Cost Performance application, the indirect cost management group (data providers) extract data from reports in accounting (file keepers), who maintain the data with a system written by IS (program keepers). The coordination of priorities and communication of requirements among these groups is time consuming.

EIS DEVELOPERS

The role of the EIS developer is to create and maintain EIS applications. He or she must organize the data providers' raw files into an EIS database and translate executive desires into menus, reports and graphs. The result is an application that accurately reflects business information in a meaningful way to executives.

To perform this role effectively, an EIS developer must have a unique set of skills in his or her personal repertoire. At NAA, we look for individuals in IS or other departments who demonstrate the four following qualities:

- *Technical Skills.* Programming skills are not necessarily the most important aspect of a good developer. Nevertheless, if applications are to be developed quickly, the EIS developer must be able to efficiently use the tools available.

- *Business Understanding.* The development team is involved in defining solutions to high-level business problems. Team members need a foundation in business terminology and principles.

- *Toleration for Ambiguity.* From our experience with early EIS prototypes, it was evident that effective developers had to be patient with the trial-and-error method of defining executive needs. Requirements are often vague, and the target is in perpetual motion. Further, developers have to be insightful and creative. They must be able to translate hunches, suggestions and innuendo into real computer screens. And they must be willing to throw away a week's worth of programming in a heartbeat when the executive changes his or her mind.

- *Interpersonal Skills.* Perhaps most important, developers must interact well with a wide range of people. They must be equally at ease in the boardroom, a manager's office or a data entry operator's cubicle. They play the roles of teacher, salesperson, detective, diplomat and entertainer.

PROJECT COORDINATOR

Coming rather late on the scene has been the project coordinator position. Chambers and his steering committee originally played this role. But as momentum grew and the magnitude of the project became evident, these busy executives saw the need to appoint a full-time coordinator to the project.

The project coordinator position involves a delicate balancing act with all the other groups in the project. For example, there are executives who need to review applications, data providers who need to identify and prepare data sources and EIS developers who need clarifications on formats and data. The steering committee ultimately chose an experienced project manager from the engineering department to fill this position.

APPLICATION DEVELOPMENT

Although the people behind the EIS will ultimately dictate its success or failure, we discovered that applications success also hinges on careful planning. As soon as the Pilot software was installed, the developer team was organized and several days of on-site training by Pilot was arranged. The team members were introduced to the Command Center language, and, in a couple of weeks, they became familiar with the capabilities of the language and the application generator.

As the requirements book took shape, the developers began to explore the process of developing a prototype application. Over time, they formalized an EIS development life cycle intended to promote quick application turnaround. The life cycle consists of the following nine tasks:

1. *Application Sketch.* The sketch is the basic outline for the application. Developed by the task groups, a sketch consists of sample display formats (including graphs and tabular reports), a description of the levels of detail required for drilling down into data layers and any special navigational needs.

2. *Priority.* Initially, the EIS developers determined what applications to work on first, based on the technical lessons to be learned and the availability of data. In the long run, NAA's steering committee will set the priorities for our development schedules.

3. *Identify the Data Source.* Once an application is selected and sketched out, the developers investigate who the data providers will be and begin analyzing the source data. The developers determine what data are already present in automated systems and what elements still have to be automated.

4. *Develop a Prototype.* With sample data in hand, the developer begins designing and coding the EIS programs. Their complexity and novelty usually dictate how long it takes to write the report, graph and menu modules. Where possible, these modules are created in less than an hour using the application generator. Yet the generator will rarely do everything. Each of our specified applications, for example, had quirks in them that forced the development team to finish the programming using the generator's native code, a high-level language resembling Focus.

5. *Verify the Prototype.* Once an application is coded, it enters an iterative verification stage where both the data providers and executives can examine it in detail. The feedback provided by these sessions is then incorporated into any program changes.

6. *Finalize Data Import.* In some cases, there may be only one source and one way to get at it. In other cases, there may be numerous

sources and ways to find the right data. Head count information, for example, is often maintained in various flavors by the human resources department, finance and various individual groups. Whatever the case, it's up to the developer to make a final decision about the best source for data.

7. *Develop Data Import.* A prototype application often uses data from a hypothetical database. Before a prototype is approved for production, however, procedures on how to extract data from the live source files and reports must be developed.

8. *Final Check-Out.* With the EIS database loaded with live data, the application is ready for a final shake down. The data providers and executives once again review the entire process and make final suggestions and comments.

9. *Install and Deliver.* The final step in the development life cycle is to install the application and make it available to the executives. At NAA, installation is a relatively easy process of putting programs, files and procedures into the production EIS environment and following through with notification to the executives.

INTRODUCING THE SYSTEM

Introducing EIS at NAA has been a long process that is still going on. We began with preliminary prototypes and demonstrations to the executive council. Keeping the executives interested during the evaluation and development phases was a challenge for the steering committee. Until some prototype applications were available on the PCs, interest was kept alive by focusing on electronic mail and other office functions such as a software calendar, word processing and spreadsheets.

We have found executive training to be especially challenging. Perhaps it goes without saying that executives are all very busy. Even when they are interested in a topic, such as EIS, making time for it is a problem. Scheduling even an hour of training can sometimes take weeks and many phone calls.

Acceptance of the system has ranged from enthusiasm to resistance that is only now being overcome. Fortunately, Howard Chambers has been instrumental in keeping EIS focused before the executive council. He enthusiastically demonstrates EIS to the executives and to anyone else who comes into his office. John Pierro's support of the system has also been critical. He's determined that EIS will be his primary source of information within the division.

NAA will change as a result of EIS. However, exactly what form these changes will take remains to be seen. Some changes have already begun to show themselves. For instance, there is already a desire to push EIS down into the support organizations. As soon as data providers see a prototype, they recognize that sooner or later they will want to have a workstation of their own.

Important political and structural changes are also occurring. For instance, we are eliminating redundant and conflicting reporting duties among various organizations. We have also uncovered cases where the lines of communication are needlessly complex.

Additionally, we are beginning to see changes in the operational systems of NAA. Reports considered less than accurate are being cleaned up as they become sources for EIS. Batch system update schedules that once had long lead times are being tightened to make them more timely. And data that had always been assumed to be automated, but were in fact being typed on a typewriter, are being automated in new systems.

CHANGING THE EXECUTIVE CULTURE

The executive culture is also changing. The executive council is becoming more computer literate, and members are beginning to gain a personal understanding of the power and limitations of computers. The executives are also developing more reliance on information technology. Consequently, they are becoming less tolerant of fuzzy answers that do not give them the hard facts they need to make solid decisions.

The road to EIS at North American Aircraft has not been without its potholes and speed bumps. There were many things we did not know about EIS when we began. Not only was the technology new but the whole idea of executives getting information directly from the computer was a novel concept for everyone. No one was sure what could be accomplished. Having a mentor in the form of Howard Chambers who could represent our frustrations and concerns to the executive council members and translate their ideas back to us has been invaluable.

Looking back over the past year's effort, we now know that fast development of applications is key to a successful EIS. Once executives get a taste of EIS, their appetites are insatiable.

We have found four factors that contribute to feeding those appetites quickly. (1) The EIS development staff has to be assigned full-time to the project. At NAA, we have three full-time developers assigned to EIS. (2) Developers need high-yield tools that make it easy to produce the kinds of graphics and displays the executives want. (3) Open and responsive lines of communications must be established between the data providers, other team members and the executive council. (4) IS must have an open and responsive attitude toward EIS.

EIS is still in the toddler stage at NAA. Executives and developers alike are still just taking their first tentative steps in the technology. As we learn to walk, and then run, EIS will become a significant tool for communicating and managing in the division. North American Aircraft is investing in EIS today to make Rockwell more competitive tomorrow.

QUESTIONS

1. What does the author mean by the following statement, "EIS success is not guaranteed by technology alone."
2. How does an EIS "challenge traditional lines of communication?"
3. Discuss the nine steps in EIS application development. Are there differences between EIS application development and application development with other computer-based information systems? Discuss them.
4. Describe the political and structural changes that are occurring at North American Aircraft.
5. Discuss changes in the executive culture at North American Aircraft.

PART IV

THE IMPACT OF EIS

Many authors have discussed the impacts that an executive information system can have on an organization and its personnel. Many of these impacts are not measurable (for example, better decisions). The readings in Part IV present a broad spectrum of potential impacts, usually in the context of actual experiences drawn from successful EIS implementations.

Lou Wallis, in "Power Computing at the Top," illustrates the impacts that an EIS can have by describing how three top executives view their EIS. All three receive company performance data, internal communications, and environmental scanning from their EIS. Impacts that Wallis notes include reduced staff and clerical personnel, improved communications, less executive reliance on staff support, easier information access, flatter lines of control, more productive meetings, information compression, information timeliness, and improved competitive position.

Turbulent operating environments make it more difficult for executives to accurately formulate mental models of the firm, its industry, and its environment. John Rockart and David De Long, in "Moments of Executive Enlightenment," state that six attributes of EIS can enhance these mental models: improved access to external data, new ways to combine data from multiple sources, presentation of data in more meaningful formats, sophisticated analytic and modeling capabilities, identifying and testing assumptions about corporate performance, and off-hours data access.

David Friend, in "EIS and the Collapse of the Information Pyramid," argues that after an EIS is successfully developed, there is much work left to ensure its continuing success. First, the EIS should have an organizational focus rather than an individual focus. Second, EIS builders should allow for growth in the scale of EIS applications and for replacement of monthly data in favor of daily, or almost real-time, data. Third, EIS data bases should be centralized for minimum data redundancy, maximum data integrity, and maximum security.

The final three articles in Part IV illustrate EIS impacts in a variety of organizations. "Executive Information System Streamlines Greyhound Dial's Operations" describes how the EIS at Greyhound Dial uses 12 key performance factors on each of 85 lines of business to enable executives to control this diverse organization. Meghan O'Leary, in "Putting Hertz Executives in the Driver's Seat," discusses how the EIS at Hertz helps executives make decisions on a real-time basis. Hertz executives needed quality information quickly to take advantage of rapidly shifting conditions in a competitive market. Caryl Holland, in "Developing an ESS for the Michigan State Senate," illustrates how an EIS may be used in a public sector environment. She provides insights into customizing EIS for its users and enhancing executive "buy-in" to the system.

21

Power Computing at the Top

Lou Wallis

Stories abound about the many senior executives who, while paying tribute to the contributions of computer technology to their companies, break out in a rash when they get within 10 feet of a computer terminal or personal computer.

This resistance is puzzling, since top executives have signed off on billions of dollars' worth of computers for their companies and must realize that their operations would grind to a halt if deprived, even temporarily, of these facilities. But translating that into their own work is another matter. They may note the computer's handling of millions of transactions for payroll, accounting, invoicing, plus word processing and other office automation. But they view their own work as vastly different, not at all susceptible to automation. Their jobs appear fundamentally different from those many layers below them, and they fail to see how their productivity could be improved by a computer system.

For them, productivity may not be the key issue. Jim Carlisle, a consultant who helped develop executive information systems for Xerox Corporation and Westinghouse Electric Corporation, observes: "Anyone who has made senior vice president probably can't have his personal productivity improved. However, he can have his vision and comprehension of the business improved."

Others say that many attempts at executive information systems have failed because they do not meet the highly individual needs of top managers. One skeptic is Henry Mintzberg, professor of management at McGill University in Montreal, who has observed that executives

Previously published in *Across the Board,* Volume 26, Numbers 1/2, January/February 1989. Used with permission.

"are still forced to conform to the technology's capabilities, rather than being able to tailor it to their own needs. The mistaken assumption is that the technology is based on an understanding of what managers do, and it's not. The technology has simply been superimposed over the work."

Executives make important decisions, a lot of them. But as they grapple for the best outcomes, they can become exasperated, panning the dross and silt of corporate computer data bases, searching for nuggets of information. Too many information systems have been designed for everything and everybody in the company except for the high-level decision-makers, who tend to find them "data rich, insight poor." The problem of providing adequate corporate data for executive decision-makers is similar to that of the provident squirrel who intends to dine on acorns once the winter snows have arrived—that is, saving the treasure isn't the problem, it's finding where it's hidden.

But newer and better systems are designed especially for corporate decision-makers and fit the way they actually work. One type that has worked well for many managers is called an executive support system (ESS). The powerful software is sold by vendors but usually has to be adapted to the needs of each company's top managers. ESS learns what executive users want, allows users to enter information and ask questions in informal English, delivers the results in a meaningful form, and, as far as possible, eliminates the need to make adjustments to the computer itself.

Computer systems have long been able to store and retrieve financial, production, marketing, and other essential measures of company performance. These are the conventional, recognizable output from electronic data processing or management information systems (MIS). The day-to-day output of these systems are garden-variety reports of weekly, monthly, year-to-date results intended for many different people and purposes. "The monthly reports are essentially background music," says Jim Carlisle, managing director of Office of the Future Inc. "They are 10 to 15 days old on arrival. If you're budgeting monthly sales of $50 million and in 15 days you've done $7 million, you need to know now—not 15 days later." With traditional computer systems, a patient analyst can sort and probe the various data bases and standard reports, draw up the comparisons, ratios, increases, and decreases, and, if familiar with the needs of the executive, produce the same kind of quality analyses offered by executive systems.

So, why should a company switch to ESS if traditional systems have worked for years? Some companies have turned to ESS because it is designed to help executives make decisions by giving them immediate access to any information that they deem helpful. ESS takes into account that one executive's needs are not necessarily another's, because analysis, reflection, and decision-making are personal arts. By contrast, little of the costly and imposing structure of corporate computing run by MIS was especially designed for, or is very useful for, making decisions. Rosabeth Moss Kanter, of the Harvard Business School, reminds us: "Information quality requires focusing on what's important, not what's available. Stored information represents potential, but is useless unless it can be actively communicated to those who need it."

Many corporate leaders have tried to do something about the shortcomings of MIS, not just for themselves but for their entire organizations. Determined not to be outflanked by the upwardly techno-mobile, some chief executives have led the charge for installing flexible information systems and convincing people to use them.

Three executives who have had positive experiences with ESS are Paul A. Allaire, president of Xerox, William D. Smithburg, chairman and chief executive officer of the Quaker Oats Company, and Finn M.W. Caspersen, chairman and chief executive officer of Beneficial Corporation. Each has for some time been using an executive support system developed by his company, getting three kinds of support from it: (1) company performance data—sales, production, earnings, budgets, and forecasts; (2) internal communications—personal correspondence, reports, and meetings; (3) environmental scanning—for news on government regulations, competition, financial and economic developments, and scientific subjects.

What follows does not pretend to be a balanced appraisal of executive support systems, but rather conveys how three executives have profited from their use.

WHY XEROX STARTED AT THE TOP

Paul Allaire began by insisting that Xerox would not cram a new system down the throats of executives, telling them, "Use it or else." In 1983, Allaire returned from Britain where he had been managing director of Rank Xerox Ltd. and took over as corporate chief of staff. To begin development of ESS, Allaire brought Kenneth Soha to headquarters from the company's plant in Rochester, New York, where he had directed the information systems group. David T. Kearns, Xerox's CEO, had asked Allaire to reduce the cost of staff work at corporate headquarters and improve its effectiveness; Allaire believed that information technology had a major role to play. He thereby became the executive sponsor of ESS, and Soha became the operational sponsor and director of the system. Allaire describes their early actions: "We hired a consultant, Jim

Carlisle, and looked at the start of the art of ESS. Looking at all of the systems that we could find in operation, we concluded that none were much good for us. So we decided to build our own."

In 1983, Xerox embarked on the development of its ESS, which was to serve more than 400 people at corporate headquarters in Stamford, Connecticut. It was to link strategic planning with electronic mail, changing the way top executives communicated and worked with one another. Soha's supporting operation grew to more than a dozen people with an annual budget of $1 million by 1988.

"We decided that ESS had to be evolutionary, not forced," says Allaire, who was promoted to president of the company in 1986. "But we had to start at the top, so we had to prove how it could help [executives] do their jobs. Bill Glavin, our vice chairman, at first said: 'I came from a systems environment, but I'm not going to use the system. I'll give it to my secretary.'" Allaire continues: "We said, 'Fine, we'll put it on your secretary's desk, and if you want a printout of anything, here's how you get it.'" Glavin eventually became one of the system's biggest fans.

"Compared with people, technology is cheap, and one of my objectives every year is to reduce spending on corporate staff," Allaire says. "We have some fairly stringent targets on that." He estimates that for each of the past three years, ESS has helped reduce staff expenses at headquarters by 5 percent. "I felt sure that technology could help reduce staff, the big expense item. But we realized we couldn't just present the system and say, 'Here's the answer to your prayers, and, by the way, take a 10 percent cut in your people.' You have to provide tools and let people decide how to use them most efficiently."

One explanation for the success of ESS at Xerox is that, early on, the principal developers, especially Allaire and Soha, did not just throw money at a vague set of problems. Improving communications and the planning process were always uppermost in their minds. Allaire explains: "Right away, we realized that electronic mail was going to be a big item. Here's an illustration: We have what's called the extended management committee meeting. When I was in Britain, I had to come to the United States for these meetings once a month. The reading material I had for the meeting was supposed to come a week in advance, but sometimes it was only three days. I still needed time to analyze it and comment on it, have my staff go over it. So I sometimes faced the prospect of reading it in a hotel room the night before the meeting, which was clearly ridiculous. Now, it's all on the ESS. The manager in Britain may actually have the material before it's available here. The meetings themselves are more productive because the action items that result from decisions go on the system and are likely to be waiting for the British manager upon his return from the United States."

One of the first things put on the system was the management data book, which contains information on sales, customer service, personnel, and finance, including items such as currency rates. Xerox ran into a stumbling block, however, with the data book. Although the data was on the system, executives had to proceed through it page by page, just as with a book. They had to conform their thinking to the structure of the data book, which was the opposite of what Allaire wanted ESS to do. Allaire reports a big breakthrough, just out and not yet generally available, that eliminates this structural problem. "Now, if I'm looking at a profit-and-loss statement and want to zero in on, say, a sales-expense item, I can point with the mouse and get more detail, perhaps geographical or historical, and plot it on a graph. I can look at it any way I want, rather than have a staff person tell me what I should be looking for. I can take a trend that concerns me, bring it up on the screen, put a note on it, and ask my marketing people, 'What's going on here?'"

Part of the pleasure of being president of a company must be to be able to pick up the phone and get anyone on the other end. Is Allaire more likely to use the system, instead of buzzing someone for the information? "Oh yes! In the past, one of the frustrations of managing has been that when you know you need some information and call someone—and we still do—they ask how soon you need the information. I say, 'Right away,' and they say, 'You'll have it this afternoon.' Now, that's pretty responsive. But I find that, when you're working on a project this morning and in the afternoon you're out with a customer, then when you return to the office and get the information, you may end up asking yourself, 'What the heck was I thinking of when I asked for this?' So, ESS allows you to work on a project or a decision, complete it right away, and be less reliant on staff support. You have flatter lines of control, and you can be more effective because you have the information you need. You can be more creative as well."

How often Allaire turns to ESS depends on the job at hand. "The fact that it isn't turned on doesn't mean it isn't working," he says. "My secretary's system is on all the time, and she can pick up anything urgent for me. I would say that some days I may not use it at all, but other days I use it most of the day."

Strategic planning at Xerox turned out to be one of the applications of ESS that got executives involved because it performed an essential task better. Shortly after ESS development began, Xerox's new resource management statement (essentially, a five-page summary of each business unit's plan) was put on the system. David Bliss, an executive in Xerox's corporate-strategy office, said that Allaire asked his operation to find a way to improve the planning process and reduce the time spent on it. An obvious target was the different formats each business-unit manager used to present the unit's plans. This made it difficult to compare one plan with another and kept senior executives scrambling to understand the details of each plan (Kenneth Soha describes this as the executives having to play on each unit's home field).

Four of the five pages of the new computer-based planning format consist of a summary of a unit's plan, such as projected sales and earnings, while the final page is reserved for senior management to respond to the plan with decisions or comments. Top management receives the plans on the ESS for a "prereading" three to five days before a scheduled meeting. The pertinent information is greatly condensed, and senior executives can easily compare one plan with another because of the consistent format.

Paul Allaire also developed the business priority list, a 15-item list used by those who report to him. The list keeps Allaire's people focused on important programs and provides progress reports. It is used to set agendas for meetings and is the basis of the direct-action list that prioritizes short-term tasks. Allaire reflects: "The list would be much harder without the ESS. The system permits us to store the items on the list in different ways and follow deadlines. Could we do it without the system? Well, we didn't. It also helps us to discipline ourselves and documents meetings immediately."

What has been the impact of ESS on meetings? "I'm not sure we have fewer meetings, but they are more productive," Allaire says. "If we feel that an issue can be decided on material already available, we don't have a meeting. If more information is needed, it's available before the meeting. The result is that we very rarely have a meeting at which we don't have enough information to make a decision."

One benefit of ESS is that when executives must travel they can still use it, wherever they are. "When you travel, it is very valuable," agrees Allaire. "If I need a document, I can call my administrative assistant and have it sent. The bad part is that you can't hide. People can get messages to you anywhere! I don't use it much at home, frankly. I live only 10 minutes away from the office, and I have to go through a modem to reach the office system. So, if I'm going to work on something, I'll just come in."

The easy flow of information from person to person is another benefit of ESS. But confidentiality of communications is obviously necessary, too—especially at the senior-executive level. ESS has security safeguards to protect that confidentiality. At Xerox, "need to know" is still invoked, and executives see essentially what their bosses want them to see. Nevertheless, since those who report to Allaire are on his system and thus receive similar information, was he worried that he might be second-guessed, perhaps limiting his freedom to make decisions?

"No, that doesn't bother me at all," he replies. "I'm glad to have the information, some that I didn't have before. People have more confidence in the decisions we make, confidence that the decision-makers are using relevant information and aren't up there in an ivory tower, not knowing what's going on in the world."

VISION AND KNOWLEDGE AT QUAKER OATS

"It didn't take any particularly creative thought to realize that executives can enhance their information flow in a way that enhances their decision-making," explains William Smithburg, CEO at Quaker Oats. "All businesses live and die with information, and historically, it's been in a stack of paper somewhere and in files and books."

Smithburg began his initiation into computers in 1982 when he asked that a PC be installed in his office and hooked up to the Dow Jones Service and The Source (an on-line public-access company offering an array of computer data bases and bulletin boards). But, he says, "it eventually took several years to master the idea of computerizing all the information that used to come into our offices on paper. We wanted it in a more digestible and accessible form. I wanted access to all the information without picking up the phone to call my controller. The problem is that the executive wants to describe the end result, 'Give me this, give me that,' rather than delving into the process, which is really what makes it productive in the end."

Smithburg continues, "I remember when one of my business-unit executives came into my office, saw my PC, and asked what I did with it. I proceeded to pull up all kinds of information on his operation, and he was stunned. He rushed back to his information-systems people and said, 'Do you realize what Smithburg has in his office, on his computer? I've got to have the same thing!' Actually, there has been a productive migration of systems, both up and down, within the company."

Using the system didn't come easy at first, Smithburg says. "The main source of slowness was that I had to get up to speed on what I needed. And information systems had to understand better what executives need from a data base; they needed to learn how executives use information to make decisions. The first year or so, my use of the PC was not particularly successful, because all I really used it for was accessing Dow Jones and similar things—valuable, but not worth the cost of putting it in my office. So we needed more. An information-systems person would say, 'Okay, you draw a chart and show us what you want and we'll get it in that box.' But that's not what you want. Then someone said, 'Why don't we ask planning to see what kind of information they want, and maybe we can enhance the flow from them to you.'

"That proved to be very beneficial. The ESS didn't really click until one or two people in information systems clearly understood my personal operating style and what I needed for decision-making. Now they are very client oriented. They say, 'Tell us how you use information and make decisions, and we'll get you a product.'"

An article in *Advertising Age* noted that one of Quaker Oats' strengths was its ability to adapt to change in the marketplace. Frank Morgan, the president, was quoted as saying that Smithburg brought a visionary quality. Had ESS contributed? "I think so," Smithburg says. "I use ESS more for environmental scanning than for management and control. A vision for the future requires knowledge of the present and the recent past, and executives need to be able to get that at will. In days of drought in farming areas, for example, I can get into the ESS and find agricultural information quickly that will influence our costs for raw materials."

With ESS, Smithburg and other senior executives can dig deeply into marketing data to check into, say, sales of Quaker Extra cereal versus sales of Total Oats, a competitor's product. "Sometimes you just feel like wading into the data," Smithburg says. His purpose, however, is to improve his own decisions, not to second-guess another department's. "I might look at more data because curiosity gets the better of me, but not because I want to get involved in managing a business that others run. Quite often I go back and check my assumptions on the ESS, because I can't remember everything I see. I'll look to see if I'm correct and check on a few hunches."

ESS offers two valuable features: compression and freshness of information. Which means the most to Smithburg? "Freshness is important," he replies, "especially for financial data. But for me, compression is the plus. It really helps me focus on the broad issues."

ESS allows the creation and use of graphs to express data visually. Yet, although research has shown that use of graphs instead of numbers increases comprehension, it means a shift in habits for many executives. "Graphs are fine for presentations, but I don't use them on my computer much," Smithburg says. "I know what I'm looking for, and I get the numbers. When I was a brand manager I came up with presentations called super charts. These had everything on them, market shares, advertising expenses, advertising campaigns, and so on. Now I can get that completeness using ESS."

Overall, Smithburg thinks ESS has improved his productivity. "I pick up the phone less, a lot less, than I used to. There are times when you're curious about what's happening, but you don't want to meddle. When important people are freed from this, they can do the more valuable diagnostic work. It makes them more productive. I may be working at home on a Sunday night preparing for our management committee meeting on Monday, and I need to check some backup material on products. If I couldn't access my ESS, I would have to phone my controller at home.

The vast majority of my time is spent communicating, in meetings, at lunches and breakfasts, on the telephone. It's not reflection time or analysis time. The best time for thinking is at home."

Smithburg agrees that ESS can affect working relationships. "I view the company not as a holding company but an operating entity in which senior executives understand the businesses they run," he says. "I expect them to know what is going on. When I prepare for a meeting, if I can access the right information, I can be more responsive to the upward flow of communications. The presenters see executives who are well informed and up-to-date."

Business leaders must have persuasive powers. Does ESS diminish the need to persuade—do the numbers themselves create agreement? "We used to say that you could make data talk," Smithburg replies. "But there's good data and bad data. The difference now is that we are all looking at the same numbers and the emphasis is on analysis and decision-making. In effect, the data can persuade because they are analyzed well."

Smithburg thinks better information is a competitive asset. "We now ask ourselves: 'Are we competitive with our information systems?' Twenty-five years ago we wouldn't have asked that. It's important now because it is a real asset. I can't pinpoint a decision for which I am sure ESS made a contribution. But I'm sure there are countless examples of when it has. It's become part of our culture. Like the car phone, I don't know how we ever lived without it. ESS is not magic, not a black box, but in general it has exceeded my expectations."

Business has come under heavy criticism for concentrating unduly on the short term, and ESS would seem to make that even easier, but Smithburg doesn't place the blame on the computers. "Business has been criticized for this. Like any fundamental contribution, computers have a dark side, and overemphasis on data has been one result. The information churned out by securities firms can be awesome, and even inhibiting. I was once in a meeting at a securities firm where they had all kinds of computers and began to throw all kinds of data on the screen. It was almost too much. It was approaching 'analysis-paralysis.' But you can't blame the computers, they just do what they're told."

Smithburg thinks the prospects for ESS are very bright. The better that senior executives understand the systems, and the better information systems understand the executives, he says, the better they can work together. "It's really an investment decision. You have to get what's useful and necessary, not pie in the sky," he says. "If you aren't careful, the expenses can go through the roof. You don't need a Rolls Royce to go to the grocery store. I can't overemphasize how necessary prioritizing is to get what you really want and need. It's very hard, very demanding work to do that."

A MILLION-DOLLAR SAVINGS AT BENEFICIAL

"If I get a hard copy of a memo, I send it back. I get 100 to 120 pieces of mail a day, nearly all of it electronic."

Finn Caspersen, the CEO at Beneficial, explains why neither "trickle-down" nor "trickleup" ESS implementation was acceptable to him and why personal use of ESS by all of the company's executives is essential to make it work. "The system identifies whether the manager or the secretary answers my memos," says Caspersen. "I simply remind the sender that if I can trouble myself to send a memo, they can trouble themselves to answer it personally. That usually does the trick."

Caspersen admits that initially he underestimated the usefulness of ESS. "I thought it would be a nice tool to contain secretarial costs, but it has now got to the point that I don't think we could operate without it," he says. "I recently came into the office and the computer system was down between 7 and 8 A.M. That was not acceptable to me. You have to educate your systems people that downtime is unacceptable. Three hundred people depend on that system. Now someone comes in at 6 to be sure it's working.

"The system is really just a conduit for information. I don't type 'what-if' scenarios in the wee hours of the morning, and I don't do much primary analysis. The CEO's job is to maintain communication with individuals in the company, move decisions through committees or meetings in a timely fashion, and implement decisions. If I want to ask the senior-management committee for their advice, I only have to type 'SM' on my terminal, type the question, and out it goes to 18 people. I can do the same thing for the board of directors. This has really speeded up communications. Reliability and accuracy have grown tremendously. In only two instances in five years can I remember when a message I sent didn't reach the person intended, and that might have been my fault. I'm not sure."

Outside the office, the system can also be helpful. But Caspersen notes, "I have used the system traveling, and frankly, I've had problems with it. I used a lap-top computer and modem and found it hard to use in hotel rooms. The phone lines are too noisy and sometimes hard to connect. I don't use it that way anymore; I just call my secretary. I do have the ESS in my vacation home and have a dedicated phone line for that; it works fine. And when I visit other Beneficial offices, I often log onto the system."

Users claim that the rewards of networking go far beyond sending an electronic reminder of when the next meeting is going to take place. "ESS is useful in unanticipated ways," says Caspersen. "Let's suppose a broker calls in and says, 'I have a block of 100,000 shares of stock for sale. Would you like to buy it?' There might be five or six people in the company who would be interested. But reaching them by telephone could take half an hour. With electronic mail, we have the answer for the broker almost instantaneously."

Has ESS changed the way companies operate, the way they organize or structure their important functions? In many instances, it has simply automated activities, but in others it has been more fundamental. Caspersen thinks the latter applies to Beneficial. "I do think it has changed the way we do business. The system has an ingrained prejudice against long-winded memos and works best with terse, data-filled content. It has increased our executives' productivity tremendously. Most of them have the system at home, and as a result, they often work in the evening and on weekends. Most of the executives will be on-line with the system at least once each weekend. They can access files and communicate with other executives, who, if you tried to reach by phone, might not be there to receive the call."

The pace of change in today's world has become a cliché, but Caspersen sees a genuine need to make decisions faster "because competitors are making faster decisions." He continues: "The pace of new-product introductions is faster and profit margins are narrower, so the margin of error is smaller. As your business matures, your profit margins can go down and you have to make better decisions. You just can't afford to be the last to respond to important changes. We use the Lexis and Nexis on-line data bases for monitoring changes that can affect us. Lexis is for the legal department, and Nexis is for general news."

Executives invest heavily in meetings, some of which are unproductive. Beneficial uses ESS to eliminate some of the wasted time. "Meetings are more effective because of ESS," says Caspersen. "We have a meeting scheduling system that works well. If you want a meeting with six people who must attend and nine others who it would be nice if they attended, the system will round up their schedules and indicate the date. Not only can all the documents necessary for a decision at a meeting be prepared and distributed, you can tell if each person attending has received the material. You can also choose areas in which you may sacrifice some of the give-and-take of a meeting to make a quicker decision. For instance, I can send out a memo to six people and ask for their thoughts. All respond, and I make the decision. If someone objects, they can append it to the request and then we may have to have a meeting. Obviously, some of the meetings become unnecessary."

Some companies note "soft-dollar" benefits from ESS—such as nonmeasurable increases in the effectiveness and professionalism of their executives—but cannot easily document "hard-dollar" savings. Caspersen believes Beneficial realizes real savings. "We have actually decreased the number of secretaries. We had Deloitte Haskins & Sells do a study for us, and they found that there was a $1 million savings in the first year that the system was in operation and a nine-month payback for the cost of the equipment. Now, I'm not sure if that is accurate, and we have spent more since, but I'm sure the system is helpful."

Beneficial is sufficiently convinced of the value of ESS to invest more money. "We are building a new system called Bencom III," Caspersen explains, "which will change the way we do business throughout the company. Not only will it make the field locations more efficient, but by pushing a button, I can inquire about the productivity of a single office if I need to."

Caspersen realizes that since others see a lot of his memos and decisions he is, to an extent, working in a fishbowl. But he sees a brighter side to this. "Some people may want to hide behind the statement that 'I have superior information that you don't have.' But I don't operate that way. I think it's an advantage for all to see the data that decisions are based on. I'd rather have people knock holes in my argument, and if you make a mistake, you make a mistake. The more people that have a chance to speak their piece, the less likely you are to make a wrong decision."

Is old-fashioned persuasion no longer necessary? Not according to Caspersen. "The facts alone won't make the decision to carry it out," he says. "People have to be motivated. As CEO, you have the power to send out a memo to 20 people and say, 'Do this,' and then you can relax and read the *Wall Street Journal*. But if you know someone has a tough job to meet a deadline, you don't just demand cooperation, you call and say it's important and, 'How can I help if you need it?' I find that you really have to lean over backward to avoid saying something in a cold, impersonal way because the system makes it so easy to do that."

Given Caspersen's ESS experience at Beneficial, what would he say to fellow CEOs thinking of acquiring an ESS? "I would tell them it's like getting another three or four secretaries, each with 20 years' experience, and a couple of MBAs thrown in. It's just great. I must admit that I cheated initially, in order to be able to lead and be experienced. I didn't want to look like a fool using it and making blunders. I had a system installed at home three months ahead of the others and worked on it every night until I felt comfortable with it."

If he could have known the benefits of the system beforehand, Caspersen says he would have pushed his managers to adopt the system even faster. "I would be very strict about getting all to use it and insisting that executives use it, not just their secretaries. You don't have to type; I don't type that well. I still believe that it must be done from the top down. There will always be a few who can't change—a secretary who finds long-standing methods comfortable and can't adapt, the executive who deigns not to type on a keyboard. It pays to find that out early rather than several years later. It is absolutely a leadership issue from the CEO on down.

"Those who kept an open mind learned to use it effectively, even if they were at first opposed to it. There's no place for the executive who calls his secretary, presents the document to her, she bows twice, retires, and prepares it. Frankly, we lost a few people who couldn't change, and it's just as well. Although there was both surprising acceptance from some quarters and surprising rejection from others, overall, it went better than I hoped. But it does require firmness. It's an open-and-shut case. There's a natural ambiguity about anything new, but I would probably push it faster if I had it to do again."

CEO-COMPATIBLE SYSTEMS

For executives such as Caspersen, Smithburg, and Allaire, ESS undoubtedly works. But how transferable are their personal and company experiences to others? The answer, some say, lies not just in the technology available or the executives' ability to describe their work and needs, but deeper in the company, in its information systems. To satisfy their ordinary computing requirements, companies have developed systems and attitudes that create inflexible structures, enforce conformity, and are intolerant of ambiguity. These are far from ideal qualities in an ESS. The work of top executives is fairly unstructured and nonroutine; facts are necessary but not sufficient to make good decisions. In addition, a lot of good ESS software is sold by outside vendors such as Execucom, Comshare Inc., and Pilot Executive Software, which can lead to the not-invented-here syndrome.

Essentially, information systems should see ESS development not as catering to the personal whims of top management but as a means of enhancing their work, to the benefit of the whole company. Giving senior executives the information they need can have greater impact than automating the work of several hundred people below them. Top executives don't want their work to be easier—they thrive on difficulty. But they do want to be more effective, and ESS offers possibilities for doing that.

For some firms, the improved communications from ESS justifies use of the system. It's much harder to prove that better top-level decisions result. In the rarefied realm of decision-making, art overshadows science. ESS may not change that. Do shortcomings of current ESS and their rate of improvement justify reluctance to use them now? Probably not.

QUESTIONS

1. If you were an executive who wanted to implement an ESS, what steps would you take prior to its introduction to help insure its success?

2. How would you "sell" your Board of Directors on the need for implementing an ESS?

3. After successful implementation of the ESS, you find your Chief Financial Officer, who is 62 and strictly a "hands-off" person, refuses to use the electronic mail feature. How would you handle this situation?

4. Would you answer any or all of the first three questions differently if you were in charge of a not-for-profit organization rather than a profit-oriented firm? Justify your answer.

5. You leave the firm you are with and become the top executive of "XYZ" corporation. XYZ has successfully implemented an ESS that it quite different from the one you used previously. Would you adapt to the new ESS or would you have the new ESS adapted to you? Justify your answer.

22

Moments of Executive Enlightenment

John F. Rockart
David W. DeLong

Popular applications of executive support systems (ESSs) by senior management include electronic mail, which can improve communication, and retrieval of internal and external information to strengthen management's planning and control responsibilities. In the long term, however, the most significant benefit of ESSs may be the delivery to their users of enhanced mental business models.

Noted management theorist Henry Mintzberg asserts that one way executives use the information they collect is "to develop mental images—models of how an organization and its environment functions."[1] Mintzberg contends that mental models help executives deal with the inherent complexity of their jobs. "In effect," he says, "managers absorb the information around them into a series of mental models of the internal workings of their organizations, the behavior of subordinates, the trends in the organization's environment, the habits of associates, and so on. When choices must be made, these models can be used to test alternatives." Mintzberg concludes that the effectiveness of manager's decisions is largely dependent on the quality of their models.[2]

This article examines how ESSs are used consciously and unconsciously to enhance managers' conceptual maps of their business environments. Because cognitive modeling is still a somewhat mysterious process, there is little hard evidence that executives use ESSs to enrich their mental models. In fact, enhancing their personal understanding of their business was rarely cited by executives in our research as a primary motivation for developing an ESS. The evidence is limited to a few cases:

- Scientist George Hatsopoulos, chairman of Thermo Electron, in Waltham MA, says that improving his mental models was a primary objective in using his ESS—Hatsopoulos developed computer-based models of his firm's operations and the industries in which it competes as well as the U.S. economy. He adjusted his business thinking in light of what he learned by watching the flow of data through the models.

- The chairman of a large manufacturing company developed a series of forecasting models using historical company data and such business indicators of consumer confidence as housing starts—These models allow him to assess sales forecasts from different perspectives by accounting for different variables. Over time, the computer models have helped the chairman identify relationships among the factors that affect company sales. The models also help him challenge subordinates' assumptions and ensure that their forecasts are as realistic as possible.

Validation or simplification of the world that exists "in their heads" can be a major benefit of an ESS for some executives. The desire to improve their mental models, however, is rarely referred to directly. Instead, such responses as "I need to improve my understanding of the business" or "it gives me a better grasp of what's going on in the company" are used to explain the desire of senior executives to develop personal information systems.

FUNDAMENTAL BUSINESS UNDERSTANDING

Applications that enhance a manager's fundamental business understanding take many forms; our analysis of executives' comments suggests that six attributes of ESSs are most important in enhancing mental models:

- Improved access to external data
- New ways to combine data from multiple sources
- Presentation of data in more meaningful formats
- Sophisticated analytic and modeling capabilities
- The ability to identify and test assumptions about corporate performance
- Off-hours data access.

Access to Data

Improved access to external data can improve managers' environmental scanning by providing more relevant data quickly. Senior executives do much of their own scanning. Most consider it a primary task of management. In his study of Silicon Valley executives, Omar E. El Sawy notes:

> CEOs in the high technology environment are very systematic scanners, and the surveillance activity, although seeming haphazard to the outside observer, is in reality well planned. They monitor information sources that they know are likely to yield strategic information. There are certain habitual sources that the CEO monitors and consults, especially for verification.[3]

The increased speed and payoff of computer-based scanning helps executives justify performing this task themselves instead of delegating it to employees. Senior managers often find great value in filtering external data through their own mental models. According to Derwyn Phillips, executive vice-president of Gillette North America, in Boston:

> I find the external information, such as world news and competitive information, very helpful. I can scan the headlines and read the stories that look interesting. I don't have to wade through a lot of irrelevant material. Also, I find that the system focuses my attention, and I actually have better comprehension and retention of the information.[4]

The CEO of a high-technology firm says that he does a lot of scanning himself because there may be subtleties that others won't see.[5] And according to Lee Paschall, former CEO and president of American Satellite Company, in Rockville MD:

> If someone else did my information screening by clipping articles that he or she felt were pertinent to me, I would lose a lot of control. That person would have to judge what's important to me, and he or she simply wouldn't have my level of experience to know what nuance in a story may have long-term implications.[6]

These comments represent the attitudes of a growing number of senior managers who use ESSs to collect information about the external environment. El Sawy found that chief executives resist delegating environmental scanning because their cognitive maps are more complete and more sophisticated than those of subordinates. As a result, senior managers perceive information differently from employees at lower levels.

El Sawy differentiates between personal information communicated specifically to an individual and impersonal information found in periodicals and speeches. He and other researchers observe that managers rely more heavily on personal than impersonal sources for strategic information.

The ability to combine impersonal external sources with more personal staff analyses is a feature of a small but growing number of ESSs. For example, executives at ConAgra, a diversified food and agricultural products company in Omaha, have direct access to commodities markets information and to Dow Jones News/Retrieval. Reports are also provided by internal financial and economics research departments on critical factors, such as weekly crop conditions and interest rates.

At Phillips Petroleum, in Bartlesville OK, staff analysts summarize relevant economic and political news from around the world three times a day for top management. Executive vice-president Robert Wallace, who accesses these updates regularly through his ESS, says:

> I'm normally in my office by seven forty-five in the morning, and the first thing I used to grab was the *Wall Street Journal*. Now, the first thing I look at is the business highlights worldwide on our system, so that by eight o'clock I have literally looked at all the critical external factors for our business. I've been clear around the world with that business summary, and I have a very good feel before my day starts for what kind of environment I'm operating in right now. That is extremely valuable for an executive at my level.

Computer-based executive support can be an advantage in processing external information. Access to external data bases not only provides standard information faster than printed matter (e.g., news summaries and stock quotes), but as Lee Paschall contends, it also makes available additional information that previously was too time consuming to obtain. He says:

> When we put together a long-range plan for American Satellite, I used the data base to search through two years of information about fiber optics. It would have been hopeless to try to find all of this information by hand. We got a complete story of what has happened in fiber optics; we determined the plans, financing, and actual implementations of various fiber networks. I was able to give the board a very comprehensive report on where fiber optics is going and what they should do about it.[7]

El Sawy points out that the importance of environmental scanning should increase as the business environment becomes more complex and interconnected. Thus, the use of ESSs in collecting this type of strategic information will increase as well. But two things must happen first.

The software used to access external information must improve. Executives need an interface that allows them to log onto external data bases quickly and to search for information without having to remember large sets of commands. Although much of the current software has been awkward for the casual executive user, new interfaces that require a minimum number of keystrokes to access and search commercial data bases are being offered. Much of that external access is now provided indirectly by ESS support groups that bring information onto executives' information systems.

In addition, high-level, industry-specific data bases that support use of ESSs by executives must be made available. Most commercial data bases today contain information that is too raw and unsynthesized to be of much value to executives. To minimize this problem, some IS departments synthesize external data to make it more useful to executives, and some small vendors have sprung up to provide similar services.

One such company, Strategic Intelligence Systems, in Burlington MA, offers competitive intelligence data bases that cover 18 industries, including financial services, aerospace, and food. Updated monthly, these data bases abstract and analyze information from more than 500 publications. Topics include market activity, industry trends, legislation, and new product development. "This enables us to scan many more publications," says Jim Figura of Colgate-Palmolive, in New York, "but the biggest barrier in this area is getting expert knowledge out of the executive's head in a very abstract and free-flowing form and down to the people scanning the data sources so they can recognize what is useful."

New Ways to Combine Data

Access to external data is only one ESS capability that improves executives' business understanding. Combining data from multiple sources also enables executives to enhance their grasp of their businesses by exploring new cause-and-effect relationships. Gerald Viste, former president of Wausau Insurance Companies, in Wausau WI, describes this benefit:

> We have extended the resources of the [ESS] to include a large library of public data on our competitors and the industry. This has been particularly useful when matched with our internal data and has significantly deepened our insight into the problems and opportunities that challenge us as managers. We also couple the information from DRI's [an econometric research service] industry model with these other resources. Was this same information available before we had terminals in our offices? Of course it was. But it was a burdensome task to assemble it from the volumes of books and reports into formats that matched the problem areas under scrutiny.[8]

In another example, a vice-president for product development and marketing uses a multiple-source management review system. Product and sales data is extracted from a corporate data base that consolidates product information from around the world. Expenditures are pulled automatically from the general ledger system. Data on product quality is extracted from another system, and still more information, such as product development milestones, is collected manually from department files. This information is synthesized monthly into a set of standard-format graphs and charts.

The vice-president says this about the use of the system in management review meetings:

> Looking at data on the screen, we have an immediate perspective on the trends that are taking place, because we see the information for previous months and previous quarters, so there is generally instant agreement about the trends and where things are going.

Meaningful Formats

Presenting data in flexible formats that can combine text, numbers, and graphics helps many executives understand their businesses by highlighting trends they might not recognize as tabular data alone. Ronald Compton, president of American Re-Insurance Co, in New York, explains it:

> I'm a very visual person; my first love is photography. So graphics is a wonderful tool for me. I can understand graphs quickly, and so can others. I always say that graphs is a language you can teach anybody. Before we got this system, it could take an entire day at looking at tables to see the trends that are contained in one graph.[9]

Another executive observes:

> I think graphically. It's so nice to be able to easily graph out the data in which I'm interested. And it's especially nice to be able to adjust the display to see the data in the exact perspective that best tells the story.[10]

The new presentation formats—particularly graphics—have had an important effect on the way executives think about information. But graphics is not the only formatting advantage provided by a computer. The CEO of a major food distributor took advantage of his computer's ability to combine tabular, textual, and graphic data on the same page to satisfy his idiosyncratic way of viewing performance data.

Graphics are typically used for standard performance reports or to present the results of ad hoc queries. The president of Citibank Columbia found that a graphic display of profits versus goals and forecasts provided a picture over time and revealed business dynamics he had not previously recognized. Derwyn Phillips, Gillette's executive vice-president, implemented his ESS largely to view performance reports graphically. Phillips believes that executives focus too much on minor variances when looking at numbers. The key is to see trends, not minor blips, he says, and graphs help management do that. This search for understanding—the ability to recognize trends and patterns in the data that inundates executives' desks—is described by Horton in his profile of eight chief executives:

> Despite the prodigious amounts of data that arrive at the CEO's desk, there is an unquenchable thirst for more. The volume and fire-hose velocity of this information would overwhelm most executives, but the successful chief develops the capacity to stand to the side, sampling chunks of data as they rush by, looking for patterns and incongruities. To draw meaning from a mass of data in motion requires a capacity to synthesize—an ability to convert data into information and information into knowledge.[11]

Wausau president Gerald Viste sums up the benefits of graphics in this process:

> Although the flexibility and efficiency with which one can develop tabular reports is a convenience, the ability to graph the data is of far greater importance. I have found that graphic presentations are much more effective than the tabular format in determining stability or volatility, direction, change, and observations in our operations. To see data as a graphic time series rather than as a column of comparisons really highlights significant situations.[12]

Sophisticated Analyses and Modeling

In addition to providing data from new sources in new formats, ESSs strengthen business understanding by providing analytic and modeling capabilities. These systems allow for the exploration of the cause-and-effect relationships that underlie a firm's business environment. They bring enhanced spreadsheet analysis and DSS modeling capabilities to senior managers (though the actual number crunching may still be done by employees). Some comprehensive models have been built for, or by, senior executives; however, most analytical work addresses specific problems. Owen Butler, former chairman of Procter & Gamble, in Cincinnati, exemplifies executives who learned to program and build financial models on their own. He says:

> It's much more efficient to think through a problem at the same time that you are working on it; in this way, you interact directly with the thought process. Sometimes I get to the point where I realize I want to change a

model and I can do it right then and there. If someone else was building it, this wouldn't be possible.[13]

The exploration of alternative scenarios online is an infrequent ESS application, but we did find several examples. In Akron OH, the president of Firestone Tire & Rubber Co works closely with his controller, who accesses an ESS to explore future business scenarios (e.g., If we raise our equity in our French affiliate, what effect would that have on Asian operations?). This approach to what-if scenarios allows management to use actual financial data base information without disrupting official financial and accounting data.

John Dembeck, vice-president and treasurer of the Olin Corporation, in Stamford Ct, has had similar sessions with his chairman:

> The chairman frequently comes into my office and poses a question or problem. We look at the screen together. In this way, we try a wide range of alternative scenarios. If an analyst were coming in here to make a presentation relating to a problem we gave him, we would probably be much more limited as to how many alternatives we gave [sic] him. If we constantly changed our minds, he'd go crazy. And we might be embarrassed to ask for an analysis of some of our wilder ideas.[14]

All of these executives perform analyses that would be impractical without a computer. One bank executive, however, qualifies his praise on his newfound cognitive capability. "Where we used to do what-ifs in two days," he says, "we now do ten in an hour. It doesn't necessarily lead to better decisions, but you feel more secure."[15]

David Davis, president of a $100 million British firm, adds, "Until the last few years, I viewed most of the complex quantitative techniques that I learned at business school as spare baggage; I now find that I have used more of them in the last year than I had in the previous ten."[16]

Does increased analytic and modeling capability help managers improve their mental models of their businesses? We do not know. But an increasing number of senior managers believe that it does. And the concept behind modeling—to abstract the fundamental structure of a complex environment—points in that direction.

Identify and Test Business Assumptions

The ability to uncover and test business assumptions is a major, but usually unforeseen, benefit of ESSs. An ESS provides data that might challenge the assumptions that underlie managers' mental models. By definition, changing assumptions means altering an executive's understanding of a business. For example, a large food distributor designed a system at its CEO's request to improve the firm's management control process. But the reports generated by the system also challenged the CEO's assumptions about the company's future direction. "When I looked at graphs of revenues in our SBUs [strategic business units]," he says, "and saw the three core businesses standing out, while the other units were flat and the new businesses were negative, I realized we needed to put more support into the core businesses. The system changed my assumptions about diversification because it confronted us with hard data."[17]

An ESS enables senior management to question its assumptions and those of its subordinates more readily. But what is the relationship between assumptions and mental models? G.E. Wagner answers:

> . . . A mental image of the business environment is developed. That image is an imperfect simplification of the environment, based on limited input and mental processes; it is a mental model that guides the organization's actions. My definition of assumptions is that they are the components of that image. In this sense, assumptions include beliefs, values, hopes, dreams, comfortable illusions, and familiar habits of thought. Many assumptions together—in an individual's mind or in the collective mind of a managerial group—form the mental images on which decisions are based. My point is that a deep, fundamental need of senior management is for technology to help externalize, communicate, understand, challenge, arrive at consensus upon, and own assumptions.[18]

Assumptions are the building blocks of mental models. When assumptions are challenged, the model may be affected. Henderson, Rockart, and Sinfonis have argued that ESSs primarily manage executives' assumptions about their businesses, noting that:

> The management of assumptions . . . cannot be delegated. The assumption set is the domain of executive management, and the responsibility for ensuring the validity of assumptions rests clearly with executive management. We suggest that a major implicit reason for existing ESSs is to support executives in the analysis of critical assumptions.[19]

The management of assumptions may be a reason for an ESS, but it remains implicit with only one or two exceptions. Yet as an ESS by-product, it can be significant.

Sometimes executives use ESSs to challenge assumptions directly. For example, at Thermo-Electron, chairman George Hatsopoulos had doubts about one division's claim of an 80 percent share in a specialized market segment for industrial furnaces. Hatsopoulos built a data base to check the claim and discovered that the division management's assumptions about market share were wrong. The share was smaller in the industrial furnaces segment but greater in another part of the market. As a result, the division shifted its strategy to build on its market leadership.[20]

Off-Hours Data Access

Many executives are frustrated by their dependence on others for information they need on specific business issues. An ESS gives an executive access to corporate or external data on demand—even after regular working hours—without relying on staff or secretarial support. One senior manager describes how this helps:

> Some of my best ideas come at fallow times between five in the evening and seven the next morning. Access to the relevant data to check out something right then is very important. My home terminal lets me perform the analysis while it's at the forefront of my mind.[21]

For an executive, the ability to check a particular item late in the evening can mean the difference between pursuing a line of thought and putting it aside. Because many executives believe that they do their best thinking outside the workday routine, immediate access to corporate data can facilitate this cognitive process. Ronald Compton, president of American Re-Insurance Co, expresses this idea succinctly: "An idea could come to me at any time," he says. "With a PC at home, a lap portable to carry along when I travel and when I'm on my sailboat, and one here at the office, it's always close at hand."[22]

Support for all-hours thinking will not directly improve an executive's business understanding, but information access—especially when some of a manager's most reflective thinking is done—is certain to be valuable.

A FIRST STEP

We know enough about mental models to talk about them as a critical factor in executive work and, thus, ESSs. Cognitive modeling remains enough of a mystery, however, that consciously designing an ESS to help enrich an executive's mental model is still very difficult. To date, information systems that help executives improve their comprehension of business reality have almost always been designed with other more concrete goals in mind. Yet, when asked, executives frequently point to uses that indicate a significant role for ESS in supporting, testing, and communicating their cognitive maps. Identifying benefits is the first step toward recognizing the real value of computer systems for senior managers.

REFERENCES

1. H. Mintzberg, *The Nature of Managerial Work* (New York: Harper & Row, 1973), p. 70.

2. Mintzberg, pp. 89–90.

3. O. E. El Sawy, "Personal Information Systems for Strategic Scanning in Turbulent Environments: Can the CEO Go On-Line?," *MIS Quarterly* (March 1985), p. 58.

4. Quoted in an interview with Donald Palmer, Controller, Gillette, NA (Boston, MA: Pilot Executive Software, 1986).

5. El Sawy, p. 56.

6. Quoted in N. D. Meyer and M. E. Boone, *The Information Edge* (Agincourt, Ontario: Gage Educational Publishing, 1987), p. 227.

7. Quoted in Meyer and Boone, p. 226.

8. G. Viste, "Executive Use of Interactive MIS" (Speech to American Assembly of Collegiate Schools of Business, Phoenix AZ, May 3, 1984).

9. Quoted in Meyer and Boone, p. 217.

10. J. F. Rockart and M. E. Treacy, "The CEO Goes On-Line," *Harvard Business Review* (January–February 1982), p. 86, reprinted by permission.

11. T. R. Horton, *What Works for Me* (New York: Random House, 1986), p. 388.

12. Viste, p. 6.

13. H. Fersko-Weiss, "Personal Computing at the Top," *Personal Computing* (March 1985), p. 71.

14. Meyer and Boone, p. 215.

15. P. Nulty, "How Personal Computers Change Managers' Lives," *Fortune* (September 3, 1984), p. 44.

16. D. Davis, "Computers in Top Management," *Sloan Management Review* (Spring 1984), p. 63, reprinted by permission.

17. See R. O. Mason and I. F. Mitroff, *Challenging Strategic Planning Assumptions: Theory, Cases and Techniques* (New York: John Wiley & Sons, 1981); P. Wack, "Scenarios: Uncharted Waters Ahead." *Harvard Business Review* 63, no 5 (September–October 1985); P. Senge, "Catalyzing Systems Thinking Within Organizations" (Working paper, Systems Dynamics Group, MIT, Cambridge MA, 1987).

18. G. E. Wagner, "DSS: Dealing with Executive Assumptions in the Office of the Future," *Managerial Planning* 30, no 5 (March–April, 1982), p. 4.

19. J. C. Henderson, J. F. Rockart, and J. G. Sifonis, "A Planning Methodology for Integrating Management Support Systems" (*Working Paper no 116*, Center for Information Systems Research, Sloan School of Management, MIT, Cambridge MA, September 1984), pp. 15, 23.

20. M. Bralove, "Some Chief Executives Bypass, and Irk, Staffs in Getting Information," *The Wall Street Journal* (January 12, 1983), p. 22.

THE IMPACT OF EIS

21. Rockart and Treacy, p. 86.
22. Meyer and Boone, p. 218.

QUESTIONS

1. What do the authors identify as the most important benefit of executive support systems? What is their rationale for choosing this particular benefit?
2. What are the six key attributes of executive support systems that help to produce the benefit in question 1?
3. Compare and contrast each of these six key attributes in the context of transaction processing system (TPS), management information systems (MIS), decision support systems (DSS), and executive support systems.

23

EIS and the Collapse of the Information Pyramid

David Friend

As a participant in the market for executive information systems, one of my most important jobs is to understand why some EISs flourish while others languish. It is not too difficult to measure success or failure in the EIS industry because these attributes can be expressed in a number of quantifiable ways—growth in number of users or hourly use per week, for example. What I find most challenging, however, is the interpretation of these measures—that is, discovering and defining the market place forces that drive these trends.

Much has been written and said about how to start an EIS. My objective here is to describe what it takes to get the job finished. The data that others and I have gathered about that process from actual EIS users suggests some rather heretical conclusions about how a successful EIS will ultimately function.

In a 1982 article written for *Computer Decisions,* I argued the case for small EISs narrowly focused on the issues relevant to individual managers. "*Simplicity* is the key word where EIS is concerned," I wrote. "EIS is really a small-scale problem." Similarly, when John Rockart and David DeLong published *Executive Support Systems: The Emergence of Top Management Computer Use* in 1988, one of the key factors in EIS success was the focus on an "executive sponsor" whose needs shaped the EIS design.

EIS theory current at the time held that by reducing the amount of information in the system to only that needed by the executive sponsor, the system would be small, manageable, and relevant to the end user. A

Previously published in *Information Center,* Volume 6, Number 3, March 1990 by Weinzarten Publications Inc. Used with permission.

much-cited example of an early EIS success was Northwest Industries, whose system contained:

- 350 monthly financial and operational line items
- 45 economic and key ratio time series
- Several externally subscribed data bases, including Standard & Poors, Compustat, and DRI.

By today's standards, this was a very limited system. And, it is interesting to note, the EIS died almost immediately after the retirement of its executive sponsor.

INDIVIDUAL FOCUS VS. ORGANIZATIONAL FOCUS

The Northwest Industries example highlights one of the principal causes of EIS failure: an *individual*, rather than *organizational*, focus. By addressing individual needs instead of those of the organization, the EIS does not become part of the corporate culture and remains tied to the continuing sponsorship of the executive.

Many IS professionals, and many vendors, for that matter, still hold to the "small-scale" model of EIS. While I still believe this model of EIS is valid, it is not the model that will ultimately define the EIS market place. Part of the explanation for the persistence of the small-scale model is the tendency to define EIS from a "who uses it?" perspective. From this perspective, an EIS is defined as "an information system for executives."

But an EIS can also be defined by what it is. Such is the technologist's view of EIS, and it promises a very different scenario for the future of the EIS industry. The "what is it?" perspective holds that EIS is hypertext navigation, point-and-click user interaction, integration of text and time series data, flexible data views, multiple data sources, and so forth.

One of Pilot's customers (whose EIS, incidentally, can produce somewhere between half a million and a million different data screens) recently told me the following: "We don't even call this an EIS. We call it our 'CIN,' for 'corporate information network.' It is the company's definitive source for near real-time operational data. We think it is totally illogical to limit EIS technology to executives. Our CIN is not peripheral to the business like many EISs are, used by few and ignored by most. It is central to the business. If you have to use the EIS acronym, it ought to mean 'everybody's information system.'"

In the "what is it?" view of EIS, the system becomes a potent weapon in an organization's information technology arsenal. It can be used to address a class of information delivery problems whose characteristics include touch-screen or mouse-driven graphical interfaces and techniques for navigating through data bases and the like, without respect to the title or position of the user. In fact, the whole notion of executive sponsorship is less important here than is the sponsorship of MIS leaders who can project the capabilities of EIS tools on to solutions for existing information technology problems.

In many respects, the mission of EIS technology is quite similar to the mission of 4GLs a decade ago. The difference is that 4GLs produced paper reports or dumb-terminal screens, where EIS offers a highly interactive on-line environment with navigational and graphical interfaces. The real question facing the EIS industry, however, is can EIS do for on-line data what 4GLs did for paper-based reporting?

GROWTH IN SCALE

If the technology to solve a problem exists, then people will eventually bring the problem and the technology together. Increasingly, MIS professionals are discovering what EIS technology can actually do and are therefore starting to think of it in terms of what it is, rather than by whom it is used. Users have grasped the original, limited concepts behind EIS and are now attempting to extend those concepts well beyond their original scope. In many cases, however, their existing EIS technology is not up to the task.

As the world changes its perception of EIS from one of abstract business theory to that of a practical technology application, two important trends are taking place. The first is a dramatic growth in the scale of EIS applications. The second is the downgrading of monthly data in favor of rapidly churning daily, or near real-time, data. Any EIS that cannot adapt to the demands of large-scale and near real-time response will more than likely fail.

Most EISs start small, with few users, limited scope, and small data bases. In fact, many EISs start with no data base at all and are merely executive "slideshows" on a PC. However, if these initial efforts show the promise of EIS technology, many forces begin to mandate a rapid growth in scale. Unfortunately, many EIS builders never plan for this growth and, as is the case with living organisms, growth constraints eventually lead to the death of the EIS.

The reasons for this scenario should be obvious. A senior executive who is able to ask specific, probing questions of a subordinate will immediately create a new customer for the EIS. A mid-level manager with an EIS will create peer pressure, as well as pressure from his subordinates, and so on. One Pilot customer responsible for his company's EIS, in fact, told me recently that senior management's use of the system has created a near-riot among middle managers who are clamoring for their own access to the EIS. If demand such as this remains unsatisfied for any length of time, affected middle managers will become enemies of the EIS and will welcome, or perhaps abet, the EIS's demise.

Another factor in the growth of EIS scale is the invalidity of the classic information hierarchy, which shows EIS atop an information pyramid based on operational data at the bottom and decision support systems in between. This model does not conform to facts gained from field research. There is no evidence to suggest that executives need or want a high-level overview based on highly aggregated data. To the contrary, even the highest-level executives have demonstrated an insatiable appetite for operational detail, which means that no matter how much information is contained in an EIS, much more always seems to be missing. An effective EIS, therefore, needs to penetrate to what may seem an excruciating level of detail. Granted, most of the information at the detail level will not be used, as executives tend to focus on a narrow set of currently important issues such as new product launches or plant profitability problems. Unfortunately, this focus is not constant and changes suddenly and unpredictably as new issues arise. For this reason, the EIS needs breadth as well as depth.

Can any organization afford to build a system of this magnitude for just a few executives? I don't believe so. If one does, the system will always be vulnerable to cost accountants who challenge its cost-effectiveness. For that reason, EISs will eventually have to be shared by a large number of users, and must be treated as a corporate information resource, and not as a personal system for the CEO.

THE MOVE TO REAL-TIME RESULTS

I hold it as a maxim that no matter how up-to-date information is, it is never as up-to-date as it should be. It used to be that executives would accept a 10-day turnaround of their monthly financials. Now, however, we see executives who get upset because yesterday's sales results are 30 minutes late on the EIS. The world of near real-time control has spread from manufacturing to marketing to finance to nearly every other aspect of corporate life.

As information systems move toward near real-time access with enormous depth and breadth, managers can turn their focus to the specific rather than the general. In fact, as one senior executive told me, a "general" focus does not really exist in business. "General" is the aggregate impression one gets from many specifics.

As the pace of business change accelerates and managers "de-layer" their organizations to diminish the bureaucracy, they have no choice but to turn to information technology for solutions. Executives demand the ability to control their businesses in smaller increments of time and scope. Business schools refer to this phenomenon as "micro-management." The result is more differentiated regional marketing, faster product evolution, lower inventories, greater manufacturing flexibility, and the mass production of customized products.

Where most EISs have focused on the events of the recent past, future EISs will concentrate on the here and now. Today, it is a luxury to have the time to dwell on past performance or even think beyond the immediate future. As an example, most serious business planning efforts occur off-site, so that the intensity of day-to-day business does not impinge on the process. Time horizons have shortened for everyone—engineers must get products to market faster, marketers must respond more quickly to competitors and changes in purchase patterns, and executives must refine their ability to control all these accelerating practices.

Evidence of this strong interest in near real-time data comes from International Data Corp.'s August 1989 survey of 93 companies planning to implement an EIS. Of the 93 respondents, 10 wanted real-time data, 2 wanted hourly, 44 wanted daily, and 17 weekly. Only 10 were interested in monthly data.

ABILITY TO GROW IS CRITICAL

As we have seen, business forces are causing EIS users to migrate from a simple environment, oriented to specific individual managers, to much more complex environments, supporting multiple departments or business units and drawing on an abundance of data bases and data sources. The result is that while most EISs start small, they will ultimately have to grow to survive. A vendor's ability to overcome real impediments to such growth will be the most important factor in its continued success in the marketplace.

The number of screens capable of being produced by an EIS is a critical indicator of its ability to accommodate the growth necessary to keep the system vital. Today, most EIS systems are based on monthly updates for the use of one to five people. However, the systems are increasingly extending their reach to larger user populations and supplying more frequent updates. As we inevitably push toward millions of systems, each serving hundreds of users with daily (or more frequent) updates, the impediments to growth are increasingly being tested and understood. If anything about an EIS makes it difficult to follow this natural expansion, the system will probably stagnate and die.

I will cite a few examples of this trend toward increasing depth, breadth, and update frequency.

- About 18 months ago, this west coast pharmaceutical company implemented an EIS with four to six users and an application involving financials that were primarily monthly. Today, it has 12 users supported by 1 and a half developers, and plans to expand to 50–100 users shortly. Important applications today include *daily* sales by product, *daily* inventory by product, and *daily* top customer report, as well as sales required to meet projections.

- This major insurance company's first EIS failed. It had two users and focused on monthly financials. A restart of the EIS project commenced about a year ago and today the system encompasses 80–90 users, supported by two to three developers. The focus today is on *daily* commission sales by product, region, and agent.

- This major metropolitan hospital began its EIS with only monthly financials and five users. Today, about 20 people use the EIS, which tracks *daily* and weekly census and supplies information on length of stay, patient demographics, number of admissions vs. discharges, capacity utilization, DRG case mix, payor mix, and insurance sources, as well as various key ratios and analyses.

- This major west coast bank implemented an EIS about two years ago with five users and monthly financials only. Today, the monthly financials are gone and have been replaced by *daily* data on deposits, loans, fee income, and staffing.

- This worldwide engineering firm started its EIS with monthly financials and a small user base. In less than two years, the system has grown to 65 users, still supported by only 1 and a half people.

Each of these organizations initially implemented an EIS as a "front end" to the monthly financials. The functional capabilities were simple and oriented to display and presentation. From that point, each faced three possible growth paths:

1. Same small number of users with more applications,
2. Same number of applications rolled out to more users,
3. Growth in both users and functionality.

It is my belief that the first two paths eventually lead to system failure.

IMPORTANCE OF THE DATA-DRIVEN FOUNDATION

As these systems grow, a self-generating, data-driven foundation becomes extremely important because most impediments to growth manifest themselves in terms of maintenance and support problems.

At present, it is not uncommon to find a ratio of one support person for every three to five executive users. A recent study at the University of Georgia suggested the same EISs have annual maintenance and support costs in excess of $10,000 per user, exclusive of hardware. While it is possible to extend such systems to a larger number of users by "throwing bodies" at the maintenance and support problem, the real answer is to find technological solutions to maintenance and support costs that allow growth in the user base without a commensurate growth in costs.

One of the most obvious ways to attack the maintenance and support costs is to centralize the maintenance of EIS data bases. IDC's August 1989 survey of its IBM 370 panel showed that most MIS managers agree with this notion. When asked where they would want their EIS data base to reside, 54 percent said "host only." Only nine percent suggested they would want their EIS data to reside at the workstation only. Yet many EISs today require downloading of data or screens to individual PCs. While easier to implement, such systems do not appear to spread as quickly as systems featuring cooperative processing and a shared central data base.

The advantages of centralized control of EIS data bases are obvious—minimum data redundancy, excellent security, and high data integrity. Interestingly, the IDC survey also showed data integrity to be the *most critical* system-level feature, with 65 percent of respondents saying that data integrity is crucial to EIS success.

One important note: Many people in the EIS industry mistakenly refer to data down-loads from a host to a workstation or LAN server as "distributed data bases." Distributed data of this kind is rife with problems, including integrity and security issues.

To keep data bases from becoming an obstacle to near real-time data access, the EIS data base should avoid batch processes wherever possible. In many cases, this will mean building the EIS on top of existing data bases.

Some EIS vendors now have the capability to build systems that run against existing SQL data bases such as DB2, SQL/DS, and Ingres. Dynamic access to these data bases that eliminates the necessity for a separate EIS data base is key to the success of the EIS implementation, as maintenance of existing EIS applications will flow from updates to the data. This is a critical consideration, since converting an EIS from monthly to daily data delivery can multiply many maintenance problems twentyfold. A smooth data flow from production sources all the way to the EIS end user is a top-priority concern.

DEVELOPMENT AND MAINTENANCE AIDS

CASE-like tools such as code generators and off-the-shelf EIS applications represent other ways to keep ahead of the costs associated with a growing EIS.

Code generators allow a developer of modest skill to create and maintain applications at a fraction of the cost of hand-coding techniques. These advanced tools should deliver at least a threefold increase in developer productivity.

Off-the-shelf applications that fit a variety of EIS requirements are offered by most vendors today. Because many of these applications are supported by the vendor, they offer the advantages of low startup costs, low maintenance, and high reliability. Their only drawback is that they may not exactly fit the user's requirements. However, most of these applications are modifiable to fit a fairly wide variety of problems.

GROUPWARE

Finally, I would like to mention the role of groupware in facilitating the growth of EIS.

It takes a great deal of time and effort to develop formal systems capable of tracking worldwide sales or monitoring a multinational company's cash balances on a daily basis. If these issues were not enduring business concerns, there would be no point in addressing them with professionally-managed systems.

At the other extreme from these ongoing business concerns are what I would call "transient" issues-problems or questions that need a single answer and then are likely to disappear. These issues are increasingly being addressed with electronic mail, voice mail, and nontechnical solutions such as face-to-face meetings around the water cooler.

Between the two are issues that will be around for a while but not long enough to warrant a formal MIS tracking system. These temporary issues grab an amazingly large part of the executive's attention and include such items as labor disputes, investment opportunities, hostile takeovers, disasters, new product launches, new plant construction, and financings. Most executives are driven by a handful of such issues at any one time, and as some are resolved, others emerge.

At the most senior levels, ongoing issues addressed by formal MIS systems become a backdrop that puts temporary issues into perspective. However, it is precisely these temporary issues that have the heat of the moment.

Electronic mail is actually a trivial example of the groupware that can be brought to bear on these short-term issues. However, more sophisticated products are now being introduced that allow issues to be set up and tracked without the necessity of MIS intervention and expense. These new products will improve the ability of EIS to address the issues that managers face on a daily basis.

Lotus Note ...

RECOMMENDATIONS

Like many of life's adventures, EIS is full of surprises. Just when you think you're done, you discover that you've just begun. Managers planning for EIS implementation would do well to keep the following recommendations in mind:

- Prepare for growth in scale,
- Prepare for near real-time access,
- Prepare for a large user base, and
- Consider how your chosen EIS technology will stand up over time.

The key to long-term success with EIS is to think ahead, beyond what may be reasonably anticipated today.

The history of the computer industry has been one of surpassing all reasonable expectations. Who would have believed even 10 years ago in the possibility of many things that we now take for granted?

When I started in the EIS industry, common wisdom held that executives would never have computers in their offices. Now, however, the executive without a computer is quickly becoming the exception rather than the rule.

QUESTIONS

1. What was the cause of the demise of the EIS at Northwest Industries?
2. In this author's view, what is the mission of EIS technology?
3. Why does an EIS need breadth as well as depth?
4. What approach does this author suggest for the maintenance and support of EIS data bases?
5. What is the most critical success factor in EIS success?

24

Executive Information System Streamlines Greyhound Dial's Operations

Execucom Systems Corporation

Here's a recipe for potential corporate disaster: mix equal measures of intense competition and unfavorable tax legislation, add an unpredictable level of deregulation and smother with an increasingly demanding financial market. Shake it up and what do you get? The situation in which Greyhound Dial Corporation found itself in 1986.

But through a combination of dieting—divesting itself of unprofitable assets—and the judicious use of the latest information technology, the Phoenix, Arizona-based corporation is a radically different and quantifiably more profitable company in 1990 than it has been at any time in its 80-plus year history.

The image of a corporation is often a lot more durable than the corporation itself. Many people still think that Greyhound Dial operates the intercity bus transport system, when in fact it sold off its U.S. bus operations in 1987. While it is the leading manufacturer of intercity coaches and transit buses in North America, Greyhound Dial is staking its future on a careful mix of consumer products and services. Under the Greyhound Dial umbrella are such popular names as Dial soap, Purex bleach, Brillo soap pads, 20 Mule Team Borax, Armour Star canned meats and Lunch Bucket microwaveable meals. Services include Dobbs International Services, the second largest inflight caterer to airlines and Premier Cruise Lines, the Official Cruise Line of Walt Disney World.

Previously published in *Planner* Volume 12, Number 2, 1990. Used with permission of Execucom Systems Corporation.

The current makeup of the Greyhound Dial Corporation can be traced to the monumental changes buffeting American industry throughout the 1980s. Increased competition from overseas, the rising costs of capital, shifting tax codes, an emphasis on services deregulation and changing consumer demographics created opportunities for organizations with infrastructures appropriate for rapid decision-making.

"The whole makeup of Greyhound Dial changed in the 1980s," says Assistant Controller Mike Brown. "We were going through a tremendous period of restructuring. As a result, it became vital from the corporate level to manage, track and operate the various lines of business that are important to Greyhound Dial."

PROFOUND CULTURAL CHANGES

Two consequences were the result of this perception. First, Greyhound Dial went through a profound cultural change that saw an increased role for both the Controllers and Information Services divisions. Second, Greyhound Dial significantly enhanced its investment in information technology, especially in terms of software and networked PC workstations for the executives.

TOP DRIVING FORCE

The driving force for such changes as the increased scope of the Controller's division and rapid development of CIS came from the very top: Greyhound Dial Chairman John W. Teets. Teets realized that to bring the return on equity up to his expectations Greyhound Dial would have to act decisively. He wanted his managers to base Greyhound Dial's future on unshakable facts and defensible predictions. Prior to 1987, Greyhound Dial simply did not have the data collection and analytical tools in place to give top managers such information. Its existing planning system, a main-frame-based electronic spreadsheet, was limited to tracking only 35 businesses.

The first high-level decision for the system was approved in June, 1987. Chairman Teets imposed an aggressive schedule for the system. It had to be up and running to accept 1988 plans by November 1, 1987; further, it had to be in place to accept actual 1988 financial results starting with the February 15, 1988 collection of January end-of-month data.

"At Greyhound Dial we ask executives to be more than managers," Teets explains, "They are expected to be leaders of change. An investment in technology was critical to our ability to control that change. Specifically, it has paid off in improved timeliness, content and consistency of vital information and has provided our executives with tools for planning, analysis and control."

A process started in the summer of 1987 resulted less than three years later in a fully operational executive information system that gives top executives up-to-date information on Greyhound Dial's diverse mix of operations.

One obvious result of Greyhound Dial's evolution is the Corporate Information System (CIS), an Executive Information System which tracks 85 major lines of business that reside in approximately 35 subsidiaries. The system shows top management the dynamic relationships among internal financial data and operational results. This information is then tied to other data and displayed in a way that makes the information quickly understandable.

CIS collects financial data on a monthly basis from Greyhound Dial's subsidiaries. Much of the data is in the company's McCormack & Dodge General Ledger and Accounting systems. To make the data immediately useful to executives, the system migrates selected views of the data to IFPS, Execucom's financial modeling and database system. Greyhound Dial uses IFPS to develop planning and analysis, budgeting, forecasting, consolidation and reporting applications.

For systems of this complexity, many companies take three years just to come up with a prototype. What did Greyhound Dial do to speed up the development process? First, the development team was workable in size. That meant that the initial user community was narrowly defined as the Controllers and Treasurer's Strategic Planning Departments. Greyhound Dial recognized that the variables introduced by too many end user communities would have made the three-year schedule unworkable. The design of the system will accommodate the needs of such users as the Tax and Property Departments in the near future. Other members of the development team, lead by Information Services Director Lynn Lahman, included auditors from a Big Five accounting firm, who managed the collection of data into the general ledger, and consultants from Execucom, who managed the extraction and processing of data into IFPS.

MEANINGFUL INFORMATION

CIS takes current and historic information and presents it in a concise fashion to top Greyhound Dial executives. In addition to basic analytical details such as income statements, balance sheets and cash flow statements, the system provides more sophisticated analyses.

For example, since companies are now increasingly evaluated in terms of their ability to generate cash, Greyhound Dial added a free cash flow calculation to track how much cash each line of business generates from operations. Another CIS calculation is a valuation model. This model allows Greyhound Dial to valuate each of its subsidiaries assuming different costs of capital.

A more general and under-estimated benefit, Brown emphasizes, is that CIS helps ensure that everyone at Greyhound Dial is working with the same financial vocabulary. The system imposes a measure of standards and agreements to guarantee that apples are compared to apples and oranges to oranges. "Every user is tied into the same historic database. IFPS makes sure that everyone talks about the same thing," he adds.

Consistent with the belief that a standard reporting structure makes for less confusion, Greyhound Dial designed a uniform set of reports to apply to every subsidiary. Thus top management knows that the same categories of information will appear in the same place on the report for every company. It required considerable programming to make a uniform set of reports possible, but that upfront investment has paid off handsomely by allowing users to generate ad hoc reports that are easier to interpret. Users take advantage of a menu-driven front end to generate analyses and to selectively print reports of summary information.

KEY PERFORMANCE FACTORS

For each of the 85 lines of business tracked by CIS, the system examines unique Key Performance Factors, the financial relationships that are key to the operations of those individual lines. The system tracks up to 12 Key Performance Factors on a monthly basis for every one of Greyhound Dial's lines of business.

These Key Performance Factors are used in preparation of Greyhound Dial monthly books: a tightly controlled analytical tool that goes to top management on a need-to-know basis. Developed with Lotus 1-2-3, Wordperfect, IFPS and Execucom's Impressionist business graphics package, these monthly books are up-to-date summaries of Greyhound Dial's operations. Greyhound Dial's new information capabilities allow it to issue the monthly books by the eighth or ninth workday of each month.

Greyhound Dial's ability to graph financial activity extends to the boardroom. Workbooks for Greyhound Dial's Board of Directors are generated directly from CIS using Impressionist. Impressionist enables Greyhound Dial analysts to visually analyze and interpret data. It includes a chartbook of more than 100 types of business graphics and a graphics editor that permits free-form drawing.

INVESTMENT IN CIS

Greyhound Dial's investment in CIS to date is approximately $1.45 million, which includes the cost of upgrading the company's PC environment by

30–35 IBM PS/2 personal computers and a Local Area Network. By all accounts, the money is considered well spent. "CIS leverages our investment in technology by allowing us to spend our time and creative energy where we can add the most value to the organization," Brown notes. "We buy and sell companies at the same time we're operating other companies. CIS gives us the opportunity to quickly evaluate the progress of our individual companies and lines of business."

Greyhound Dial exploits the modeling capabilities of IFPS in a number of ways, Brown explains. Executives can quickly see the effects of combining segments of various operating companies. What would be the effect on capacity utilization, an executive might ask, of consolidating two facilities? "These 'what if?' exercises allow us to explore various combinations of company structures," Brown says.

Similar modeling techniques help Greyhound Dial pinpoint candidates for acquisition or divestiture as it can quickly forecast the effects of a proposed action. "We're not going to buy or sell a company if it does not appear that it will result in an incremental increase to the value of the Greyhound Dial Corporation," Brown insists.

CONCLUSION

Greyhound Dial's strategic planning process, supported by CIS, ensures a thorough periodic review of the short and long-term objectives of each operating company and provides a framework on which to build practical and measurable plans. The return on equity goal for all subsidiaries is at least 15%. Many Greyhound Dial companies regularly surpass this goal.

Something must be going right. At a time when practically every large Phoenix-based company reported depressed earnings, Greyhound Dial reported net operating profits up 17% for 1989.

The information system revolution for executive management is changing the way executives are operating their businesses, often replacing seat-of-the-pants intuition with carefully calculated analytical, financial modeling and demographic information.

"By leveraging our management experience and making an investment in technology to gain competitive advantage, we will continue to maintain a sound overall financial condition and enhance shareholder value. Our record demonstrates that we are producing positive results," Teets concludes.

It is debatable whether all this technology was created to meet pent-up information demands by executives or whether the technology itself created a class of executives equipped to take advantage of the unprecedented information services available through PCs. But regardless of the way the situation is analyzed, the net outcome is that everyone—the executives, the organizations for which they are responsible, and the shareholders who ultimately pay the cost and reap the benefits of the technology—is enriched.

QUESTIONS

1. What was the situation at Greyhound Dial in 1986 that led to the CEO's statement, ". . . we ask executives to be more than managers. They are expected to be leaders of change." Include the firm's information systems situation in your answer.

2. How has the company's EIS helped corporate executives become leaders of change? How has the EIS helped turn the company around?

3. How did Greyhound Dial implement their EIS so quickly?

4. What are the benefits of the firm's EIS?

25

Putting Hertz Executives in the Driver's Seat

Meghan O'Leary

Hertz's car-renting competitors might be interested to discover that they're not the only ones who try harder. As the number one car-rental company in the nation, The Hertz Corp., located in Park Ridge, N.J., dominates an intensely competitive industry where a marketing plan is more likely to depend on the weather than the economy. The ability to sift through electronically gathered information about cities, climates, holidays, business cycles, tourist activity, past promotions and market forecasts allows a company to make the almost instantaneous marketing decisions that have become a requirement for playing the game.

In order to maintain its lead on the competition, Hertz's marketing department has implemented a mainframe-based decision support system (DSS) and an executive information system (EIS)—a PC-based front end to the DSS that gives executives the tools to analyze the mountains of demographic data and make real-time marketing decisions.

The system's information reach extends to Hertz's nationwide network of rental locations and culminates at the company's executive offices in Park Ridge, where its creators, Staff Vice President of Marketing Planning William J. Carroll and Director of Marketing Services and Pricing Systems Scott H. Meadow, oversee its operation.

Hertz's EIS began somewhat unexpectedly three years ago as Carroll was interviewing Meadow for the position he now holds. When Carroll had finished asking questions, Meadow had one of his own. He wanted to know what Carroll wanted in a computer system. Carroll's answer, and his subsequent hiring of Meadow, resulted in the DSS (built around

Previously published in *CIO Magazine*, Volume 3, Number 5, February 1990 by CIO Publishing Inc. Used with permission.

System W from Comshare Inc., of Ann Arbor, Mich.) that formed the backbone of the EIS (Comshare's Commander EIS was added in 1988).

With the EIS, Meadow and Carroll gave their DSS a front end in the form of tools that executives could use to analyze and extrapolate on valuable sales and marketing information from across the country. This includes not just information from Hertz's own rental agreements, accounting departments and fleet purchases, but computer-reservation-system reports on how many calls are made to Hertz's 800 number and airport reports on comparative revenues for the various car-rental companies stationed there.

The major force behind the company's EIS—besides the energy and vision of Meadow and Carroll—was the clear need for more information, better information and immediate information. There was no army of technology-resistant executives to convince, because Hertz executives understood the mercurial and demanding nature of their industry as well as Meadow and Carroll did. Their understanding of the competitive value of information opened their minds to any tool that would make it easier to get information and interpret it.

The car-rental industry is a deadly competitive one, according to Carroll. "You have four or five major firms vying for major market share." Car-rental prices have risen little over the past decade, forcing companies to cut costs and increase sales to maintain healthy profit margins. "It's an easy business to enter, but a difficult business in which to grow and become successful," he said.

As a result, according to Meadow, the decision-making processes at a company such as Hertz are marketing-oriented and based on future expectations rather than known quantities. For instance, a manager may decide to lower prices and add cars in Florida during March in hopes of attracting vacationers at the height of the season. Another may discount weekly rates during the holidays in order to win over some of the plane- and train-boarding crowd. Whatever the marketing ploy, the expectations are based on analysis of past market behavior, seasonal and regional business highs and lows, and the success or failure of past promotions. And no matter how painstaking the market analysis or how complete the market history, consumer behavior is hard to predict.

"We knew we had a need," Carroll said. "It wasn't an apparition in St. Patrick's Cathedral."

As a result of filling that need, Carroll has masses of marketing and rental information at his fingertips. But you wouldn't know it from his Spartan, nearly paperless office. "Look around," he said to a recent visitor, gesturing to the uncluttered workspace, "I didn't just empty it out before you got here."

The absence of paper is evidence of the EIS's streamlining effect, which allows Hertz executives to make marketing decisions based on their immediate observations of the dynamic car-rental market. "Timing is critical," said Meadow. "We were able to [analyze information] before, but when [a marketing executive] asked a question, he had to go to a systems analyst, tell him what he wanted," and then wait for the result. Now marketing executives can answer their own questions and plug in their own variables.

"Decisions are going to be made whether you have information or not," Meadow continued, and they're going to be made at the company's convenience. "A CEO . . . can't wait for information. [Waiting] makes it useless information."

By allowing Hertz to keep track of and respond to current market conditions, the system also allows the company to take into account the possibility of certain conditions occurring again. This ability is at the heart of the company's yield-management system, whereby it may choose to offer special rates or unlimited mileage in order to boost sales in slow times and keep rates steady at times when demand has been high in the past. While these kinds of decisions were possible in the past, executives had to wait days or weeks for paper reports from MIS. According to Carroll, "The system gives you the opportunity to accumulate information about [possible] future trends [and] to take some of the risk out of those decisions."

Despite the obvious importance of a marketing-oriented system in a marketing-oriented company, Meadow emphasized that cooperation between marketing and IS was essential to the project. The IS department was concerned at first that the host-based DSS might overload their mainframe enough to slow-down other non-marketing applications. The EIS portion of the system concerned IS less because it was PC-based. (Meadow contends, in fact, that off-loading data analysis to PCs "benefited the mainframe side.")

To the IS department's credit, it tempered its concern about resources with a clear understanding of Hertz's business objectives. "The absolute need to have the kind of information that we could get with the EIS and the DSS associated with it was . . . [so] overwhelming . . . that everybody in MIS kind of rallied around the banner," Meadow said. Not only did marketing get its system, but it maintains it with a smaller technical team than was originally planned, according to Meadow.

Hertz's EIS stands out as much for its modesty as for its excellence. Despite the unquestionable benefits of their system, Carroll and Meadow don't push the EIS's technology as much as they push its output. Although every Hertz executive uses the system in one form or another, according to Meadow, they're not all hands-on users. In the executive suites, some managers access the EIS through personal computers on their desks. Others, who may not need or want a computer, choose to rely on paper reports generated by the system. One of the better-known examples of this is

Hertz's chairman, Frank A. Olson, who prefers paper printouts of EIS-generated reports to a high-tech interface.

"Frankly, at this point, a chairman can be provided the information without having the system on his desk," Meadow said. "He [still] has access to better information more quickly than before." Form takes a back seat to function in this case.

This conservative approach in no way stunts the system's growth, Carroll and Meadow agreed. "The system becomes [more widely] available because it's needed," Carroll said.

"We're constantly enhancing it," said Meadow, adding that the system's assimilation into the corporate culture is intuitive because it conforms to the way Hertz executives work. "People find new applications and suggest them. Without adding more software or people, you can leverage [the EIS] with a small change or adjustment."

Carroll and Meadow are quick to point out that the number of people using an EIS isn't the sole measure of the system's success. As to what is an accurate measure for Hertz of the system's success—"That's a tough question to answer," Carroll replied. "We can't say 'It was this sum of revenue, or that market share we captured.' It's hard to quantify in terms of dollars and cents, but we're doing better than our competitors."

The reason for this, and the real measure of the system's success, according to the two men, is that the EIS allows Hertz to use its information and IS resources better. Executives can manipulate and refine data to be more meaningful and strategically significant to them. In addition, "our [mainframe] programming resources can be routed to other projects," Meadow said. "With powerful PCs, you can offload analysis and ad hoc stuff that would normally eat a mainframe alive." Hertz's EIS allows executives to draw in the mainframe's information resources, store the needed data on their PCs, and analyze and what-if to their hearts' content without tying up valuable mainframe time.

As a result, Hertz's EIS has a conserving, streamlining effect, triggering a kind of creative growth among executives, according to its creators. Meadow pointed out that EISs are often described purely in terms of critical success factors—the types of information they must provide in order to fill the executives' needs. But Meadow contends that an EIS has an elusive creative effect that is quite apart from the specific pieces of information it provides.

"A tool like this begins to create a synergy in decision-making," he said. "It triggers questions, a greater influx of creative ideas, and more effective marketing and cost decisions." The fact that the car-rental industry relies on successful marketing decisions makes a company such as Hertz particularly conducive to this kind of synergy, he added. According to Meadow, the decision to use an EIS does not guarantee success. The key, in Hertz's experience, is "how you use it."

QUESTIONS

1. What are the benefits of the EIS to Hertz? Pay particular attention to the business that Hertz is in and its peculiar needs.
2. Discuss the interrelationship of Hertz's DSS and EIS.
3. Discuss the part played by Hertz's information systems department in the development of the EIS.
4. How does Hertz measure the success of its EIS?

26

Developing an ESS for the Michigan State Senate

Caryl Holland

INTRODUCTION

Senators at the Michigan Senate have been supported by an executive support system (ESS) for the past nine months. The ESS has progressed from providing operational session functions, to a more sophisticated local area network (LAN) information retrieval and communication system. Although system usage was not mandatory, thirty-four out of thirty-eight senators use the system during session.

During the first phase, the Senate developed a base system, using state-of-the-art technology, that could be enhanced as needs changed. Senators could vote, view current amendment under consideration, and access Michigan Compiled Laws and Bill Status via personal computers from their desks in the Chamber.

The next phase came after three months of operation when additional features were added to support senators. These enhancements included: referral of bills to committee, daily calendar, an intercom messaging system, and access to the senator's office information.

Currently, new development efforts are in process including the ability to select and view any amendment submitted for consideration with their corresponding fiscal notes, and partisan analysis. Additional ESS enhancements consist of: a rule-based system for drafting amendments, a parliamentary procedure support system, access to outside news services, and legislative databases.

Caryl L. Holland, "Developing an ESS for the Michigan State Senate," Transactions of the Eleventh International Conference on Decision Support Systems, 1991. Used with permission.

SYSTEM OVERVIEW

Hardware

The senator's workstation configuration is a 16MHz IBM PS/2 Model 70, with a 60-Mbyte hard disk and 4 Mbytes of RAM. The senators may use a keyboard or mouse, as well as touch-screen input to perform functions on a Sharp LCD flat screen, mounted in a custom-made wooden frame.

Software

The senator's basic workstation software consists of: MS-DOS 4.1, Microsoft Windows v2.11, and Novell Netbios v2.15. Custom messaging, security, and a windows-based legislative application software achieve near real-time operation for voting. Access to LAN based applications are also available including: word processing, spreadsheet, database, personal information management systems, and electronic mail.

Network Connectivity

An IBM Token-Ring local area network, running Novell's NetWare v2.15 network operating system connects the workstations in the senate chamber. A fiber optic backbone connects the chamber to other Senate offices located in three buildings.

System Interface

The system interface provides an electronic interchange between a software based voting system, chamber gallery wall displays, computer workstations, and backup voting hardware. Messages are transmitted between workstations and the voting system processor via the Token-Ring network. The display boards, backup voting hardware, and voting system processor also transmit messages via a daisy chained signal cable.

DEVELOPMENTAL PROCESS

Committed Leadership

The Senate was fortunate to have progressive leadership with respect to computer technology. The Senate Majority Leader, Senator John Engler, wanted to develop a pre-eminent legislative information system optimized to serve office management functions in a distributed, networked environment.

Executive Sponsor

The Senate's executive sponsor was the Secretary of the Senate, Willis H. Snow. The executive sponsor played an important role by managing political resistance during the development process. The executive sponsor also spent time building senator support and providing feedback which impacted system design and implementation.

Development Goals

Four objectives were accomplished in the development of the ESS. (1) The ESS provided critical operational functions for voting and displaying information. (2) The ESS was designed to enhance the capabilities of a rule-based organization. (3) A platform was chosen that could meet changing needs and utilize new technology. (4) The ESS provided connectivity to the entire organization leveraging the investment of installed Office Automation Systems.

Furniture Design

Modern computer technology had to be incorporated into a Senate chamber restored to the late 19th century. It took six months to design a wooden side-console to accommodate the computer, voting equipment, and other electronics, while providing workspace for the senator. The furniture design was critical to the acceptance of the ESS. If senators did not feel comfortable working at the computer, more than likely they would not use the system.

System Prototyping

At the beginning of the design process, screen layouts were developed using Dan Bricklin's Demo II software. These layouts facilitated feedback sessions where senators offered suggestions on screen format and functionality. In subsequent meetings, a prototype system was used to enhance senator involvement in the design process. Senators performed functions, by touching the screen, enabling them to interact with the system as they would in the chamber. This approach allowed spontaneous reactions, which proved invaluable during the development process.

Operation Simplicity

It was estimated that eleven out of thirty-eight senators had minimal computer experience and three with exceptional skill level. Therefore,

Table 26–1. *Features of the Executive Support System at the Michigan Senate*

Application	Description
Session voting	A vote window displays "YEA"/"NAY" buttons, vote-time remaining and running tallies. The vote list may be viewed alphabetically, by Yeas and Nays, and by party.
Request to speak	The Senator may request to speak by pressing the "speak" button. A "speaker's list" automatically updates on each computer and wall display boards.
Request a page	The senator may request a page by pressing the "page" button. A seating chart automatically updates on the sergeant-at-arms station. Upon dispatch, the senator's page button changes shading, indicating a page is on the way.
View current amendment	The senator may view the current amendment being discussed by pressing the "current amendment" button. The amendment text is displayed in a window that can be scrolled for viewing.
Daily calendar	The senator may view the daily senate calendar prior to session beginning or during session. The calendar text is displayed in a window that can be scrolled for viewing.
Referral of bills to committee	The senator may view bills referred to committee by pressing the "referral of bills" button. The text is displayed in a window that can be scrolled for viewing.
Chamber intercom	The senator may send messages to other senators, as well as the secretary, presiding officer, and sergeant-at-arms. an individual or group of individuals may be selected. Also, messages can be created and stored for later use.

the ESS had to be simple to use; yet capable of supporting applications for advanced users. The main system features were developed to require only touch screen input to perform legislative functions. This method of user interaction requires very little, if any, application training. Other off-the-shelf applications may be accessed via a menu option by using the keyboard or mouse.

Consistency

Throughout the development process, it was important to maintain a consistent look and feel when accessing information. Scrolling buttons were designed for advancing text line-by-line, or page up and page down, as well as directly accessing the top and bottom of the document. Button shape, size, and location remain consistent from screen-to-screen. Button shading was also an integral aspect of the design process, indicating access to information, activity pending, or no action taken.

Application Overview

Senators can access information that was distributed in paper format. The benefit of having on-line access to information over paper-based systems is the timeliness of material delivery. Table 26–1 describes the current features of the executive support system.

SUMMARY

The Michigan Senate is a pioneer of legislative executive support system development. Senators are supported in carrying out operational functions, and have access to an information retrieval and communication system.

The result of our effort has improved senator efficiency. Senators can monitor inter- and intra-office communications, on-the-floor communications, and access outside legislative data. Information is now, just a finger tip away.

ESS development takes commitment, dedication, and enthusiasm of individuals involved in the process. There needs to be a resolve to tackle difficult problems, and executive creativity when viewing the overall project. ESS developers must be willing to accept feedback and make necessary changes to meet the needs of the executive.

An ESS is unique in its design and function. It should reflect an appropriate amount of status and prestige for those executives who use it. The ESS must be simple to use and fully equipped to accommodate executives with exceptional personal computer skills. When possible, the system should permit some degree of executive customization. This personal touch establishes executive ownership of the ESS, increasing the probability of a successful system implementation.

QUESTIONS

1. Discuss the evolution of the Senate's ESS functions.
2. What were the four objectives in the development of the ESS?

Index

B

Batch-EIS, 133–142
Beneficial, 310–313
Benefits of an EIS, 9, 25–26, 243–244,
   282–283, 316–324

C

Capabilities of an EIS, 7–8, 99
Command Center, 218–225
Commander EIS, 218–225
Compass, 246–255
Comshare, 218–225
Cost of an EIS, 12, 95, 225
Cost/benefit analysis, 95
Critical success factors, 131, 166–168

D

Data, 5–6, 25, 93, 111–112, 207–208,
   289–290, 332–333
Data keepers, 292
Data providers, 291–292
Data sources, 93, 111–112
Data timeliness, 94, 251–252,
   330–331
Development framework, 85–87
Development process, 93–100,
   112–114, 147–158, 294–295
Dialog, 99–100

E

Executive information systems:
   applications:
      aerospace, 13–30, 177–188,
         279–297
      banking, 245–252

car rental, 343–346
consumer products and services,
   191–200, 337–342
copier manufacturer, 303–307
finance, 310–313
food products, 307–309
government, 349–353
mining, 191–200
benefits, 9, 25–26, 282–283
capabilities, 7–8, 99
characteristics of, 4–8, 15, 81–83,
   161–162
comparison to ESS, 83
comparison to MIS and DSS, 14–16,
   128–133
costs, 95, 225
data, 5–6, 24, 93, 111–112,
   207–208, 289–290, 332–333
definition of, 82–83, 161
development framework, 85–87
dialog, 93–100
executive support, 239–240
evolution, 96–97, 243, 259,
   275–276
failure reasons, 84, 118–119, 237,
   274–275
growth of, 329–332
hardware selection, 29
keys to success, 28–30
motivation for development, 93–94,
   119–125, 250, 280
response time, 100
resistance to, 114, 259
security, 24, 206
software, 96, 191–193, 211–236
Evolution, 96–97, 243, 259,
   275–276

Executive sponsor (champion), 29, 90,
    108–109, 118, 239–240, 251,
    258–259, 270–271
Executive culture, 20–24
    uses of EIS, 3–4, 13–14

F

Feature analysis and capability
    review, 197–200, 226–233
Fisher-Price, 152–158

G

Greyhound Dial, 337–342
Groupware, 334

H

Hertz Rental Care, 343–346

I

Impacts of, 296–297
Information:
    hard, 184–186
    media, 59–62
    requirements, 29, 163–188,
        240–241, 247
    soft, 185–186, 281
    sources, 57–59
    value, 56–57
    volume, 55–56
Information systems personnel,
    92–93, 259, 272–273
Information requirements
    determination:
    methods, 168–173, 179–188,
        240–241, 247
    strategies, 163–166

L

Lockheed-Georgia, 13–30, 177–188

M

Managerial roles:
    decisional, 45–47, 53–54, 63–65
    informational, 43–45, 53–54, 63–65
    interpersonal, 42–43, 53–54

Managerial work, 35–41
Marine Midland Bank, N.A., 245–255
Michigan State Senate, 349–353
Management Information and
    Decision Support (MIDS) system,
    13–30, 177–188
Mental models, 315–324
Motivation for development, 93–94,
    119–125

N

Northwest Industries, 8–10

O

Online-EIS, 133–142
Open architecture, 204
Operating sponsor, 90, 259, 271

P

Pilot Executive Software, 218–225
Protyping, 29, 112–114, 214–216,
    283, 294–295

Q

Quaker Oats, 108–109, 307–309

R

Response time of an EIS, 100, 252
Rockwell International Corporation,
    279–297

S

Screen design, 18–24, 253
Security, 24, 206
Software, 96, 191–193, 211–236
Software selection, 29, 191–200,
    285–286
Spread, 97
Strategic business objectives (SBO)
    method, 150–158
Stowe Computer Corporation,
    260–277
System objectives, 240
Support staff, 24, 29, 91–92, 242,
    292–293

T

Training, 21–22
Transition paths from MIS to EIS,
135–142

U

User expectations, 71–76, 203–209

W

Western Mining Corporation,
196–200

X

Xerox, 303–307